The Second Umayyad Caliphate

HARVARD MIDDLE EASTERN MONOGRAPHS
XXXIII

The Second Umayyad Caliphate

The Articulation of Caliphal Legitimacy in al-Andalus

Janina M. Safran

DISTRIBUTED FOR THE
CENTER FOR MIDDLE EASTERN STUDIES
OF HARVARD UNIVERSITY BY
HARVARD UNIVERSITY PRESS
CAMBRIDGE, MASSACHUSETTS
LONDON, ENGLAND

ISBN 0-932885-24-1
Library of Congress Catalog Number 00-102672
Printed in the United States of America
00 01 02 03 04 6 5 4 3 2 1

Dedicated to My Parents

Contents

Acknowledgments

This book began with a question in class: "What about the caliphate in Spain?" A moment of curiosity about the "marginal" Umayyad caliphate in the West eventually developed into an abiding interest in the political culture of al-Andalus.

I am grateful to Roy Mottahedeh, Paula Sanders, William Graham, Everett Rowson, and Kristen Brustad for their instruction in Islamic history and religion and Arabic literature and language, and for their inspiration. Over the years I learned much from discussions with fellow students of the Middle East and the Islamic world and from friends with other interests, and I thank you all. I would like to thank a few in particular who listened, probed, and prodded as I began my initial research: Michael Propokow, Joseph O'Donnell, Ben Westervelt, David Bush, and especially Caroline Castiglione and Jim Gelvin.

I am indebted to those who read all or part of the manuscript at different stages and offered their insights and criticisms: Roy Mottahedeh, Susan Miller, Dede Fairchild Ruggles, Tim Gianotti, Dan Beaver, Jim Gelvin, Thomas Glick, and Maribel Fierro. Maribel Fierro, who has written extensively on politics and religion in Umayyad al-Andalus, has been a tremendous resource. She has directed me to Spanish and French scholarship and demonstrated a genuine commitment to international academic exchange. All the shortcomings of the book are, of course, my own.

I benefitted greatly from a semester leave granted to junior faculty for research and writing and thank the dean of the College of Liberal Arts of the Pennsylvania State University and the head of the History department for this privilege.

The reader will find some material from chapters one and two published in two articles: "The Command of the Faithful in al-Andalus: A Study in the Articulation of Caliphal Legitimacy," *International Journal of Middle East Studies* 30 (1998), 183–198; and "Ceremony and Submission: The Symbolic Representation and Recognition of Legitimacy in Tenth-Century al-Andalus," *Journal of Near Eastern Studies* 58 (1999), 191–201. I thank the editors of these journals for their interest and the readers of the article manuscripts for their contributions.

Finally, I would like to thank Barbara, Abby, Liz, Anita, and Nadav for their enduring patience, renewing interest, and enthusiastic support, expressed in many ways over many years. I thank Dan for his rigorous standards and careful comments and especially for his partnership.

The Second Umayyad Caliphate

Introduction

I proclaim to all who are near and far and warn of certain truths in which I sincerely believe:

The sun of a caliphate has risen in the west which will shine with splendor in the two easts.

Syria will rise at its appearance, for it had claims to her from long ago,

And the darkness of unbelief will be dissipated with the imam's compassionate direction of the true religion.[1]

—Verses by ʿAbd al-ʿAzīz ibn Ḥusayn al-Qarawī praising the Umayyad caliphate of al-Andalus in the court of the second Andalusi-Umayyad caliph

I

The political history of Islam, from the death of the Prophet Muḥammad in the fourth decade of the seventh century until the Mongol conquests of the middle of the thirteenth century, has been defined by the institution of the caliphate and measured by successive caliphal dynasties and the reigns of individual caliphs. In the most common periodization, the first four caliphs—the *rashīdūn* or "rightly guided" caliphs, all close companions of the Prophet—presided over the polity Muḥammad had created in Medina and directed the conquests that brought Arabia, most of the eastern domains of the Byzantine empire, and the lands of the former Sassanian empire under Muslim rule. The Umayyads established their dynastic rule over the Islamic empire and extended it, governing from Syria for nearly a century (661–750) until they were overthrown by the Abbasids in a revolution carefully planned and promoted in ideological terms. The period of Abbasid rule (750–1258) is often characterized as the apogee of Islamic civilization, and in many ways the Abbasids defined the institution of the caliphate. The ways they elaborated their authority, asserted their claims to legitimacy, and styled their rule inspired the imitation of contemporary and future provincial rulers and rivals.

This chronology of Islamic history obscures the many contests for political power and the challenges to established authority that helped shape the historical development of the caliphate and the language of political legitimacy. It represents, first of all, a Sunni view of history. The Shi'a have alternative interpretations of the history of the Muslim community and privilege a chronology defined by the imams. Considered in a context of political competition, the chronology outlines a more specifically Abbasid view of history. In the tenth century the Isma'ili Shi'i Fatimids and the Sunni Umayyads of al-Andalus (Islamic Iberia) challenged Abbasid legitimacy. Each of these dynasties claimed the exclusive right to the Command of the Faithful and promoted distinctive interpretations of the past and visions of the future to support their claims.

Umayyad history did not end in 750 for descendants of the Umayyad caliphs of Syria and their supporters. Only a short time after the Abbasid revolution one of the Banū Umayya secured his rule in al-Andalus and a new seat for his dynasty in Cordoba. In 929, the eighth Umayyad ruler of al-Andalus reclaimed his dynastic right to the caliphate and the inheritance of his ancestors. While he characterized his caliphate as a restoration, he effectively established a second Umayyad caliphate in a new geographical and historical context.

This book examines how the Umayyad caliphs of al-Andalus defined their authority, articulated their legitimacy, and challenged the claims of the Abbasids and the Fatimids. While the basic principles of the Islamic caliphate originated in the political decisions of Muḥammad's companions following his death, historical claimants to the office invested those principles with particular meaning according to the circumstances of their rule and, especially in challenge to the existing order, reinterpreted the conventions of caliphal legitimacy. The concept of the caliphate proved historically malleable within parameters determined by the early community.[2]

As Sunni tradition relates, when the Muslim community of Medina originally agreed, after some deliberation, to preserve the unity of their polity and acknowledge the leadership of one man among themselves as Muḥammad's successor, they established the ideal of the caliphate as unitary and universal. In the understanding that Muḥammad was the "seal of the prophets" or the last of God's messengers to humankind, the caliphate was conceived of as a trusteeship. The caliph was a political and military leader with ultimate responsibility for the temporal, but also spiritual and moral, welfare of the community (*umma*). Accounts of the leadership of the *rashīdūn* caliphs record that in the decades after Muḥammad's death the caliph's mandate included protecting the interests of the Muslims, championing Islam against unbelievers, and upholding the principles of Islam within the community. The *rashīdūn* caliphs were respected for their personal closeness to Muḥammad and their participation in his mission, and this was the basis for their nomination or election to leadership. However, the legitimacy of individual caliphs, even among the *rashīdūn,* came to be contested over issues of performance and succession, and these issues continued to inform the articulation of legitimacy in the era of dynastic rule and competition.

Research by scholars such as Moshe Sharon, Jacob Lassner, and Elton Daniel on the Abbasid revolution, the propaganda campaign that supported the revolution, and the subsequent historiographical elaboration of Abbasid ideology has given us insights into the Abbasid definition of the caliphate and the terms and themes the Abbasids used to justify their rise to power and legitimate their policies.[3] Work on Isma'ili doctrine and cosmology has greatly informed our understanding of the Fatimid caliphate. Heinz Halm, for example, demonstrates how the Fatimids developed and expressed their distinctive ideology in the context of the establishment their regime.[4] The Syrian Umayyad conception of the caliphate has also received careful attention in recent years. Given that the historiographical treatment of the Syrian Umayyad caliphate was subject to Abbasid ideological shaping, scholars such as Patricia Crone and Martin Hinds, Wadad al-Qadi, Khalid Yahya Blankinship, and others have investigated how the Umayyads themselves articulated their legitimacy and defined their authority. They recovered the Syrian Umayyad conception of the caliphate by examining extant redactions of letters, panegyric poetry, and the Umayyad commitment to holy war.[5] More specialized scholarship—for example, on symbols, ceremonial, art, and architecture—has further refined our understanding of how these different dynasties and their individual rulers promoted their caliphal rule.

A comparable study of Andalusi Umayyad caliphal ideology will enlarge our understanding of the Islamic concept of the caliphate and the political contests of the Islamic world in the tenth century and develop a dynamic view of Andalusi political culture. The neglect of the subject in English-language scholarship may be a consequence of a traditional academic focus on the Islamic heartlands and a corresponding orientation to the Abbasid view of history. Few writers in the Abbasid empire wrote of al-Andalus, and those who did dismissed the significance of the rival caliphate because its domains were limited and did not include the holy cities; in other words, the Andalusi caliphate did not have the territorial basis to claim unique and universal leadership.[6] Some modern scholars have thus described or treated the Andalusi Umayyad adoption of caliphal titles and prerogatives as an act of vainglory with no ideological significance.[7] One can, however, turn to Ibn Ḥazm (d. 1064), an Andalusi scholar and Umayyad partisan, for an alternative perspective on the problem of universality. He writes it was licit for someone to use the exclusive title of Imam or Commander of the Faithful if he had the legitimate *right* to rule all of the believers, even if a large number disobeyed him or did not recognize his authority.[8] The theoretical ideal of the caliphate should be investigated in context as an ideal interpreted and tested by the caliphs and their supporters in al-Andalus and North Africa and not applied as an abstract standard.

The Umayyad caliphate appears quite different if one approaches it from the Andalusi evidence. Scholars in a number of fields who focus their research on al-Andalus using Andalusi sources, often writing in French or Spanish, tend to assume the ideological significance of the Umayyad caliphate in Andalusi politics and culture. The English-language scholarship that draws on this abundant research and examines Andalusi sources, such as Hugh Kennedy's recent survey, *Muslim Spain and Portugal: A Political History of al-Andalus,* or more specialized studies—for example, of monuments, panegyric poetry, or numismatics—is informed by this alternative perspective.[9]

Political narratives and studies of Umayyad rule identify the caliphate with greater centralization, not withstanding debates about the degree of its success, and with a new manifestation of sovereignty. One can see this reflected in monographs that approach the Umayyad polity from a number of different angles—for example, in Pierre Guichard's work on the tensions between "western" and "eastern" social structures and ethnic divisions in al-Andalus, Manuel Acién Almansa's argument about 'Umar Ibn Ḥafṣūn's rebellion against the Umayyad regime, Eduardo Manzano Moreno's study of the frontiers, and most recently, Mohamed Meouak's analysis of administrative elites.[10] The investigation of caliphal ideology complements scholarship on the state, contributing another view of how the Umayyads refashioned their regime and promoted its interests. David Wasserstein and François Clément independently demonstrate the continued significance of Umayyad caliphal ideology for the definition of rulership and legitimacy in the decades after the collapse of the

Umayyad regime in their work on the *ṭa'ifa* kingdoms (1002–1086).[11] How then did the Umayyad caliphs define and promote their authority and legitimacy?

While large-scale studies like Evariste Lévi-Provençal's grand *Histoire de l'Espagne musulman* provide details of some of the more tangible ways the dynasty asserted and styled its power, a number of recent focused studies specifically explore Umayyad representations of legitimacy in a range of forms and contexts.[12] To provide only a few examples, Maribel Fierro explores why 'Abd al-Raḥmān III adopted the caliphal title when his predecessors had not and develops an argument from statements of the first caliph's territorial ambitions; Miquel Barceló investigates caliphal receptions and develops a ceremonial profile of the court; a number of scholars—including Antonio Vallejo Triano, Manuel Acién Almansa, Christine Mazzoli-Guintard, Jerrilynn D. Dodds, D. Fairchild Ruggles, and Nuha Khoury—analyze the palace city of Madīnat al-Zahrā' and the Great Mosque of Cordoba as expressions of Umayyad legitimacy.[13] The insights provided by these scholars have yet to be integrated into a coherent framework in which the subjects of their research are viewed as part of an ideological system.

One scholar, Gabriel Martínez-Gros, has devoted a monograph to Umayyad caliphal ideology, *L'idéologie omeyyade: la construction de la legitimité du califat du Cordoue (X–XI siècles)*.[14] Beginning with the premise that 'Abd al-Raḥmān III supported his caliphal claims ideologically, Martínez-Gros turns to an examination of literary evidence, primarily historical texts. His approach and conclusions are original and problematic. He proposes that a coterie of pro-Umayyad writers, profoundly influenced by Fatimid ideology, produced texts encoded with esoteric or *bāṭinī* meaning to elaborate Umayyad ideology, and he presents an explication of the "hidden" meaning of the texts he has selected. There is no evidence that Andalusis read or wrote texts for esoteric meaning, however, and given the impossibility of corroboration, some of Martínez-Gros's identifications of signs and interpretations of meaning, while intriguing, seem tendentious. His treatment of contemporary texts as a body, however, invites reconsideration of the historical production under Umayyad aegis as part of the discourse of Umayyad legitimacy.

This book recovers the Andalusi Umayyad argument for caliphal legitimacy by revisiting the textual evidence, including explicit statements issued by the caliphs themselves, following the model of inquiry into the ideology of the Abbasid, Fatimid, and Syrian Umayyad caliphates. The close examination of caliphal rhetoric provides a framework for the reconstruction of Umayyad caliphal ideology, understood as a "system of interacting symbols and interworking meanings" largely defined by the court and the caliph at its center.[15] The study incorporates and interprets the relevant scholarship on specific aspects of Umayyad rule and political culture within this framework with some elaboration, as well as an analysis of Andalusi historiography.

II

Islamic rule in the Iberian peninsula began in the early eighth century, after Muslim expeditionary forces from North Africa conquered al-Andalus, and it ended some eight hundred years later when the Catholic monarchs Fernando of Aragon and Isabel of Castile conquered Granada in 1492. Within that period, the Umayyad dynasty established its capital in Cordoba and both asserted and defended its rule for 275 years (756–1031). While the Umayyads experienced periods of relative strength and the expansion of their political influence and periods of weakness and the contraction of their power, they proved to be the only Muslim dynasty able to claim continuous authority in al-Andalus over so many generations. When ʿAbd al-Raḥmān (III) al-Naṣir li-Dīn Allāh proclaimed himself caliph in 929, the Umayyads had ruled the peninsula as amirs for more than a century and a half. The proclamation of the caliphate, however, marked a new era in the history of the dynasty and the period of its greatest power and glory.

'Abd al-Raḥmān III ascended the throne in 912, after thirty years of rebellion throughout the peninsula had completely undermined Umayyad authority and reduced the dynasty's effective power to the capital city of Cordoba and its immediately surrounding region. The new amir spent much of the first two decades of his reign in the field fighting to impose his sovereignty over the territory of Muslim settlement, bounded to the north by the Tagus and Ebro Rivers. While 'Abd al-Raḥmān III did not use military might to attain the throne, he did use it to win a domain, and in this sense he established a new regime. He supported his new regime with an ideology that established and supported his right to rule.

The decades of rebellion had seen the breakdown of ties between the capital and the provinces. Historically, in the frontier region to the north powerful families took advantage of every opportunity to maximize their autonomy and expand their territory, and this became increasingly true in the late ninth century. Beginning in the 870s, for example, the Banū Marwān based in Badajoz in the Lower March and the Banū Qasī in the Upper March expanded their domains in defiance of Umayyad authority; they even captured Umayyad governors and commanders. Then, shortly before the amir 'Abd Allāh came to the throne (r. 888–912), a rebel from Ronda, 'Umar ibn Ḥafṣūn, began to raid the heartlands of al-Andalus and came to dominate the region around Malaga. When 'Abd Allāh proved ineffective against him, numerous towns and rural districts also revolted against Cordoba. 'Umar ibn Ḥafṣūn's leadership allowed for some political coordination and the association of various political, economic, and social interests.[16]

After defeating the Banū Ḥafṣūn, lesser rebel leaders, and the frontier lords, 'Abd al-Raḥmān III consolidated his power through practical measures such as the expansion of his administration and personal army. He also endeavored to generate loyalty by distributing benefits and cultivating an ideological platform for his regime. This ideology raised him above his subjects and distinguished him from other contenders for power. As caliph, 'Abd al-Raḥmān III claimed divinely ordained authority and exclusive legitimacy and promoted himself as a unifying symbol, the focus of not only political but also religious identity.

By declaring himself Commander of the Faithful, 'Abd al-Raḥmān III defined his polity in distinctly Islamic terms and identified his rule with the long history of the institution of the caliphate and the models and precedents of historical and contemporaneous claimants to the title. He thus evoked a cluster of expectations, ideas, metaphors, terms, symbols, and ritual forms, all elements of an idiom he could use in his own way to express and promote his authority and legitimacy. For example, as *khalīfat Allāh,* God's deputy, he could describe the campaigns he waged against those who did not recognize his authority as holy war. He defined his ambitions in a language that bespoke divine will and the advancement of truth and not stark concerns of power. Communication with others in this idiom affirmed common cause and facilitated the process of incorporating former enemies and new allies into the regime by providing conventions for expression and behavior. So, for example, the protocol that governed certain difficult moments—such as an enemy's surrender to an Umayyad commander or submission to the caliph —depersonalized the experience and imparted it with gravity.

'Abd al-Raḥmān III used this idiom not only with the commanders and officials directly involved in his rule and the politics of his caliphate but also with his subjects, especially the inhabitants of the capital, to represent his authority more broadly. The idea that successful rule depended on the satisfaction of one's subjects was proverbial in the Islamic world of the tenth century, as this aphorism found in the "mirrors for princes" advice literature suggests: "Islam, the ruler, and the people are like the tent-canopy, the poles, and the pegs. The canopy is Islam, the poles are the ruler, and the pegs are the people. None is good without the others."[17] According to advice offered by the first caliph's tutor and court poet, Ibn 'Abd Rabbihi, a wise ruler must recognize that he depends on his subjects and their good will.[18] By publicly promoting himself as caliph, 'Abd al-Raḥmān III could secure acquiescence to his rule and even inspire emotional allegiance. At the same time, to support his claim to be the one legitimate leader of the Muslims, he had to be able to elicit public recognition of his rule.

'Abd al Raḥmān III generated the ideology of his caliphate in part by describing his actions and policies in terms of his caliphal authority and legitimacy, whether it was to his military commanders and ministers in letters and orders or to his subjects through public announcements. In words and writing, those who communicated with him, those who promoted his regime, and even those who passively supported his rule then used the same terms, themes, and metaphors, elaborating them and giving them currency. All these words contextualized symbols, symbolic actions, and rituals and helped explain their meaning. At the same time, symbolic actions like the founding of a new palace city by 'Abd al-Raḥmān III or the enactment of a ritual like the *taslīm,* the formal salutation of the caliph, gave further dimension to Umayyad caliphal ideology. Additional meanings could be conveyed through form, like the arrangement of positions in a caliphal reception; the experience of the viewer(s) or participant(s) in ritual or ceremonial events, for example, on the occasion of a procession through the capital; and the evocation of associations with reiterated themes and other symbols.[19]

The new caliph devoted considerable resources to the glorification of his rule and the promotion of his prestige. This no doubt satisfied his ego and desire for immortalization and demonstrated that he was what he claimed to be: the supreme power and the agent of reward and punishment in the kingdom. The lavish display of power was not exclusive to caliphs in the Islamic world at this time, of course, but it was necessary to support the grand claims of caliphal ideology. 'Abd al Raḥmān III had to convey the power of the Umayyad caliphate and provide evidence of its divine favor to his subjects, and in the context of the tenth century he also had to address the example of his rivals. He and his successors participated in a "competition of display" with the Abbasids and especially the Fatimids in neighboring North Africa.[20] Finally, we can see in the way he expended his resources—the establishment of the new palace city outside of the old capital, the growing pomp of the court and its ceremonies, the elaboration of protocol—an effort to remove the caliph from the mundane realm and enhance the iconic qualities of his office.

'Abd al Raḥmān III's efforts to promote his rule were consistent with the practices of the Umayyad amirs who preceded him in al-Andalus but differed in scale. His ancestor 'Abd al Raḥmān (I) ibn Mu'āwiya al-Dākhil established Umayyad rule in the Iberian peninsula in the middle of the eighth century with the help of Umayyad loyalists and clients. He drew on dynastic prestige, and the amirs who succeeded him continued to emphasize their dynastic legitimacy. Although they refused to acknowledge the authority of the Abbasid caliphate, the amirs stopped short of adopting caliphal titles and prerogatives. In fact, the Muslims of al-Andalus lived in an anomalous situation; they recognized the authority of a caliphal dynasty but did not formally acknowledge any living caliph.[21]

The Umayyad amirs ruled over a largely Christian population with the support of their clan and its partisans and by means of a network of alliances with both Muslim and Christian elites. They did not command either the authority or the resources to support a claim to the caliphate or rival the Abbasids. Nor did they have a constituency for whom the identification of their rule in these terms would make a significant difference. Instead, they demonstrated they were good rulers dedicated to defending their subjects and their welfare and to upholding justice and religion. Thus they waged war in the frontier region of the north, undertook public works, held audiences for the redress of grievances, and in most cases sought the counsel of the *'ulamā'* or religious scholars. Over time, the amirs also demonstrated an interest in the display of power and authority by renovating the palace of Cordoba and developing a court protocol.

'Abd al Raḥmān III built on the foundations of Umayyad legitimacy in al-Andalus. He based his right to rule on dynastic legitimacy and claimed to be a good Muslim ruler but went further and declared himself to be the caliph of God and the instrument of divine will. In a sense, he stepped into a role waiting to be filled. The internal circumstances of his rule help explain 'Abd al-Raḥmān III's interest in developing the caliphal ideology. His dramatic reestablishment of Umayyad authority by strength of arms provided him with a foundation for the glorification of his reign but also the need to bind officials, officers, governors, notables, and subjects of diverse ethnic backgrounds (Arab, Berber, "Slav," Iberian), as well as new allies and former enemies, to his regime.[22] The fact that the majority of the population of al-Andalus was now Muslim provided an important social context. To fully understand why and how he defined his caliphate, however, we must return to the wider political context of the tenth-century Islamic world.

The Fatimids declared their imamate-caliphate and established themselves in Tunisia in 909. In accordance with Shi'i belief, they based their legitimacy on descent from the Prophet Muḥammad through his daughter Fāṭima and his son-in-law 'Alī and on a conception of the imam as divinely inspired. By the tenth century, Sunni-Shi'i sectarian differences were marked, and the Isma'ilis were in the process of elaborating their own theology and system of law. The Fatimids expressed grand expansionary ambitions in terms of the spread of the true faith, but the Sunnis condemned them for espousing deviant beliefs and practices.

The rise of the Fatimids thus posed a military and ideological threat to Umayyad rule in al-Andalus. By 929 'Abd al Raḥmān III had a strong army that had proved itself, the territorial base to support substantial revenues, and an ideology that identified him as the defender of the faith. As caliph, he claimed to embody the unity of the Sunni community in opposition to the Fatimids and thus rallied support for his regime and interests in both al-Andalus and North Africa. The weakness of the Abbasids at this time—who were unable to prevent or redress the factionalization of the Muslim community or check the recent advances of the "infidel" Byzantines and "deviant" Fatimids—allowed him to make his claims more persuasively.

The emergence of the Fatimid *dawla* or state may have served as the catalyst or inspiration for 'Abd al Raḥmān III's revival of his dynasty's claims to the caliphate and certainly informed how he represented his legitimacy and authority. Because the institution of the caliphate was understood to be unique and universal, 'Abd al Raḥmān III challenged the authority of both the Abbasids and the Fatimids in the representation of his own caliphate both explicitly and implicitly, verbally and symbolically. As we have seen, he asserted historical and exclusive dynastic legitimacy, presented his performance as ruler as evidence of his divine favor, and identified himself as the one true guide to salvation. We will see further that the Andalusi Umayyads, who opposed the Abbasids on historical and genealogical grounds and claimed the role of Sunni defenders of the faith for themselves, defended an understanding of the caliphate and the true faith they shared with their Abbasid rivals. In practice, opposition to the Fatimids prompted the more distinctive representations of their rule. The immediate instances and specific words and means in which the Andalusi Umayyad ruler defined his caliphate and opposed his rivals gave his caliphal claims their rhetorical power.

III

'Abd al Raḥmān III and his successors themselves actively promoted their legitimacy through a variety of means and forms, but the concepts and themes they disseminated became interpreted and diffused more widely by others, whether they were participants in the regime, proponents of culture, or otherwise active within the Umayyads' political sphere. To understand how the Andalusi Umayyad caliphs articulated their legitimacy and generated an ideology that infused and defined the political culture of al-Andalus we can approach the investigation from two directions: the direct way that the caliphs promoted their legitimacy on the one hand, and the indirect way that Andalusi historiography reflected and reinforced Umayyad legitimacy on the other.

This book is thus divided into two complementary sections. Part 1 provides the reader with the chronological framework of the caliphate as it explores how the caliphs ʿAbd al Raḥmān III (r. 912–961) and his son and successor al-Ḥakam (II) al-Mustanṣir Billāh (r. 961–976) explained, projected, and promoted their right to rule. Chapter 1 presents the assemblage of terms, themes, and metaphors the caliphs used to argue their legitimacy, examining them in their immediate historical context to explain their significance and recover their rhetorical impact. Based on written evidence generated by the caliphal court—redactions of complete or partial excerpts of caliphal proclamations, correspondence, and panegyric poetry—this chapter provides the verbal articulation of caliphal ideology necessary to appreciate the visual means and forms discussed in the next chapter. Chapter 2 investigates how both monumental construction as well as public ceremony and ritual action visibly represented and reinforced Andalusi Umayyad caliphal authority, drawing the reader into the experience of caliphal rule. The discussion demonstrates how the ideological competition between the three caliphates of the tenth century stimulated and informed the elaboration of political culture in al-Andalus. Chapter 3 ends Part 1 with a discussion of how a client of the dynasty subsequently manipulated elements of Andalusi Umayyad caliphal ideology to support his rule.

Part 2 of the book analyzes Andalusi historiography, exploring how partisans of the Umayyad dynasty expressed the caliphs' legitimacy in historical terms. Like their Abbasid and Fatimid rivals, the Andalusi Umayyads viewed history as an important medium for the assertion of legitimacy, and promoted historical revisionism. As the first half of the book demonstrates, the Andalusi Umayyad caliphs claimed to have revived the caliphate of their Syrian ancestors. They staked their legitimacy in the past, argued for the historical continuity of their authority, and pointed to the record of their reigns as evidence that God was on their side. Chapter 4 investigates how contemporary Andalusi historians anticipated ʻAbd al Raḥmān III's caliphate and restoration of his dynasty's fortunes in their representations of the Muslim conquest of the Iberian peninsula and the foundation of Umayyad rule. Chapter 5 highlights how, in a more general manner, the historiography of the caliphal period expressed confidence in Umayyad rule and celebrated the strength of Islam on the peninsula and illustrates how later historians reflected back on the caliphate as a golden age. The Andalusi Umayyad caliphs presided over a political culture that supported and reinterpreted their view of their rule. The historical texts under examination were both products of the culture and purveyors of ideology. The discussion of historiography thus deepens our understanding of the persuasive power of Andalusi Umayyad legitimacy.

Part I

MAKING THE CLAIM: CALIPHAL ARTICULATIONS OF LEGITIMACY

· ONE ·

Defining the Caliphate

With him the age gone by has returned, and the worn-out reign has been renewed.[1]

—Ibn 'Abd Rabbihi (d. 940)

At the age of twenty-one, 'Abd al-Raḥmān III (r. 912–961) ascended the throne in the palace, or *qaṣr,* of Cordoba as the designated successor of his grandfather, the amir 'Abd Allāh. He was the eighth Umayyad to rule the Iberian peninsula since his ancestor 'Abd al-Raḥmān (I) ibn Mu'āwiya escaped death at the hands of the Abbasids and established his reign in al-Andalus in 756. 'Abd al-Raḥmān III's predecessors on the peninsula had ruled as independent amirs and styled themselves "the sons of caliphs" and "kings," neither recognizing the authority of the Abbasid caliphate nor asserting their own counterclaim to the leadership of the Muslims.[2] In 929, however, 'Abd al-Raḥmān III took the dramatic step of assuming the title of Commander of the Faithful (*amīr al-mu'minīn*) and asserted the prerogatives of *khuṭba* and *sikka.*[3] Now every Friday, by his command, in every congregational mosque of his domains, the preacher (*khaṭīb*) followed the sermon (*khuṭba*) with an invocation of God's blessing on the caliph, referring to him by his title of Commander of the Faithful and his *laqab* or regnal name, before the assembled male population. This was one widely recognized way for the caliph to broadcast his title and assert his sovereignty; another was to strike gold coins inscribed with his name and title (*sikka*).[4] The coins of the realm of the independent amirs had been silver dirhams bearing dates and the location of the mint but not the names of the rulers. For 150 years, since the fall of the Umayyad caliphate in the east, no gold coins had been struck in al-Andalus.[5] When 'Abd al-Raḥmān III put gold dinars into circulation bearing his names and titles, he announced his caliphal status and the dawning of a new era.

'Abd al-Raḥmān III's symbolic actions declared his caliphal pretensions to the inhabitants of al-Andalus and all in contact with them. How did he invest the symbols with meaning? How did he articulate his right to rule the Muslims and define his authority as Commander of the Faithful?

'Abd al-Raḥmān III and his successor al-Ḥakam II represented and elaborated their caliphal legitimacy through public proclamations and correspondence. This book's narrative discussion of the evidence closely examines how the caliphs chose certain occasions to make statements about their rule and how the words they used spoke to specific circumstances at the same time that they evinced broader themes. The basic related themes of the argument for Umayyad legitimacy were constantly reiterated in reference to Umayyad rule of al-Andalus and Umayyad policy in North Africa. They included the following assertions: the caliphs inherited their authority; their commitment to the unification of the community and their dedication to the suppression of heresy and the restoration of the Islam of the righteous ancestors demonstrated their leadership of the Muslims; their success and the prosperity of the kingdom proved God's favor. The evidence of the caliphal texts alone quickly disposes of the idea that the Andalusi Umayyad caliphs did not claim responsibility for the spiritual as well as temporal welfare of the Muslims or that they "lacked the attributes usually associated with the command of the faithful."[6] Here, and in the discussion that follows, we also show how even though the Andalusi Umayyad caliphs denied the legitimacy of the Abbasids and Fatimids, their self-representation involved both renunciation of the rival caliphates and identification with them, both differentiation from and assimilation of their models.

TRIUMPH OVER BOBASTRO

'Abd al-Raḥmān III came to power after half a century of rampant rebellion had reduced Umayyad rule to Cordoba and its immediate environs.[7] The new ruler embarked on a virtual reconquest of the peninsula and finally secured control over the heart of al-Andalus with the defeat of the Banū Ḥafṣūn in 928. 'Umar ibn Ḥafṣūn and then his sons had fomented revolt for decades from their mountain fastness of Bobastro, south of Cordoba, defying Umayyad rule and Umayyad armies and even marching on the Umayyad capital.

'Abd al-Raḥmān III identified his defeat of the Banū Ḥafṣūn and triumph over the previously invincible fortress of Bobastro as a signal event in the history of the peninsula. In a letter announcing the victory, read in all the congregational mosques, he described how Bobastro had served as a base for the sedition that had spread throughout the land, laying waste to crops and depopulating cities for fifty years. In his words, no one had been able to overcome the rebellion or prevail over Bobastro until God granted him success. He recounted how, since the first days of his reign, he had dedicated himself entirely to the suppression of every revolt, fortress by fortress, campaign by campaign, pursuing his enemies to every mountain crag and peak, gradually imposing obedience and restoring security and tranquility. Bobastro represented the culmination of his efforts and he described his systematic tightening of the stranglehold on the fortress until surrender was inevitable. Finally, he reported on the evacuation of the inhabitants and the destruction of all the buildings and gardens so that it was rendered "emptier than the desert and more desolate than a tomb."[8]

'Abd al-Raḥmān III used his military triumph as the basis for reviving Umayyad claims to the caliphate, proclaiming himself Commander of the Faithful after this victory and those that immediately ensued and taking a *laqab* that celebrated his military prowess: al-Nāṣir li-Dīn Allāh, Champion of the Religion of God.[9] In his announcement to the governors of the realm informing them of his adoption of the title of Commander of the Faithful, he pointed to his reconquest of the peninsula as evidence of divine favor and of his worthiness for the office: "God has favored us, He has shown His preference for us, He has established our authority and has allowed us to realize His success with ease. He has achieved His wishes through our rule, spread our fame to the far horizons, and extended our command over the land. He has hung the hope of the two worlds on us and brought those who deviated back to us so that they rejoiced in the shadow of our rule."[10] 'Abd al-Raḥmān III followed the logic of his assumption of the caliphal titles by challenging the legitimacy of the Abbasid and Fatimid caliphates. He asserted in his announcement: "Anyone else who uses the title [of *amīr al-mu'minīn*] is an imposter who appropriates what is not rightly his."[11]

The two extant public circulars in which 'Abd al-Raḥmān III described the conquest and destruction of Bobastro prepared the way for his announcement of his adoption of the caliphal dignity and demonstrate how he developed his reconquest of al-Andalus into a foundation for his caliphal legitimacy. In these circulars, 'Abd al-Raḥmān III represented his pursuit and defeat of the rebels that plagued Umayyad rule of al-Andalus as holy war against the polytheists (*al-mushrikūn*). Many of the supporters of the Banū Ḥafṣūn and their allies were from families that had recently converted to Islam from Christianity or were in fact Christian, and contemporary historians reported that when the bodies of 'Umar ibn Ḥafṣūn and his son Ja'far were exhumed, their burial positions proved that they had apostatized to Christianity.[12] 'Abd al-Raḥmān III also identified 'Umar ibn Ḥafṣūn as a former partisan of the Shi'i cause, claiming in his announcement of the destruction of the congregational mosque of Bobastro that the name of the Fatimid imam had been invoked from its pulpit.[13] Whatever the confessional allegiances of the Banū Ḥafṣūn over the course of their rebellion, ʻAbd al-Raḥmān III referred to Bobastro as the base of polytheism and the strength and refuge of Christianity and more generally as the abode of unbelief and falsehood (*dār al-kufr wa-l-ifk*), the place of error (*buqʻat al-ḍalālā*), the pulpit of discord (*minbar al-khilāf*), the den of iniquity (*maʻdin al-ghawāya*), and the city of criminals (*madīnat al-mujrimīn*).[14] In short, he defined his enemies as the enemies of God and himself as the warrior against the polytheism (*shirk*), hypocrisy and apostasy (*nifāq*), and schism (*shiqāq*) that filled the land.[15]

ʻAbd al-Raḥmān III professed his determination to bring those who deviated back to the true path and to destroy those who refused, as service to God. He attributed his success to God's help and suggested that he earned God's favor through his devotion to His service: "Praise God who has decreed glory to whomever obeys Him and humiliation to whomever resists. . . . He does not cease to promote Islam and the person who upholds it, and favors and assists him who propagates and supports it."[16]

ʻAbd al-Raḥmān III's representation of his military campaigns as holy war to extend the domains of the faith and to return those who were misguided to the fold established his credentials as a good Muslim ruler. Court poets celebrated and promoted every one of his campaigns in terms such as those Ibn ʻAbd Rabbihi used on the occasion of ʻAbd al-Raḥmān III's departure for campaign in Monteleon: "Your armies are divine help and support, extending God's mercy to the horizons." When the Umayyad ruler set out for the territory controlled by the Banū Ḥafṣūn, the poet said: "God has shown Islam a path and the people have entered into the religion in a rush."[17] Commemorating ʻAbd al-Raḥmān III's capture of Carmona, the poet proclaimed that his patron "straightened the path of righteousness from its deviation" and that through his efforts "religion revives after stumbling . . . , infidelity has been shaken to its foundations, and the head of hypocrisy has been cut at the neck."[18] On hearing the news of ʻAbd al-Raḥmān III's triumphant entry into Bobastro, the poet Abū ʻUthmān ʻUbayd Allāh ibn Yaḥyā ibn

Idrīs proclaimed: "Truly this is how God champions His champion!"[19]

'Abd al-Raḥmān III used the occasion of his victory over Bobastro to expand his spiritual and political claims. He presented his success in holy war as proof that God had chosen him to be caliph and Commander of the Faithful. The opening passages of the first announcement of the conquest of Bobastro provide this interpretive context for the news and develop its significance as evidence of 'Abd al-Raḥmān III's specifically caliphal authority. The text begins by recalling the history of God's agency on earth: God sent the prophets and revealed the books and then sent Muḥammad as the seal of prophets, the messenger of the rewards and punishments to come, and the guide to the truth; after Muḥammad's death, God established the caliphate (succession) of the Prophet and the imamate of His religion. The text goes on to define the attributes and responsibilities of the caliphs: God chose the preferred of His creation—the best of His worshipers, who were God-fearing and pleasing to Him, who commanded authority and inspired trust, who followed the traditions (*sunan*) and extinguished sedition (*fitan*). Then the text underscores 'Abd al-Raḥmān III's own qualifications by stating that ever since God had honored him with His caliphate and distinguished him with the imamate of His worshipers, he never ceased to combat His enemies. Finally, the text presents the account of his efforts described above.[20] With these passages, 'Abd al-Raḥmān III established himself as the latest heir to a chain of authority going back to the Prophet and represented the defeat of the rebels to his rule as the fulfillment of his caliphal mandate to suppress sedition.

'Abd al-Raḥmān III's representation of his military successes as evidence of his caliphal authority achieved a certain currency and was reflected back to him in the words of those who submitted to his rule. When the lord of Alhama and his son sought a grant of security in exchange for their obedience, for example, the son referred to 'Abd al-Raḥmān III's success in restoring security to the kingdom as an indication of God's favor and acknowledged him as the divinely appointed heir to the caliphate of the rightly guided imams.[21]

The Andalusi Umayyad caliph articulated his legitimacy in terms of his prosecution of holy war but, more particularly, emphasized his aggressive defense of the faith and the community against deviance and factionalism. In this way, ʿAbd al-Raḥmān III expressed his authority in terms that spoke to his immediate environment but also addressed and reflected his rivalry with the Fatimids and, less directly, with the Abbasids. This other dimension of his rhetoric emerges more clearly as we examine how ʿAbd al-Raḥmān III represented his authority and justified his ambitions to the Berber allies he cultivated in common cause against the Fatimids.[22]

CAMPAIGNS IN NORTH AFRICA

The general historical context in which ʿAbd al-Raḥmān made his bid to the caliphate was essentially defined by the growing power of the Ismaʿili Shiʿi Fatimids and the apparent weakness of the Abbasid caliphate. The Fatimids emerged in North Africa at the beginning of the tenth century and, with the help of the might of the Kutāma Berbers, conquered Ifriqiya from the Aghlabids, a dynasty of independent governors who formally recognized Abbasid suzerainty. In 910 the man who called himself ʿAbd Allāh Abū Muḥammad and declared himself Commander of the Faithful and the Imam Rightly Guided by God, al-Mahdī Billāh, had the *khuṭba* said in his name in the former Aghlabid capital of Raqqāda and in Qayrawān.[23] The Fatimid movement (*daʿwa*) and newly founded polity were expansionary. By the next year al-Mahdī (r. 909–934) was organizing campaigns eastward, intending the conquest of Egypt and perhaps aspiring to the conquest of Baghdad and even Constantinople, in fulfillment of the prophecies about the arrival of the messianic figure of the Mahdi that had been circulating in Shiʿi circles at least since the ninth century.[24] At the same time, the Fatimid caliph kept a vigilant eye on the western fringes of his domain and sent his armies to suppress rebellion and the encroachment of hostile tribes.

The Fatimids posed a threat to Umayyad rule in their growing strength in North Africa and their secret missionary activities in al-Andalus.[25] In 917, in response to an appeal for help, 'Abd al-Raḥmān III became involved in North Africa in support of Berber tribes resistant to Fatimid rule, sending them generous gifts, supplies, and military and naval support. His involvement intensified after he became Commander of the Faithful and secured the allegiance of the Zanāta tribal chief Muḥammad Ibn Khazar and his brothers and son. Other allies soon followed, including the Miknāsa chief Mūsā ibn Abī al-'Āfiya, former Fatimid governor of Fez, and their alliances extended 'Abd al-Raḥmān III's suzerainty over the far western Maghrib.[26] In 931 his forces occupied the strategic port of Ceuta, which opened the way to further expansion. In his correspondence with the Berber chieftains, the Andalusi Umayyad caliph declared his intentions to extend his rule across North Africa and beyond to the holy cities, Egypt, Syria, and further east, challenging the similar ambitions of his Fatimid rivals and asserting his own claims to universal rule. His allies communicated their shared commitment to the propagation of his authority to the east and the west, over desert and plain, land and sea, even to the "farthest ends of Iraq."[27]

'Abd al-Raḥmān III presented himself in this context as the defender of the true faith against deviance, of the religion of the Prophet against false prophecy, of the Sunna against heretical innovation, and of the Qur'an against corruption, while his correspondents addressed him in the same terms, describing their dedication to the fight against the traitor of the faith, the great impostor, and pledging the elimination of that faction of error (*al-ḍalāla*) and unbelief (*al-kufr*).[28] Defense of the faith meant active engagement with, and pursuit of, the enemy. As 'Abd al-Raḥmān III wrote, conquest and the extension of his sovereignty were part of his divine mission to purify the faith of all corruptions and bring about the revival of the religion (*iḥyā' al-dīn*).[29]

Echoing and appropriating the messianic propaganda of his Fatimid rivals, he suggested that his role in this mission was anticipated by well-known signs (*al-āthār al-mashhūra*) and frequently mentioned traditions (*al-riwāyāt al-madhkūra*) and that his sense of destiny guided him in his expansionary efforts.[30]

In his mission against the Fatimids the caliph presented himself as upholder of the one true faith, and in this sense he defined the way to salvation. The correspondence between the caliph and his allies clearly associated recognition of ʿAbd al-Raḥmān III's legitimacy with the straight path and refusal to do so as deviation. In a passage in a letter to the Miknāsa chief Mūsā ibn Abī al-ʿĀfiya, urging him to call the people to obedience to the Commander of the Faithful, ʿAbd al-Raḥmān III identified himself as the One Who Upholds the Truth, the Champion of the Religion of God (al-Qā'im bil-Ḥaqq, al-Nāṣir li-Dīn Allāh). ʿAbd al-Raḥmān III's *laqab,* al-Nāṣir li-Dīn Allāh, is here coupled with a *laqab* that recalls that of the Fatimid heir-designate, al-Qā'im bi-Amr Allāh, with its eschatological connotation of the one who will usher in the *qiyāma* or day of Resurrection.[31] By appropriating his rival's name, ʿAbd al-Raḥmān III intimated that he, not the Fatimid, was God's chosen leader of the Muslims and that he, not the Fatimid, was the long-awaited Qā'im who would restore them to the faith after they had fallen into error. This meant, in fact, the intended defeat of the impostor and his misguided followers and the restoration of the community to the traditional interpretation of the faith. In his letter, ʿAbd al-Raḥmān III elaborated that he was the one who sustained the right path (*hudan*) of the rightly guided caliphs, the one who rejected all innovation (*bidʿa*), extirpated all error (*ḍalāla*), and clarified all doubts (*shubha*). To follow him was to follow the right path; to obey him was to please God. Only someone who had separated from the truth would turn away or refuse to do so.[32]

In this context too, ʿAbd al-Raḥmān III staked his claim to be Champion of the Religion of God on the traditional legal and religious authority of the four rightly guided caliphs who succeeded the Prophet and on the historical authority of the Umayyad dynasty whose caliphate he claimed to restore. As the eleventh-century historian Ibn Ḥayyān records, ʻAbd al-Raḥmān III wrote to the Berber chieftains across the straits of Gibraltar reminding them of their historic loyalty to the Umayyad dynasty. He received, in response, recognition that the Umayyads had introduced the Berbers to Islam and that he was therefore their master (*mawlā*) and other earnest affirmations of the legitimacy of his *dawla*, or reign, and that of his ancestors.[33]

As he intimated when he announced his adoption of the caliphal titles and prerogatives, ʻAbd al-Raḥmān III challenged the legitimacy of the Abbasids as well as the Fatimids. Over a century and a half after the Abbasid revolution toppled the Syrian Umayyad caliphate, ʻAbd al-Raḥmān III described his territorial ambitions in North Africa and further east in terms of the recovery of his lost patrimony—the inheritance that had been unjustly denied him by the Abbasids.[34] This representation of the caliph's cause and characterization of Abbasid rule shaped the way ʻAbd al-Raḥmān III's allies communicated with him. When the Zanāta chief Muḥammad ibn Khazar acknowledged the Umayyad's caliphate, he explicitly rejected the possibility of Abbasid leadership (because it was illegitimate) in this time of crisis. He wrote that he had been inclined to turn to the Abbasid imam for help against the evil spread by the Fatimids, until God intervened and "I realized, Commander of the Faithful, that you are the most legitimate claimant to the caliphate [*āḥaqq al-nās bil-khilāfa*], that it is your inheritance, and that no one can challenge you in this unless he rejects the truth and renounces God and His Prophet."[35] Ibn Khazar then assured the caliph that he dedicated himself, thereafter, to the recovery of the territorial inheritance of ʻAbd al-Raḥmān III's ancestors, "the honored, pious, and good caliphs."[36]

ʻAbd al-Raḥmān III defined his authority to the North Africans in terms of his dedicated championship of the true faith, on the one hand, and his dynastic inheritance, on the other, at a time when the Abbasid caliphate appeared particularly weak and could not either offer the kind of support and protection the Umayyad caliph could provide or challenge his dynastic claims.[37] The Abbasid caliph al-Muqtadir (r. 908–932), a puppet of his courtiers and commanders, failed to suppress the Fatimid movement or to protect Mecca from destruction by the Qarmatians in 930, exposing the weakness of his rule and undermining Abbasid legitimacy.[38] The situation only deteriorated after his assassination. For more than a decade the caliphate was manipulated by generals who raised and removed caliphs while the authority of the government of Baghdad did not extend much beyond Iraq, until the Imami Shi'i Buyids became the masters of the Abbasid caliphate in 945. This context lent the Andalusi Umayyad's claims to the Command of the Faithful added currency within his sphere of influence because his rule, in contrast, was strong, and the prospects of his dynasty ascendant.

'Abd al-Raḥmān III became actively involved in the politics of North Africa after he had assumed the caliphal dignity, revived the fortunes of his dynasty, and demonstrated his authority at home; his involvement abroad grew out of a momentum he had generated on the Iberian peninsula.[39] The Berber chieftains who sought his help against the Fatimids or responded favorably to his calls for allegiance were attracted by what he could offer, already impressed by his achievements and the strength of his firm rule. As Ibn Khazar put it, 'Abd al-Raḥmān III's reign (*dawla*) offered security and peace in this world and the next to whomever would grab hold of it.[40]

'Abd al-Raḥmān III articulated his legitimacy in two realms, the domestic one of al-Andalus and the larger one of the Dār al-Islām, but addressed both as he did so. His representation as a Mahdi-like figure is an example of the multireferential quality of his appeal. As we have seen, 'Abd al-Raḥmān III manipulated the eschatological elements of Fatimid propaganda to promote his own cause in North Africa, claiming that it was his reign, not that of the Fatimid imam al-Mahdī or of al-Mahdī's son al-Qā'im, that was anticipated by signs and prophecies and that he, not the Fatimid, would recover the legacy of the Prophet and destroy the impostors. His rule in al-Andalus supported this manipulation. According to Isma'ili doctrine, the Mahdi would come to power and, by the sword, put an end to the *fitna* (violent discord) that had divided the Muslims since Muḥammad's death, restore the purity of the faith after its degradation, and fill the world with justice, harmony, and prosperity; Fatimid propagandists represented their caliph in these terms.[41] 'Abd al-Raḥmān III represented his rule similarly: by his sword he put an end to *fitna,* and through his reign God purified al-Andalus of all evil and established the religion there as it had been when He perfected it for His worshipers; his rule brought widespread justice, prosperity, and tranquility.[42] This vision of the new regime bringing the restoration of the original principles of the faith echoed the (unfulfilled) promises of the Abbasid *da'wa* and revolution as well, giving 'Abd al-Raḥmān III's words a double resonance.

The caliph's partisans echoed the theme: 'Abd al-Raḥmān III reunited the community, eradicated the corruptions of the faith, restored justice, and revived the land as rain after drought.[43] His rule was divinely sanctioned; he was God's caliph, chosen over all creation, marked by visible signs and the divine illumination in his face.[44] By his sword, he "sewed this world together after it had been split apart," and through him "God allayed the blaze of civil strife [*fitna*] and the people became united in reconciliation and the sheep and wolf grazed together after the wars had lain down their arms."[45] The court poet Ismā'īl ibn Badr likened 'Abd al-Raḥmān III's armies to those of the Last Day and averred that God had decreed that they would always triumph over his enemies.[46] According to the contemporary historian Ibn Maslama, God illuminated the darkness with the caliph's reign, or in the words of Ismā'īl ibn Badr, "he is the full moon of kings, the radiance of his sunna dispels the darkness from the religion and the world."[47]

'Abd al-Raḥmān III's ability to impose order and command respect after decades of strife invited his representation as

Mahdi-like, particularly as the period of *fitna* had generated anxiety about the fate of the Muslims on the peninsula—anxiety that found expression in apocalyptic predictions.[48] 'Abd al-Malik ibn Ḥabīb's ninth-century history, for example, contains numerous predictions of the imminent apocalypse, including the devastation of Cordoba. One prediction implicitly associates the destruction of al-Andalus with the reign of the amir 'Abd Allāh, 'Abd al-Raḥmān III's predecessor.[49]

'Abd al-Raḥmān III could promote his rule in these terms and remain within the bounds of what had become Sunni precedent. After all, propagandists for the Abbasids had also described their cause in similar language (originally adopted from Shi'i messianism) and portrayed their caliph as a Mahdi figure. 'Abd al-Raḥmān III, in his own efforts to establish the legitimacy of a newly proclaimed caliphate, now used the messianic language of revolution to mark the transition in al-Andalus from a state of disorder and corruption to a state of restored order and renewed faith. Although the Shi'is had endowed the term *al-Mahdī* with special meaning and apocalyptic connotations, in its meaning of "rightly guided" the usage of the term had Umayyad precedents. Some of 'Abd al-Raḥmān III's caliphal ancestors in Damascus were celebrated as rightly guided (*mahdī*) imams who showed humanity the way to salvation after *fitna,* like a beacon in the darkness, and in this way appeared as redemptive figures.[50]

'Abd al-Raḥmān III exploited Fatimid propaganda about the arrival of the Mahdi to exalt his reign, identify it with future promise, and express competition with his rivals. He did not go so far as to claim transcendent authority. Recall that in communication with his allies in North Africa he defined his authority in terms that specifically denounced Fatimid ideology. He opposed the Fatimids' belief in the imam's divine inspiration, decried their rejection of the authority of the first three caliphs and the Sunna recognized by the consensus of the majority, and opposed their esoteric interpretation of the Qur'an.

Reviewing the Bobastro circulars, we can read the refutation of Fatimid ideology as a subtext and appreciate the dual resonance of the caliph's statements about his triumph over the Banū Ḥafṣūn. As we have seen, 'Abd al-Raḥmān III declared that the historical responsibility of the caliphate was to follow the Sunna (which the Fatimids rejected) and eliminate *fitna* (which they fomented). When he asserted that the caliphs of the past were all chosen by God, he countered the Fatimid rejection of the first three caliphs. At the same time, he implied that it was God's designation, not blood descent from Muḥammad, that determined who was the legitimate leader of the Muslims. He upheld a chain of authority that extended from the Prophet and the rightly guided caliphs through the Umayyad dynasty to himself, rejecting both Fatimid and Abbasid dynastic claims.[51]

'Abd al-Raḥmān III's representation of his rule always had local and universal dimensions, as specific terms and emphases came into focus, faded, or evolved in response to circumstances. Examining how he used an eight-year-long campaign against a heresy in al-Andalus to promote his legitimacy provides another view of this process. 'Abd al-Raḥmān III reiterated the familiar themes, this time addressing the problem of a charismatic challenge to the consensus and authority of the *'ulamā'* and ultimately, as he represented it, to his own guardianship of the faith. This context, like the North African context, gave the caliph the opportunity to elaborate the religious dimension of his authority. In both he identified himself with the "true faith," but in response to this challenge there is a different emphasis in the way he represented the caliphal mandate to uphold the model of the rightly guided caliphs, preserve the Sunna, and protect the Qur'an.

THE SUPPRESSION OF IBN MASARRA'S HERESY

The "heresy" advanced by the teachings of an Andalusi named Ibn Masarra included ideas historically popular in some circles in the east. Ibn Masarra aroused the suspicion of the Andalusi *'ulamā'* both for his ideas and for his withdrawal from the community. The contemporary historian Aḥmad al-Rāzī (d. 955), or his son 'Īsā (d. 989), describes Muḥammad ibn 'Abd Allāh ibn Masarra (d. 931) as a man of great erudition and persuasive powers who deviated from the faith in his belief in the createdness of the Qur'an and human free will and in his rejection of the intercession of the Prophet on behalf of the repentant sinner. In the historian's words, he seduced many believers from the true path of the Sunna, thereby undermining the unity of the community. After his death early in 'Abd al-Raḥmān III's reign, these followers of his continued to propagate his beliefs. As al-Rāzī reports, their activities aroused the consternation of the legal and religious scholars of Cordoba, who warned 'Abd al-Raḥmān III. On investigation, we are told, he dedicated his attention to the eradication of this sect (*firqa*), fulfilling his charge as caliph.[52]

In the course of this campaign, 'Abd al-Raḥmān III issued a number of circulars that described his determination to suppress Ibn Masarra's followers and advertised his efforts. Ibn Ḥayyān's history, based on the work of al-Rāzī, mentions three occasions when the caliph's orders to his minister in charge of the administration of the city (*ṣāḥib al-madīna*) were publicly read: the first in the congregational mosques of Cordoba and Madīnat al-Zahrā' (May 952), the second and third at the entrances of the congregational mosque of Cordoba (June 956 and the same letter again in November 957).[53] Ibn Ḥayyān also includes the text of a circular on the matter sent to be read in all the cities of the caliph's domain.[54]

In these texts, 'Abd al-Raḥmān III again represented himself as the champion of the faith against deviation and as guardian of the community against *fitna*. As in his announcement of the conquest of Bobastro, he portrayed himself as the scourge of God delivering His punishment (sura 11:76) and quoted a number of Qur'anic verses about the dangers of factionalism and divergent opinions, warning his audience against them: "Do you not see how those who dispute the revelations of God turn away from the right path? Those who have denied the Book and the message We sent through Our apostles shall realize the truth hereafter, when with chains and shackles round their necks, they shall be dragged through scalding water and then burnt in the fire of Hell" (sura 40:69–70).[55]

'Abd al-Raḥmān III used Qur'anic verses such as these to characterize Ibn Masarra's followers as the ignorant and unguided who "wrangle about God" and lead others astray. This was potent language, effective in condemning these Muslims as a danger to the community and the faith. By using Qur'anic terms, the caliph also created an identification between his time and the time of the revelation and, most important, between himself and the Prophet. We have already seen how 'Abd al-Raḥmān III described the caliphs as the successors of the Prophet responsible for the defense of the *umma* and the religion. Although they did not receive revelation, the caliphs, like Muḥammad, acted as guides and warners for the Muslims.

In the context of his persecution of Ibn Masarra's *firqa* in the 950s, 'Abd al-Raḥmān III expressly identified himself with the model of the Prophet—the *mahdī* metaphor was not here appropriate—and defined orthodoxy specifically as the Maliki rite or "school" of law (*madhhab*).[56] Al-Rāzī's summary of 'Abd al-Raḥmān III's circular of 952 shows us how the caliph logically connected the model of the Prophet with his promotion of the Maliki *madhhab*. As al-Rāzī tells it, the caliph reminded the audience that he was charged by God with the guardianship of His religion, just as his ancestors had been. He characterized this guardianship as condemning heresies and following the path of the community and the model of the people of Medina. He explained that Medina was the bastion of the faith and the honored refuge of the Prophet in life and death and that its people had been granted the privilege of adherence to the unanimous tradition (*al-sunna al-mujma'a 'alayhā*).[57]

By upholding the Maliki *madhhab,* which derived from Medina and followed the *sunnat al-salaf,* or the traditions of the Prophet and his upright companions and followers, 'Abd al-Raḥmān III reinforced and refined his earlier pledge to maintain the legacy of the Prophet and follow the model of the early caliphs. This act of official sanction also firmly distinguished his caliphate from any other, and it should be noted that support of the Maliki *madhhab* continued to be a distinctive feature of the caliphate after his death.

It is in this context that al-Rāzī, perhaps drawing on another caliphal circular, uses the history of 'Abd al-Raḥmān III's rule to assert the Andalusi Umayyad's legitimacy in opposition to his Abbasid rivals. In a summary of 'Abd al-Raḥmān III's persecution of Ibn Masarra's *firqa,* the historian repeats the formula that the responsibilities of the caliphate are the preservation of the tenets of the faith, following the model of the Prophet, and maintaining the norms of the Sunna. He describes how all the caliphs, following the Prophet's death until the rise of the Abbasids, protected the community from innovation and suspicious influences by "fighting for God with the sword of God so that truth triumphed over falsehood," humbling rebels such as the Kharijis and Shi'is (*al-rāfiḍa*), and extinguishing the fires of sedition.[58]

Al-Rāzī describes the Abbasids as a "deviant faction" who neglected the responsibilities of rule. As he elaborates, they failed to prevent the ignorant and perverse from spreading false ideas, as was their mandate, and as their predecessors had done. Order collapsed with the proliferation of factions, and the religion was undermined by the promulgation of innovations. In contrast, al-Rāzī points out, the Umayyads guarded the religion from such calamity in al-Andalus, where God's chosen Commander of the Faithful followed in the footsteps of the caliphs and imams, and his fathers and forefathers, upholding the Book and promoting the Sunna.[59]

Clearly echoing 'Abd al-Raḥmān III's self-representation, al-Rāzī points to the caliph's military achievements to confirm his legitimacy. He notes how, with God's help, the Andalusi Umayyad caliph fought for, and defended, the religion: no devil raised a horn that was not broken, no standard of perdition was raised that was not brought low. In him, God united the community, and when the community showed obedience to him, God extended to it security and tranquility, prosperity and felicity. His fame spread so that people in the Mashriq vied with each other, seeking his support and refuge in his domain.[60]

As the historian continues, Cordoba became the cultural center of the time, and al-Andalus became the one place where the ruler's vigilance and zeal ensured the support of God's law (the Sharīʿa) and the renewal of the religion. This he associates with the preservation of the most authoritative readings of the Qur'an, adherence to the Maliki *madhhab,* and the extirpation of all heretical innovation.[61]

Al-Rāzī's account presents a concise example of how ʿAbd al-Raḥmān III translated his strong rule of al-Andalus into a platform for his caliphate. The historian heralded ʿAbd al-Raḥmān III's establishment of political and religious unity in al-Andalus and implied that the revival of the Umayyad caliphate would see the restoration of the covenant between God and His caliphs betrayed by the Abbasids, who did not keep a firm grasp on the reins of power.[62]

With security established, prosperity followed. During the second half of his rule, ʿAbd al-Raḥmān III enjoyed the fruits of his labors, added luster to his rule, and promoted his caliphate by cultivating his capital as a center of culture and learning. He undertook monumental construction and elaborated protocol and ceremony (as is discussed in chapter 2). But even in these circumstances, he did not neglect the fundamental mandate of the caliphate: defense and support of the religion and the community. Although ʿAbd al-Raḥmān III stopped leading campaigns personally after thirty years of rule, he continued his commitment to fight God's enemies on two fronts: North Africa and the Christian territories of the Iberian peninsula. He sent armies, fleets, weapons, provisions, and money to North Africa, responding readily to appeals for help by allies and enemies of the Fatimids. The thirteenth-century historian Ibn ʿIdhārī reports that as an expression of his continuing zeal, ʿAbd al-Raḥmān III ordered that the Shiʿis be cursed publicly from all the minbars of al-Andalus in 955 and in 956 launched a naval attack on the North African coast, perhaps intending to bombard the Fatimid capital of al-Mahdiyya.[63] At the same time, he regularly launched raiding expeditions into the *dār al-harb*, or domain of war, to his north. As part of a project to secure the frontiers, he sponsored the reconstruction of abandoned border towns and fortresses that also served as bases for aggressive attacks in the Christian territories.[64] In constant contact with his commanders and allies, the caliph ensured that the news of victories was read to his subjects from the Great Mosques of Cordoba and Madīnat al-Zahrā'.[65]

THE REIGN OF AL-ḤAKAM II

Al-Ḥakam II al-Mustanṣir Billāh (r. 961–976), 'Abd al-Raḥmān III's successor, assumed the *laqab* "The One Who Seeks Victory with God's Assistance." He had gone on campaigns as a boy with his father and continued to pursue his father's policy of aggressive defense of the faith. At home he punished deviants like "Abū Khayr," who was accused of a range of unorthodox beliefs and offensive behavior, including Shi'i affiliation.[66] He conducted holy war against the neighboring Christian kingdoms, in the first few years of his reign personally commanding successful campaigns to the north, and he maintained an active involvement in North Africa.[67] Thus the articulation of Andalusi Umayyad caliphal legitimacy continued to celebrate the caliph's prosecution of holy war as news of victories continued to be read from the minbars.

The extant fragment of Ibn Ḥayyān's history of al-Ḥakam II's reign from 971 to 975, based largely on a chronicle by 'Īsā al-Rāzī, contains references to, and citations of, the caliph's correspondence with his commanders and allies in North Africa as well as a few caliphal documents. These demonstrate how the second Andalusi Umayyad caliph employed and elaborated the terms defined by his father and predecessor on the throne to justify and express his authority. The historian also records panegyric verses that give a vivid illustration of Andalusi Umayyad propaganda.

The political context of al-Ḥakam II's involvement in North Africa in this period was one of flux. At the time he ascended the throne in 961, the balance of power in North Africa favored the Fatimids. The nadir of their power had come in 945, when the Khariji rebel Abū Yazīd of the Kaydād tribe, supported by 'Abd al-Raḥmān III, reduced the Fatimid empire to the confines of al-Mahdiyya, which he kept under siege for eight months.[68] The third Fatimid imam, al-Manṣūr (r. 945–952), suppressed Abū Yazīd's revolt, and his successor, al-Mu'izz (r. 953–975), inflamed by 'Abd al-Raḥmān III's attack on the coast, gradually reduced Umayyad influence and partisanship to two strongholds: Ceuta and Tangiers. Nevertheless, al-Ḥakam II remained committed to his father's policy of supporting and sponsoring resistance against the Fatimids. Once the Fatimids decisively shifted their orientation eastward, to the Mashriq, with the conquest of Egypt in 969, he was able to reassert Umayyad interests through an accelerating commitment of resources, sending his most experienced commanders and sizable armies. In local terms, the pro-Umayyad Zanāta, joined by the Banū Ḥamdūn, confronted the pro-Fatimid Ṣanhājī Zirids, and then the Umayyad commanders Muḥammad ibn Ṭumlus and Ghālib ibn 'Abd al-Raḥmān dedicated themselves to the defeat of the turncoat Idrisids. Once significant amirs acknowledged Umayyad sovereignty, their lesser neighbors were often easily persuaded to follow suit.

Al-Ḥakam II commanded his generals to fight until all recognized his authority or fell by the sword, and in the early 970s the renegade Idrisid Hasan ibn Qannūn became the focus of his zeal.[69] As al-Ḥakam II wrote to Ghālib, he would commit every last soldier of his army and every last official of his administration to the holy war against this reprobate (*fāsiq*).[70] In their correspondence, al-Ḥakam II and his officers consistently referred to Hasan as the reprobate (*al-fāsiq*), the heretic (*al-mulḥid*), the rebel (*al-māriq*), and the tyrant (*al-ẓālim*)—terms ʿAbd al-Raḥmān III had used in his characterization of the Banū Ḥafṣūn a generation earlier. Al-Ḥakam II celebrated his eventual triumph over Ḥasan ibn Qannūn as a signal event that marked the extension of his authority over all of the western Maghrib and used the occasion to publicly articulate his legitimacy, as his father had used the triumph over Bobastro.

Al-Rāzī reports that al-Ḥakam II sent a letter announcing the surrender of Ḥasan ibn Qannūn to his governors, to be read in all the congregational mosques, and provides the text (it was written by the caliph's secretary and the prefect of Cordoba, Jaʿfar ibn ʿUthmān). This manifesto of caliphal legitimacy has a formulaic quality that is very remniscent of ʿAbd al-Raḥmān III's proclamations. Like the Bobastro circulars, the letter presents the news of the important surrender in a framing discussion of the office of the caliphate. The text explicitly establishes al-Ḥakam II's inheritance of his authority and describes his dedication to the fulfillment of his divinely charged responsibilities. Thus, after praising God, the letter begins with a brief recapitulation of the history of God's agency on earth, with a distinction between the age of the prophets (culminating in the seal of the prophets, Muḥammad) and the age of the caliphs. The letter describes Muḥammad's mission in detail before it portrays the caliphs as the Prophet's successors and God's chosen deputies who must preserve His law (*sharīʿa*) and religion against any innovation or doubt and must act as shepherds for His creatures. The first section concludes by identifying al-Ḥakam II as the latest in the chain of caliphs, each of whom inherited his role from his predecessor.[71]

Following this preamble, and again according to the Bobastro model, the letter represents al-Ḥakam II's reign as exemplary of his caliphal inheritance. As the text recounts, al-Ḥakam II dedicated himself to the office God had bestowed on him with such constancy and assiduity that the religion again flourished as it had been in the time of his forefathers. People flocked to the path he illumined for them and on which he guided them and became as brothers in their support of the truth and the pillars of the faith, while the caliph's justice brought prosperity and security to the land. Linking his rule of al-Andalus with his ambitions in North Africa, the text reports that the caliph has dedicated himself to the welfare of the Muslims wherever they may be and to the invigoration of their laws. He has decided to wage holy war against the heretical innovators, the Shi'i warriors and the imams of heterodoxy, who dared to alter these laws and violate the dictates of the Qur'an and Sunna, treating the forbidden as permissible.[72]

The balance of the letter focuses more specifically on the caliph's involvement in North Africa. It describes his cause as the rescue of those under rebel control and the "correction" of those who have deviated from the path defined by the Sunna of the Prophet and the judgments of the rightly guided (*rashīdūn*) caliphs. That is, his cause is their salvation and reconciliation to the *umma* (community). The text represents Ḥasan ibn Qannūn's submission as the triumph of the caliph's efforts: now the minbars or pulpits of the Maghrib resounded with the *da'wa* (mission) of the caliph, and the *khuṭabā'* (preachers; s. *khaṭīb*) glorified and praised God and His Prophet and called for His blessings on the Commander of the Faithful and the community of Muslims. The final paragraphs detail the submission of a number of other lords of the region who, the text reports, expressed their gratitude to the caliph for removing the harmful influence of the erroneous and misleading *firqa* by burning the minbars constructed by the Fatimids. The text goes on to say that they demonstrated their allegiance to the *madhhab al-jamā'a*, the rite of the (Sunni) community (as opposed to the Shi'i *firqa*) in the way they issued the call to prayer and conducted their prayer, in their *sikka* (striking coins in the caliph's name according to his standards), and in their legal tradition (*sunna*) and legal judgments (*aḥkām*).[73]

We have seen how 'Abd al-Raḥmān III identified himself as a prophetic warner according to Qur'anic models and the example of the Prophet in his confrontation with Ibn Masarra's followers. Here al-Ḥakam II uses the same device in another context. The letter about Ḥasan ibn Qannūn's surrender describes the Prophet's mission in a way that establishes it as a model for the caliph's own mission. In paraphrase, the text recounts that God sent Muḥammad to the people with the religion of Islam, which abrogated the other religions. He clarified the way to belief through Muḥammad and supported him with the Qur'an and the irrefutable proofs. Muḥammad called the people to God and guided them, introducing them to the prescriptions of obedience to Him and showing them the conduct they should follow to reach the Garden. He explained what was permitted and forbidden, what was required, and what was customary. He showed them the correct path and guided them along the clear road, informing them that Islam was the religion of the chosen, demonstrating His preference in His words: "Truly the religion of God is Islam" (sura 9:40), "He who looks for a religion that is not Islam will not be accepted and in the next life will be lost" (sura 3:17), and "Truly God has chosen for you a religion, do not die except as Muslims" (sura 2:26). Thus, the text tells us, Muḥammad undertook holy war (*jihād*) against whomever denied him or diverged from his path, until God made clear His favor by granting him victory. Then Muḥammad's followers multiplied, and the people came to him in a rush.[74]

The parallels with the way al-Ḥakam II styled himself are clear. He was prepared to wage holy war against all who "denied him or diverged from his path," but he also undertook to instruct the North Africans he "liberated" from Fatimid rule in the prescriptions of the faith, showing them the correct path (true Islam) and ensuring that they would "die as Muslims." In al-Andalus too he continued to call people to the faith and warn of the consequences of failing to heed the call. As is shown in chapter 2, the inscriptions on the entrances to the Great Mosque of Cordoba dating from al-Ḥakam II's reign echo the theme of the Qur'anic verses cited above, reminding passersby that Islam is the one true faith.

Al-Ḥakam II's representation of his involvement in North Africa as an act of warning and liberation was a recurring theme and one he broadcast abroad. For example, he ordered Ghālib to inform the subjugated population that the caliph would not abandon them and that he was dedicated to reuniting the community and reestablishing the religion.[75]

The caliph was, of course, interested in forming alliances and incorporating local North African leaders into his regime. He instructed his commanders to accept the petitions of those seeking to switch allegiances and recognize his authority, as long as they swore to fear God and obey His caliph. Al-Ḥakam II associated obedience to him to adherence to the true faith, which he described as upholding the Qur'an and the Sunna, or following the *madhhab* of the caliph. Like his father, he asserted the integrity of the Qur'an against Fatimid interpretation and used the word *sunna* to refer to the custom of the Prophet (*sunnat al-nabī*), the precedents of the *rashīdūn* caliphs, and the norms of the early community, in contrast to the Fatimids, who defined *sunna* and the law according to different authorities.[76] The *madhhab* of the caliph, as we know, was the Maliki *madhhab*.

Al-Rāzī gives us an idea of what was specifically required of those seeking an alliance with al-Ḥakam II in his redaction of a letter Ghālib sent the caliph informing him that the two amirs of Fez had sworn the oath of loyalty on behalf of their subjects. Ghālib reported that, according to al-Ḥakam II's instructions, the amirs had their oaths read in the congregational mosques of their districts. They thus publicly declared their allegiance and informed the populace that to demonstrate their obedience to the caliph and enter into the community (*al-jamā'a*) they would act in accordance with the *madhhab* of Mālik ibn Anas, the imam of the people of Medina; undertake the supererogatory practices of the month of Ramadan; and renounce all Shi'i innovations, corruptions, and alterations of the faith. As al-Rāzī reports, this public declaration was then confirmed with hostages and written oaths.[77]

Al-Rāzī provides the text of one of these written oaths of loyalty (*kitāb al-bay'a*) dated June 24, 974, and signed by the amir

'Abd al-Karīm ibn Yaḥyā and thirty-four others. The oath declares that the amir and his community swear loyalty to God and the just imam al-Ḥakam al-Mustanṣir Billāh, Commander of the Faithful, and that they will obey him, ally with his allies, and be enemies against his enemies, without duplicity and forswearing any other overlord. The signers then attested to their renunciation of all their Shi'i associations and acknowledged al-Ḥakam II's caliphate as the one that upholds the truth (*al-Qā'im bi-l-Ḥaqq*), a designation we have seen before in 'Abd al-Raḥmān III's assertion of his legitimacy against Fatimid claims.[78]

The document (*sijil*) conferring on the chief Abū al-'Aysh ibn Ayyūb officially sanctioned jurisdiction over his people among the Kutama, written as a directive from the caliph to his client, expresses the caliph's authority similarly. The client must swear to fear God and obey Him and, as in a chain of command, obey His caliph, and the caliph's commander, Ghālib, in matters of government and religion. The text also elaborates some of the specific obligations expected of local powers who have entered into obedience. The client is ordered to personally attend to the welfare of his subjects, treat them all with justice, and guide them in their religion according to the precepts of the Book and the Sunna. Addressing specific points of difference between Sunni and Shi'i practice of the faith, the text commands that prayer be performed according to the practice of the Prophet and the *rashīdūn* and as prescribed by the consensus of the Muslims, that the breaking of the fast of Ramadan begin at the sighting of the new moon, and that the *zakāt* be collected according to detailed instructions. Finally, the text concludes with the command to participate in *jihād* against those who dare defy the caliph's authority or refuse obedience to him.[79]

Al-Ḥakam II promised his subjects the temporal rewards of justice, security, and prosperity and the spiritual reward of salvation in exchange for their obedience.[80] This was reflected back to him by Muḥammad ibn Abī 'Āmir, reporting on the celebration of the *'Īd al-Aḍḥā* (feast of the sacrifice) in 973. He wrote that the Muslims of North Africa expressed their happiness in religion (*dīn*) and worldly affairs (*dunyā*) and their gratitude to God for gracing them with the favor of the Commander of the Faithful, the blessing (*baraka*) of his guidance (*hidāya*), and the felicity of his *dawla*.[81]

In the articulation of his legitimacy, al-Ḥakam II clearly reiterated the themes defined by his father: the inheritance of his authority through a chain of transmission extending back to the first caliphs, his commitment to the preservation and restoration of the purity of the faith, and his determination to defend and promote the unity of the community. Readiness to take up arms had become an established expression of legitimacy, evidence of the caliph's service in God's cause.

The nature of the caliph's authority, as articulated in the caliphal texts of both reigns, is sometimes defined in specific terms but in other instances is left somewhat ambiguous. Thus the Andalusi Umayyad caliphs claimed to follow the precedents of the rightly guided caliphs and dedicated themselves to upholding the Maliki *madhhab,* but they also represented their authority in unbounded terms: they alone defined the path to salvation, they perfected the religion, they were "the hope of the two worlds," and they even appropriated eschatological language and promised the renewal of the faith and the reign of the righteous. These are two rhetorical strategies employed in a range of contexts.

Contemporary *'ulamā'* represented the caliphs in the more circumspect terms of the guardianship of the welfare of the community. Biographies of Andalusi judges, for example, praise the caliphs' care in making appropriate appointments and record their supervision of the proper administration of the law.[82] Not surprisingly, these texts represent the ideal ruler as someone who seeks the counsel of the religious scholars. Accounts of instances in which the caliph is guided, or even humbled, by the words of a pious man of learning present the caliph as mortal and remind the reader that everyone, even the caliph, will face the Final Reckoning.[83] They also establish the supremacy of the Shari'a and the authority of the *'ulamā'*. Even so, the writings of the *'ulamā* convey respect for the caliphal office, and their words and actions reinforced the legitimacy of the caliphate.

Maribel Fierro demonstrates this point in her analysis of legal opinions and the way they acknowledge the unique legal status of the caliph. In one case, for example, the *faqīh* Qāsim ibn Asbagh was consulted about whether it was "harmful" to accept gifts from "infidel" rulers. He invoked a precedent that effectively identified 'Abd al-Raḥmān III as Commander of the Faithful and *wālī al-'ahd* (the administrator of the pact of the Muslims) to declare it was not harmful and to establish that such gifts belonged to the Muslims, not to the caliph personally.[84] In another case, the *faqīh* Isḥāq ibn Ibrāhīm declared that al-Ḥakam II must expiate his violation of the proscriptions of Ramadan by fasting rather than by feeding the poor because, as Fierro explains, a caliph had no private identity or personal property to give away. These opinions assume the legitimacy of the caliphate even if they try to legally constrain the caliph's behavior or appear to treat him harshly (Isḥāq ibn Ibrāhīm criticized the other *fuqahā'* for trying to ingratiate themselves with the Commander of the Faithful by recommending charity over fasting).[85] They offer an indication of how "official" caliphal ideology permeated and defined political culture in tenth-century al-Andalus.

At the other extreme, as active promoters of "official" caliphal ideology, court poets celebrated the caliphs on special occasions and developed and projected the themes of their legitimacy in the most overt language and emphatic manner. Like the public proclamations, the *qaṣā'id* or panegyric odes reified an event and interpreted it for an immediate audience as they addressed the Umayyad rivalry with the Abbasid and Fatimid caliphates. In fact, poets intended their words to reach the courts of the rival caliphates where other poets generated similar "propaganda."[86] In the next chapter we discuss some specific *qaṣā'id* in their ceremonial context, but here we can get a taste of how the poets in their verses not only incorporated but embellished and even exaggerated the various facets of Andalusi Umayyad legitimacy articulated by the caliphs.

Poets addressed the rivalry with the Fatimids and the Abbasids in a number of ways. Perhaps the most direct challenges to the Abbasids and the Fatimids were expressed in terms of territorial rights and ambitions. Just when the Fatimids were realizing their ambitions in Egypt and Syria, poets in the court of the Andalusi Umayyad caliph envisioned an Umayyad restoration in the east and triumph over the Abbasids in Iraq: "God decreed that his [al-Ḥakam II's] squadrons occupy the kingdoms of Iraq and Syria and the holy sites. / It is as if the waters of the Euphrates were already before us, tinted with the blood [spilled] by his cavalry."[87] In another *qaṣīda,* Ibn Shukhayṣ described al-Ḥakam II's heir Hishām as the most legitimate claimant to authority and denounced both Fatimid and Abbasid rivals. He consigned the Fatimid caliph al-Ma'add (al-Mu'izz) to hell and declared it better not to go on pilgrimage at all than do so in the name of a *rāfiḍī* apostate and scornfully described the Abbasid caliph al-Muṭī' as someone who sings and drinks while, in contrast, Hishām undertakes good works.[88] In the same *qaṣīda* the poet anticipated Hishām's conquest of Iraq (Babel) and the Hijaz (Yathrib) and his triumph (and that of the clan of 'Abd Shams) over the Banū Hāshim.[89]

In the following examples, the historical dynastic legitimacy of the Umayyads is juxtaposed against the violence and illegitimacy of the other two dynasties. In a *qaṣīda* recited for a caliphal reception in 971, the poet Muḥammad ibn Shukhayṣ portrayed the recent disaster of the Fatimid conquest of Egypt as a remote consequence of a historical failure to follow the model of the Umayyad caliph Marwān after the battle of Marj Rāhiṭ. (He also intimated that the deliverance of the people of Egypt might lie with the caliph al-Mustanṣir Billāh.)[90] In another *qaṣīda,* recited to commemorate the caliph's defeat of Ḥāsan ibn Qannūn, the same poet condemned all the Banū Hāshim (a clan designation that included Ḥasan's family the Idrisids, as well as the Fatimids and the Abbasids) and traced their evil to the murder of 'Uthmān (the third caliph and an Umayyad).[91]

The poets frequently celebrated Umayyad ancestry since this was fundamental to the caliphs' exclusive claims to legitimacy. They recalled both 'Uthmān and Marwān, in particular, but also invoked other Umayyad caliphs of the past. For example, verses praising the name and *kunya* of al-Ḥakam II's son and designated successor, Hishām Abū al-Walīd, explicitly recalled the Syrian caliphs Hishām and al-Walīd.[92] When Ibn Shukhayṣ described al-Ḥakam II as descended from 'Uthmān and modeled on 'Umar (the second caliph), he conveyed both the long history of Umayyad authority going back to 'Uthmān and the Andalusi Umayyad commitment to follow the precedents of the *rashīdūn* caliphs ('Uthmān and 'Umar).[93] Verses affirming the coherent succession of Umayyad rulers over the ages further promoted the idea of dynastic continuity: "whenever one of the kings of the house of Marwān sets, another rises."[94]

Poets frequently praised the caliphs as "God's favorite," an obvious way to promote one caliph against other contenders. As we have seen, the Andalusi Umayyad caliphs claimed that God chose them to be the successors to the *rashīdūn.* This emphasis on divine designation had polemical connotations in a context where other dynasties asserted close blood ties to the Prophet. Thus we should read such verses as more than simple flattery: "the office of the imam is an inspiration from God"; God formed and chose the caliphs and prophets "from the best clay"; the ruling caliph was the "chosen of God," "the favorite of God," "the best God sees among men," "the best of His creation."[95]

As did the caliphs themselves, poets developed a caliphal identification with the Prophet in their verses. For example, one poet declaimed that al-Ḥakam "undertook what Aḥmad [Muḥammad] conveyed from God and continued, enlightening those who did not conform."[96] Going one step further, poets challenged the Abbasids and Fatimids in their own terms, asserting the Umayyads' blood relationship with the Prophet. For example, verses referred to the heir-designate Hishām as "the chosen of the family of the Prophet" and as the one who had "the Prophet as his uncle and al-Ḥakam as his father."[97]

Poets readily celebrated the caliph in terms that echoed Fatimid representations of the imam and evoked the idea of the Mahdi, going much further than the caliphs did in their own writings. Every *qaṣīda* dedicated to al-Ḥakam II or his son used light imagery as a metaphor to express their divine favor and represent their guidance to salvation: their light dispelled the darkness and illuminated the way. The poets likened their subjects to the sun and the moon, to a blaze, a lamp, a beacon. In some verses, the poets endowed the metaphor with eschatological connotations, developing the idea of al-Ḥakam as the "Mahdī of Marwān" or playing with his designation as the divinely guided ruler, "al-Ḥakam al-Mahdī."[98] Thus 'Abd al-'Azīz al-Qarawī, appropriating the Fatimid representation of their first imam, al-Mahdī, as "the sun risen in the west," harbinger of the end times, recited: "I proclaim to all who are near and far and warn of certain truths in which I sincerely believe: / the sun of a caliphate has risen in the west which will shine with splendor in the two easts."[99] He recited this *qaṣīda* for the *'Īd al-Fiṭr* of 974, following the caliph's recent success in North Africa, and took the opportunity to predict the vindication of the Umayyad caliphate, echoing claims made by 'Abd al-Raḥmān III a generation earlier in his confrontation with the Fatimids: "Syria will rise at its appearance, for it [the western caliphate] had claims to her from long ago / and the darkness of unbelief will be dissipated with the imam's compassionate direction of the true religion."

The poets also, of course, celebrated al-Ḥakām II's rule in terms that reflected his own more sober representation of his authority. They praised his successes against God's enemies and his defense of the community and the faith and extolled his commitment to the Shari'a and the extension of justice to all. In a number of ways, and employing a number of phrases that correspond to epithets, they established that the caliph was God's agent, acting on His behalf with His support. For example, he was the trustee of God (*amīn allāh*), the rightly guided imam (*imām al-hādī*), the favored by God (*al-murtaḍī*), the champion of the religion of God (*al-nāṣir li-dīn allāh*), his father's *laqab*, and the one who seeks victory with God's assistance (*al-Mustanṣir billāh*).[100]

The poets praised the caliph and his heir not only as men of action but as men of piety and learning: "When he [al-Ḥākam] fasts, he fasts all day and stands all night reciting the Book, meditating on it and extracting its certain truths."[101] Charged with maintaining the standards of the faith and more specifically of the Maliki *madhhab*, the caliph was described as an ocean of religious knowledge (*'ilm*) whose mastery of *ḥadīth* (authoritative reports about the early community) and *ra'y* (reasoning applied in jurisprudence) was comparable to that of Mālik and al-Nakhkha'ī.[102] Al-Ḥakam II had ensured that his heir was trained in the Maliki *madhhab* by the most authoritative teacher, the shaykh 'Abd Allāh ibn Yaḥyā ibn Yaḥyā al-Laythī, whose father had taught both al-Ḥakam II and 'Abd al-Raḥmān III, so even while al-Ḥakam II's son was still a boy, Ibn Shukhayṣ identified him as the one who upholds the *'ilm* of Mālik and the *riwāya* (transmission) of Yaḥyā and Ibn Wahb and Ashhab.[103]

The poets followed their patrons in their projection of local successes into grander achievements. With God's will, and according to His design, first 'Abd al-Raḥmān III, then al-Ḥakam II, then later Hishām al-Mu'ayyad billāh ("Supported by God"), would triumph in the east and fully restore the Umayyad caliphate. As we have seen, poets anticipated Hishām's future conquests and celebrated him as the one who would purify the world.[104] They hinted at his special destiny, as the tenth Umayyad designated to rule al-Andalus, by referring to astrological and textual predictions associated with his reign.[105]

Al-Ḥakam II's death in 976, however, marked a shift in political power in Cordoba and an eclipse of the effective power of the caliph, if not of the ideological potency of the caliphate. Hishām inherited the throne while still a child, and the government fell subject to the tightening grip of Muḥammad ibn Abī 'Āmir, one of the men who had served in his father's administration. We will see later how the chamberlain Ibn Abī 'Āmir acknowledged and adapted the principles of Andalusi Umayyad legitimacy and manipulated its symbols to serve his own interests. First, however, we investigate how 'Abd al-Raḥmān III and al-Ḥakam II represented their legitimacy and authority in the tangible forms of monumental construction and ceremony.

· TWO ·

The Symbolic Articulation of Legitimacy: Monuments and Ceremony

'Abd al-Raḥmān III translated his military strength and dynastic credentials into an argument for his caliphal legitimacy, and, as we have seen, he and his successor, al-Ḥakam II, used every campaign against external and internal enemies as an occasion to assert Umayyad caliphal authority. Both 'Abd al-Raḥmān III and al-Ḥakam II defined themselves as caliphs to their commanders and allies in their correspondences and more broadly to their subjects and their rivals through public proclamations and the propaganda of poetry. In addition to these means, they developed and manipulated visual media such as monuments and ceremonies to project their caliphal authority and legitimacy. These devices for enhancing the prestige of the ruler had become attributes of caliphal rule in the Islamic political culture of the tenth century, and the Andalusi Umayyads accommodated the models of their predecessors and their rivals to suit their particular circumstances and convey their distinctive right to rule.

This chapter explores how 'Abd al-Raḥmān III and al-Ḥakam II used monuments and ceremony to manifest their authority and express their legitimacy—first setting the stage with a discussion of the construction of the palace-city of Madīnat al-Zahrā' and its relationship to Cordoba and then turning to the drama of court-sponsored public ceremony. This framework conveys the ideological importance of the caliphal capital and presents specific arguments about the articulation of legitimacy.

MONUMENTS

Summarizing 'Abd al-Raḥmān III's reign, the thirteenth-century North African historian Ibn 'Idhārī observed that the caliph put an end to misfortune, triumphed over enemies, and extended justice for all. He also observed that the caliph laid foundations, planted seedlings, and constructed buildings and palaces whose traces would remain until the sound of the trumpet (of the Last Day).[1] Some ten years after declaring himself caliph, 'Abd al-Raḥmān III turned to monumental construction to celebrate and promote his caliphal authority, and in this too, al-Ḥakam II followed his father's example.

'Abd al-Raḥmān III began work on a new seat for his rule, the palace-city of Madīnat al-Zahrā', in either 936 or 940, according to different accounts.[2] Ibn Hayyān states that a shift occurred in the caliph's attention with his defeat at al-Khandaq (Alhandega), north of Toledo in the territory of the king of Leon in 939. According to the historian, after this experience the caliph stopped going on campaigns and turned to supervising construction.[3] The defeat of al-Khandaq was significant not so much as a Christian victory but because the frontier lords of the Upper March proved unreliable.[4] While 'Abd al-Raḥmān III had been able to bring the Lower and Middle Marches under his direct rule by installing his own governors, he was not able to do so in the northwest. The defeat at al-Khandaq led the caliph to modify his approach to attacking Christian territories and perhaps also impressed on him a need to cultivate his prestige.[5] In doing so he could hope to strengthen bonds with the different participants in his regime and intimidate his enemies. 'Abd al-Raḥmān III's withdrawal into a newly created palace and capital should not be seen as an act of defeat but as an effort to make himself the center and symbol of the polity. The double-walled city on the hill was not a defensive refuge but a statement of power.[6]

In the decade following the triumph over Bobastro, 'Abd al-Raḥmān III began to reap the economic rewards of political stability so that by 940 he was able to direct sizable revenues toward such a major building project as the construction of a palace-city. Within a few years he was holding audiences in the hall or *majlis* overlooking the gardens of Madīnat al-Zahrā', although sources indicate that the city was only finally completed by al-Ḥakam II as late as forty years after construction began.[7]

The new caliph undertook to build himself a new capital to display his power and glorify his rule. The construction was also a symbolic act to match the precedents of his rivals, the Abbasids and the Fatimids. The second Abbasid caliph, al-Manṣūr, founded Madīnat al-Salām (the City of Peace) on the west bank of the Tigris River in 762. He conceived of the new capital as a monument to his dynasty and a signal of a new era in Islam and engineered a shift in the center of the Islamic world away from Syria and the Mediterranean to Iraq and the Persian Gulf. A century and a half later, the first Fatimid caliph, al-Mahdī, established a new capital outside Qayrawān as the base of his newly declared caliphate, and this city, named al-Mahdīyya after him, served as the seat of the Fatimid dynasty from 921 to 949. The construction of a new capital from the ground up had become one of the insignia of caliphal rule, announcing a new claimant's rise to power and projecting the endurance of his dynasty. We can appreciate Madīnat al-Zahrā' as a new capital for a new caliphate if we briefly survey the Syrian Umayyad, Abbasid, and Fatimid capitals as ideological constructs. We can then turn to a more focused discussion of the particular ideological significance of the capital in the articulation of Andalusi Umayyad legitimacy.

In Syria, the Umayyad caliph Mu'āwiya transformed Damascus, the seat of his governorship, into the capital of his empire after asserting his claims to leadership of the community in the middle of the seventh century. Damascus had a past as a

Byzantine city and was gradually and visibly transformed by Islamic (and especially Umayyad) rule until it came to represent the triumph of the Islamic conquests. Although some of Mu'āwiya's successors used their country estates and palaces as their primary residences, the Umayyad dynasty and rule remained strongly identified with Damascus.[8]

The Abbasids chose to distance themselves from Damascus for political and economic reasons but also to express their ideological break from the "corruptions" of Umayyad rule. After some effort to find an appropriate location for the seat of the new caliphate, al-Manṣūr chose to build a city on the site of the historically insignificant village of Baghdad; the new city posed a new beginning. Yet only some twenty miles from the ruins of the Sassanian capital of Ctesiphon or Madā'in, it too evoked the triumph of Islam over the infidel empires. The iconography of the plan of al-Manṣūr's double-walled city has been much discussed: perfectly round, with four axial gates leading to the palace-mosque complex isolated in the center, Madīnat al-Salām represented the *imago mundi* with the caliph at the very navel of the universe.[9] Perhaps not entirely practical, the city expressed a conception of the caliph's authority in a way unique in the experience of the Muslim community. Even when Baghdad grew beyond the bounds of al-Manṣūr's round city and caliphs moved to palace complexes they established across the river and even sixty miles up the Tigris in Samarra, the city persisted as the symbolic capital of the Abbasid caliphate. This symbolic identification continued when the caliphs fell subject to court intrigues and coups and when the practical rule of the Buyids and the Saljuqs eclipsed the effective power of the Abbasid dynasty.

By the end of the eighth century, the Abbasids set a standard in the elaboration of dynastic prestige and the demonstration of authority that included the construction of palace-cities. Thus the Aghlabids in Tunisia and the Tulunids in Egypt, for example—dynastic governors who formally recognized the Abbasid caliphate in exchange for independent rule—founded palace-cities, locating their constructions just outside established urban centers.[10] When the Fatimids came to power in the early tenth century, they naturally established a new capital, announcing their arrival on the political scene.[11]

'Abd Allāh Abū Muslim ('Ubayd Allāh) declared his caliphate in 909, assuming the prerogatives of *khuṭba* and *sikka* after his chief missionary seized power from the Aghlabids. By 912, the newly designated caliph al-Mahdī had chosen a site for his new capital, a small peninsula jutting off the coast of Tunisia, south of Sūsa and several miles from Qayrawān. The defensive siting and fortifications of al-Mahdīyya suggest the Shi'i dynasty's antagonistic relationship with the local Sunni population. Described as a "refuge-city," it was surrounded on three sides by water and a solid wall on the fourth and doubly secured by an encircling wall.[12] While we can recognize the fortified city as a refuge, we can also see in its fortifications an expression of the dynasty's determination to pursue its ambitions by force of arms. Functionally, al-Mahdīyya might be described as a base of operations for military expansion, as well as the personal domain of the caliph. The architecture within the city walls, as we can reconstruct it, expressed Fatimid pretensions by employing the local palace idiom but also Fatimid differentiation from local practice through architectural adaptation. Thus the Fatimids reproduced the model of twin palaces for ruler and heir found in the Aghlabid capital of Raqqāda, and adapted the plan of the congregational mosque of Qayrawān in the construction of their own mosque, eliminating the minaret and replacing it with a substantial projecting portal.[13] These architectural borrowings and adaptations reflected an effort to absorb and supplant local monumental traditions and represent a preliminary stage in the invention of a new Fatimid architectural "tradition."

As the Fatimids successfully pursued their military ambitions, they abandoned their first capital. Over the next fifty years, they founded al-Manṣūriyya, not far from Raqqāda and Qayrawān, and then al-Qāhira (Cairo), after the conquest of Egypt in 969. The third Fatimid caliph ordered construction of the second capital in 947, about a decade after 'Abd al-Raḥmān III began construction of Madīnat al-Zahrā', and it is striking to see how the new Fatimid capital contributed to the competing propaganda of the two dynasties. Commemorating Ismā'īl al-Manṣūr's triumph over the Umayyad-supported rebel Abū Yazīd, the new capital of al-Manṣūriyya (Ṣabra) celebrated the caliph's power in its construction and well-watered gardens and emphatically reasserted Fatimid claims to the leadership of the Muslims in its plan—a round city modeled on the Abbasid al-Manṣūr's Madīnat al-Salām.[14] Here the Fatimids appropriated Abbasid iconography to glorify their own rule, suggesting that they (not the Andalusi Umayyads) had superseded the Abbasids in the Command of the Faithful.

'Abd al-Raḥmān III founded Madīnat al-Zahrā' as a declaration of his caliphate to a wide audience, in terms universally recognized in the Islamic world. His construction also marked the transition, in al-Andalus, from the age of the amirs to the age of the caliphate. He deliberately set out to make al-Zahrā' into a capital city, distinguishing it from the recreational palaces or *munyas* in the country around Cordoba established and enjoyed by his predecessors and other prominent and wealthy men. These *munyas* were satellites around Cordoba, enjoyed as retreats from the city and the *qaṣr.* They may have been the local inspiration and point of departure for al-Zahrā', but the caliph differentiated Madīnat al-Zahrā' in planning and scale.[15] In addition to a palace complex and administrative buildings and audience halls, the city (*madīna*) came to comprise caliphal factories, stables, storehouses, a mint, baths, a prison, a congregational mosque, shops, caravansarais, houses, and gardens. According to a tenth-century report, the caliph distributed land grants to promote settlement, and over time the area became extensively populated so that the distance between Madīnat al-Zahrā' and Cordoba became fully inhabited.[16]

Madīnat al-Zahrā' rose as a monument to the caliph's material and imperial resources on stones brought from quarries all over al-Andalus and marble columns of different colors, purportedly brought from the farthest removes of the caliph's influence beyond the peninsula, and employed an army of laborers and artisans.[17] It is more difficult to read Madīnat al-Zahrā' as an ideological construct in the way one can read the round city of Madīnat al-Salām. We cannot yet fully determine the plan of the city or of most of its major buildings, with excavations still underway and textual descriptions providing an inadequate guide.[18] Constructed on the slopes of the Sierra de Cordoba, aerial photographs indicate the city was rectangular, defined by a double wall, twice as wide (about 1,506 meters) east to west as it was deep, north to south. Archaeological investigations support descriptions of Madīnat al-Zahrā' as divided into three levels, from the most exclusive to the more public. The upper level was restricted to the personal use of the caliph and his family. The middle level, bifurcated by a north-south axis, included administrative buildings, the caliph's reception halls, and gardens to the east and private residences to the west. These top two levels seem to have been contained within the *qaṣr* proper, while the lowest level of the city included another garden and housing for the majority of the population. The congregational mosque stood on the boundary of the second and third levels.[19]

The topography of the city identified the caliph as the pinnacle of the social and political hierarchy, with his palace standing at the highest point. His audience hall, designed like a camera looking out over the lower half of the city and the road and plains below, further suggested he was master of all he surveyed. The relationship of buildings to landscape maximized the caliph's views and suggested his proprietary gaze.[20] In its architectural complexity and exploitation of the topography, Madīnat al-Zahrā' recalled the Abbasid palaces of Samarra.[21] As reconstructed now (and in textual descriptions), the audience hall with the dominating view, dubbed the "salon rico" earlier in this century, is also the focus of the *qaṣr* and the city, distinguished by the flat patio before it with its quadripartite garden and a pavilion, surrounded by reflecting pools. Yet the *majlis* does not appear to have been directionally defined; that is, access to it was indirect, a possible function of the topography.[22] Instead of a straight approach to the throne room, as we see in the plans of the great Samarra palaces Jawsaq al-Khāqānī and al-Balkuwārā, the route to the caliph's hall was always ceremonially defined by rows of attendants standing to attention.

The gardens of Madīnat al-Zahrā' expressed the caliph's temporal and spiritual authority. The aqueducts, pools, and fountains, said to have rivaled those of the great kings of past ages, and the gardens that flourished thanks to the water channeled from the nearby mountains demonstrated the caliph's mastery of the environment.[23] Art historians also suggest that the gardens and pools in front of the caliph's main audience hall, and the floral and vegetal wall panels within, were meant to evoke paradise, while the *majlis*-pavilion complex itself, reflected in the water, suggested a celestial palace.[24] While paradisiacal gardens had become a standard part of "Islamic palatine vocabulary" by the tenth century, the gardens of Madīnat al-Zahrā' nevertheless supported the conception of the caliph as the Muslims' guide to salvation.[25] As the seventeenth-century historian al-Maqqarī put it, Madīnat al-Zahrā' stood as a visible reminder for God's servants of the heavenly reward awaiting the blessed after Judgment Day.[26] Given what we know about Andalusi Umayyad caliphal ideology, the themes of Madīnat al-Zahrā' might be described as the renewal of the dynasty and the fortunes of al-Andalus, the flowering of the caliphate, and the promise of reward at the Resurrection.

The name of al-Zahrā' probably reflects these themes, although its exact derivation remains a mystery. We can dismiss the story that it was named for a favorite concubine, al-Zahra ("Flower" or "Blossom"), as apocryphal but still consider the possibility that the name was intended to inspire associations with blossoming, noting that the same story celebrated the blooming (*izhār*) of the fig and almond trees the caliph planted to please her.[27] The root *z-h-r* is associated with brilliance as well as blooms and also suggests the resplendence of the site and of its founder. We should also consider the use of the name as part of the propaganda war between the Umayyads and Fatimids, for *al-Zahrā'* was an honorific name for Fāṭima, the Prophet's daughter and eponym of the Fatimid dynasty. While the Fatimids did not name any of their constructions *al-Zahrā'*, they did assign names derived from the root *z-h-r* to connote brightness and evoke the imam's divine emanation, for example, designating the mosque in al-Manṣūriyya as al-Azhar—while later in Cairo the Fatimid caliph al-'Azīz (r. 975–996) called his palatial complex al-Quṣūr al-Zāhira and renamed the primary Fatimid mosque in the city al-Azhar.[28] We may see here another example of 'Abd al-Raḥmān III's appropriation of Fatimid symbols and language to represent his own caliphate.

Madīnat al-Zahrā' objectified 'Abd al-Raḥmān III's achievements and authority as caliph. The caliph (and caliphate), in turn, became identified with this physical icon. Everyone who heard the name of Madīnat al-Zahrā' thought of the Umayyad caliphate of al-Andalus, and all who saw the city recognized it as the caliphal seat, even if the caliph was not in residence. This association is aptly expressed in verses of a *qaṣīda* recited by Muḥammad ibn Ḥusayn al-Ṭubnī to the caliph al-Ḥakam II on the occasion of the *'Īd al-Aḍḥā* of 971. Representing the idea that the caliph was the guide to salvation, the poet developed the common metaphor of the caliph as the source of light in the darkness, first likening him to the full moon directing the night traveler and then, more originally, to a radiant blaze (*ghurra zahrā'*) that sets the Muslims on a brighter path (*sabīl azhar*).[29] Here the poet identified the caliph with Madīnat al-Zahrā' and both with divine guidance, in the context of a reception in the main *majlis* of the city. Al-Ṭubnī returned to the theme on the occasion of the caliphal reception for the *'Īd al-Fiṭr* of 972, this time identifying al-Ḥakam II's heir, Hishām II, with the caliphal city. He describes Hishām as "the brightness of the world (*zahrat al-dunyā*) and the gate of its happiness (*bāb surūrhā*)."[30] The "gate of happiness" is a play on words using a near-homonym to refer to the main gate of Madīnat al-Zahrā', the Bāb al-Ṣūra.

The best way to explore the ideological dimensions of

Madīnat al-Zahrā' further is in its relation to Cordoba. The Andalusi Umayyad caliphs did not abandon the *qaṣr* of Cordoba or their stake in the original capital. 'Abd al-Raḥmān III defined the new capital of Madīnat al-Zahrā' as a twin to, rather than a replacement of, the old.[31] Unlike the first Abbasid and Fatimid caliphs, 'Abd al-Raḥmān III did not represent his caliphate as a radical break from the past but cultivated the idea of a dynastic inheritance passed from generation to generation from the origins of the Islamic caliphate through the days of the last Umayyad caliph in Syria and the reign of the first Umayyad amir of al-Andalus to his own rule. Symbolically, 'Abd al-Raḥmān III could express the renewed vigor of his dynasty and the restoration of the caliphate by founding the new city of Madīnat al-Zahrā' and assert dynastic continuity by maintaining Cordoba as the original capital. Cordoba had been the seat of Umayyad rule in al-Andalus since shortly after the conquest, serving as the seat of the governors of the Umayyad caliphs from 717 to 756 and then of the independent Umayyad amirs. In times of civil strife and rebellion, Cordoba had remained the Umayyads' stronghold and symbolized the idea of their centralized rule, and in times of security and prosperity it exemplified the success of the dynasty and the flourishing of Islam on the peninsula. Aḥmad al-Rāzī, for example, celebrated Cordoba in 'Abd al-Raḥmān III's day as the cultural center of the time and a magnet for men of learning and talent.[32]

Cordoba had historical significance for the Umayyads, and the caliphs continued to invoke and uphold that legacy after the foundation of Madīnat al-Zahrā'. All the Umayyad amirs were buried in the *qaṣr* of Cordoba and so too would be 'Abd al-Raḥmān III and al-Ḥakam II (Hisham II's death is shrouded in mystery). Alongside the construction and development of Madīnat al-Zahrā', the Umayyad caliphs continued to take a proprietary interest in Cordoba. For example, al-Ḥakam II became personally involved in such projects as repairs to the bridge, moving the *barīd* to accommodate a growth in the trade of secondhand clothes, widening the road of the eastern suburbs, widening the main street of the central market, expanding the cemetery, and establishing charitable endowments such as Qur'an schools and an alms house.[33] 'Abd al-Raḥmān III and especially al-Ḥakam II expended considerable resources on the expansion and decoration of the congregational mosque of the old capital, deepening the monument's symbolic significance and underscoring the importance of Cordoba to the representation of Umayyad legitimacy.

The Great Mosque of Cordoba is the most important surviving monument of Umayyad al-Andalus. Situated opposite the *qaṣr* on a main thoroughfare, the monument stood as a visible daily reminder of Umayyad rule. Especially as elaborated in the caliphal period, the mosque symbolized the success of Umayyad rule and the caliphs' guidance of the community and the faith, as well as their dynastic inheritance. We can appreciate the rhetorical impact of the monument most fully if we keep in mind that the mosque served not only as a place of worship and religious instruction but also as a place of congregation. Here the *khaṭīb* pronounced the names and titles of the caliph before the assembled population every Friday, and caliphal announcements were read to the public. This was the pulpit from which the caliph disseminated news of his latest triumphs and articulated his commitment to the command of the faithful.

Purportedly constructed on the site of a church, the Great Mosque of Cordoba became a visible symbol of the political dominance of Islam on the peninsula, particularly under Umayyad rule. The story of its foundation reports that the conquerors first divided and shared the space of a church in the city with the Christian population until 'Abd al-Raḥmān I bought out the Christians and razed the building in order to build a more substantial mosque. This story commemorates the amir's sponsorship of the faith as it establishes his just treatment of the Christian population.[34] Even if the true origins of the Great Mosque are uncertain, it is clear that over time, as the community grew, the Umayyad rulers extended the dimensions of the mosque to accommodate the population of worshipers.[35] Each expansion then testified to the strength of Islam and the success of Umayyad sponsorship of the faith and leadership of the community.

The extant inscriptional program on the entrances of the mosque, dating mostly from the caliphal period, also addressed the social environment of a mixed population, asserting the primacy of Islam—"The only true faith in God's sight is Islam"—while acknowledging the historical relationship between Judaism, Christianity, and Islam.[36] Thus one gate reads: "God! There is no god but Him, the Living, the Ever-existent One. He has revealed to you the Book with the Truth, confirming the scriptures which preceded it; for He has already revealed the Torah and the Gospel for the guidance of men and the distinction between right and wrong. Those that deny God's revelations shall be sternly punished" (sura 3:2–3).[37] Everyone in Cordoba, whether Muslim, Christian, or Jew, would have recognized the mosque as the place of Muslim communal prayer, but the Arabic inscriptions on the exterior sacralized the building and marked it territorially. The Qur'anic verses themselves were probably not meant to "missionize" so much as to encourage the Muslims (including converts and their progeny) in their faith.[38]

Thus we find Qu'ranic verses asserting the fundamental Islamic principle of the unity of God and warning of divine judgment: "In the name of God, the merciful and the Compassionate, this is a warning to mankind. Let them take heed and know that He is but one God. Let the wise bear this in mind" (sura 14:52).[39] Other inscriptions remind of God's mercy for those who "surrender" (*aslama*) themselves to God—in this context also meaning those who become Muslim: "In the name of God the Merciful and Compassionate, you, my servants, who have believed in Our revelations and surrendered yourselves, shall on that day have nothing to fear or regret. Enter paradise, you and your spouses, all in delight. You shall be served with gold dishes and golden cups. Abiding there forever, you shall find all that your souls desire and all that your eyes rejoice in" (sura 43:68–71).[40] Individually and as a body, by asserting the unity of God (against the Christians' "polytheist" notions) and warning of His judgment, the inscriptions over the entrances enjoined all to enter the mosque and participate in the rituals of Islam so that they could hope to one day enter paradise: "Judgment rests with God, the Most High, the Supreme One. It is He who reveals His signs to you and sends down sustenance from the sky for you. Yet none heeds except the repentant. Pray" (sura 40:12–13).[41] The inscriptions evoked the holy book they came from and guided the Muslims to their duty. At the same time, because the caliph commissioned them, they conveyed his exhortation to the community.

All the inscriptions, outside and inside the Great Mosque, associated the patrons of the mosque with the spiritual guidance of the community. Inside, extant inscriptions date from the reign of al-Ḥakam II and are found in the area around the *miḥrāb*. Here inscriptions repeat the message of the unity of God and His omnipotence, His judgment of humankind, and His forgiveness (quoting some of the same Qu'ranic verses inscribed on the gates outside) and call on His mercy.[42] The inscriptional program in its entirety, however, more explicitly asserts the caliph's guidance and leadership of the community.[43]

An inscription of the opening verses (*fātiḥa*) of the Qur'an runs along the external wall of the *miḥrāb* vestibule.[44] Appropriate for a mosque because of their reference to worship and their place in the ritual prayer, these same verses also decorated the Great Mosque of Medina reconstructed by the Umayyad caliph al-Walīd (r. 705–715)[45]: "Praise be to God, Lord of the Universe, the Compassionate, the Merciful, Sovereign of the Day of Judgment! You alone we worship, and to You alone we turn for help. Guide us to the straight path" (sura 1:1–5).[46] The caliph, in his patronage of the mosque and in his rulership more generally, identified himself with God's guidance; this association is clear as we continue to follow the inscriptions. Two bands of inscriptions (gold mosaic on cobalt blue) frame the arch into the *miḥrāb* (the *miḥrāb* is actually a room). Reading from right to left, inside to outside, the inscriptions begin with a statement of

God's omnipotence and a testament of His uniqueness and thank God and His chosen imām al-Mustanṣir Billāh, servant of God ('Abd Allāh), for the caliph's expansion of the mosque for the benefit of his flock.[47] These blue bands, naming the patron of the new area of the mosque, frame our understanding of the inscriptions within the frame and of the *miḥrāb* itself. The horizontal inscription beneath the blue frame, in contrasting blue on gold, reiterates the theme that God is one and all-knowing, while the inscriptions on the imposts of the *miḥrāb* arch reinforce the association of the caliph's name with God's guidance: "In the name of God, the Merciful and Compassionate, 'Praise be to God who has guided us hither. Had he not given us guidance we should have strayed from the right path. Our Lord's apostles have surely preached the truth' (sura 7:42). The Imām al-Mustanṣir Billāh, Servant of God, al-Ḥakam, Commander of the Faithful, commanded (God favor him for it) his client and *ḥājib* . . . to set up these two supports."[48]

Inside the *miḥrāb,* running along the edges of the dome, we find Qur'anic verses particularly expressive of Andalusi Umayyad self-representation and not typically employed in mosque decoration. Reading the inscription should prompt the reader to recall how 'Abd al-Raḥmān III used the occasion of his triumph over rebellion to articulate his claims and the terms in which he and al-Ḥakam II defined their authority. The inscription reads: "Believers, fear God as you rightly should, and when death comes, die true Muslims. Cling one and all to the faith [literally, rope] of God and let nothing divide you. Remember the favors God has bestowed on you: how, after your enmity, He united your hearts, so that you are now brothers through His grace; and how He delivered you from the abyss of fire when you stood on the very brink of it. Thus God makes plain to you His revelations, so that you may be rightly guided" (sura 3:102–103).[49] The Andalusi Umayyad caliphs identified themselves as the "rope of God"—the lifeline of the community and the faith. They were agents of unity against *fitna,* deliverers from hellfire, and champions of God's revelations.

The location of the inscriptional program in and around the *miḥrāb* reinforces the association of the caliph with the guidance or direction of the community, for the *miḥrāb* indicated the direction of prayer, commemorated the Prophet's leadership of the Muslims, and marked the caliph's place in the mosque when he attended prayer. Glittering with gold and glass mosaics and illuminated by its dome and a "lamp of a thousand candles," the *miḥrāb* was and still is a beacon in the dark and undifferentiated space of the vast prayer hall and may be seen as a metaphor for the caliph. Like the Prophet he directed the believers in the worship of God and lights the way to eternal reward.[50]

The architecture of the mosque represented Umayyad legitimacy in further dimensions. The use of local materials and the incorporation of elements from church architecture, such as the horseshoe arch, gave the mosque a distinctive quality and reflected the Umayyads' adaptation to a new environment. However, the original mosque also largely conformed to the conventional hypostyle plan of the earliest examples of mosque architecture. It had aisles perpendicular to the *qibla* wall like al-Walīd's mosque in Jerusalem and achieved height with double arches that recalled the Great Mosque of Damascus. The original structure invoked the Umayyad heritage as it established the dynasty's authority on the peninsula. Each of the subsequent additions to the mosque maintained the integrity of ʿAbd al-Raḥmān I's construction and followed his elevation, conveying a respect for tradition and continuity: ʿAbd al-Raḥmān II extended the prayer hall by eight bays to the south in 836, going out of his way to reproduce the *spolia* used in the original mosque; al-Ḥakam II lengthened existing arcades in the same direction, adding twelve bays and preserving elements of ʿAbd al-Raḥmān II's *miḥrāb;* the minister al-Manṣūr added eight aisles to the east, along the entire length of the mosque.[51]

The caliphs ʿAbd al-Raḥmān III and especially al-Ḥakam II more fully and explicitly developed the mosque's association with the great religious monuments of the Syrian Umayyad caliphate. In 951 ʿAbd al-Raḥmān III renovated the courtyard with alternating piers and columns in a sequence found in the Great Mosque of Damascus.[52] Al-Ḥakam II began work on his addition shortly after ascending the throne ten years later. He not only elongated the prayer hall, but he changed the area of the *qibla* completely, constructing an elaborate *maqṣūra,* with three domed bays enclosed by two screens of polylobed interlacing arches and the unique octagonal *miḥrāb* flanked by two functional doorways.[53] He decorated the *qibla* wall and *miḥrāb* with marble, stucco, and costly mosaic. The use of mosaic decoration, unique on the peninsula until the caliphal period, recalled most vividly the mosaic decoration of the Dome of the Rock, the Great Mosque of Damascus, the Great Mosque in Jerusalem, and the Prophet's Mosque at Medina.[54] Al-Ḥakam II's "mosque within a mosque" has been described as typologically akin to these last three mosques, all constructed by the Umayyad caliph al-Walīd in the early eighth century.[55]

By emphatically associating the Great Mosque of Cordoba with these monuments of the first Umayyad caliphate, al-Ḥakam II articulated iconographically the transmission of Andalusi Umayyad legitimacy from Syria, so important to the ideology of the caliphate. At the same time, his expansion and revetement of the original Umayyad mosque expressed the idea of dynastic renewal. Now the congregational mosque of Cordoba matched the scale, lavish decoration, and expense of those of the great Umayyad caliphs of the past. Such active celebration of the Umayyad heritage may even have found expression in the elaboration of a ritual around the presentation of a few leaves of 'Uthmān's personal Qur'an, stained with his blood, said to have been housed in the treasury behind the *miḥrāb.*[56]

The caliphal additions to the Great Mosque of Cordoba implicitly challenged the authority of the rival Abbasid and Fatimid caliphates by invoking the continuity of Umayyad rule and demonstrating the Andalusi Umayyads' power and resources. We are told that the mosaics that decorated al-Ḥakam II's mosque were a gift from the Byzantine emperor, applied under the direction of a Byzantine mosaicist, as in the days of al-Ḥakam II's ancestor al-Walīd.[57] The sight of the ornate *miḥrāb* area conveyed the Andalusi Umayyad and Byzantine association and the idea that the former had influence over the latter, at a time when the Abbasids were losing territory to Byzantine armies and the Fatimids competed with Byzantine navies.

'Abd al-Raḥmān III's addition of a tower minaret in 951 to 952 expressed his power and authority in a number of directions. The tower may have been designed to assert his challenge of Fatimid authority because the Fatimids rejected such towers, and they became a symbol of contested authority in North Africa.[58] Reportedly rising 100 cubits, topped by a domed pavilion, the minaret dominated Cordoba's skyline and projected the strength of Islam on the peninsula to the local Muslim, Christian, and Jewish populations and to visitors from abroad, including the Christian north. When we consider that 'Abd al-Raḥmān III erected the tower at the height of his persecution of Ibn Masarra's *firqa* or heresy, we can also see it more specifically as a monument to his command of the faithful and, as a beacon marking the site of the mosque, as a symbol of his direction of the community to the true religion.[59]

The caliphal additions to the Great Mosque reflected, and further endowed, the significance of Cordoba to Umayyad legitimacy, for the mosque epitomized, as it helped shape, the Umayyads' relationship to the city. The monument came to symbolize the continuity of Umayyad rule as every Umayyad amir and caliph added to, repaired, or embellished it in some way and helped identify Cordoba as their capital. The expansion and elaboration of the mosque celebrated the success of Umayyad promotion of Islam on the peninsula. As the central monument of Cordoba, the building expressed the supremacy of Islamic rule over the Roman and Visigothic past and of Islam over Christianity. The mosque's architectural and decorative references to Syrian Umayyad monuments identified Cordoba as an Umayyad city and capital.

Symbolically, Madīnat al-Zahrā' stood in relationship to Cordoba as the caliphate to its dynastic inheritance. The link between the new and the old capitals was defined in a number of ways. The caliph developed the prestige of Madīnat al-Zahrā' and established its relationship to Cordoba by commemorating the original Andalusi Umayyad capital in the new. Again, while we can not say much about the plan of either city in the tenth century, we do know that Madīnat al-Zahrā' recapitulated the relationship between mosque and *qaṣr* found in Cordoba: the two structures faced each other across a main thoroughfare, bridged by a *sabat* or passageway. Textual references make clear that the most important city gate (*bāb al-ṣūra*) and the most important gate into the *qaṣr* (*bāb al-sudda*) in Madīnat al-Zahrā' were named after their counterparts in Cordoba. The Bāb al-Ṣūra of Cordoba took its name from the image (*ṣūra*) surmounting it (statue or frieze), dating from the Roman period, and it is possible that the Bāb al-Ṣūra of al-Zahrā' also bore a figure in imitation.

We can see a similar kind of commemorative referencing in the Fatimid context. The Fatimid general, Jawhar, who conquered Egypt for the caliph al-Mu'izz in 969, constructed the dynasty's new palace-city outside Fusṭāt according to the instructions of the imam. He named the new capital al-Manṣūriyya after the Fatimids' capital in Tunisia (the name changed to al-Qāhira after the arrival of the imam in 973) and two of its gates after gates in the first al-Manṣūriyya: Bāb Zuwayla and Bāb al-Futūḥ. Unlike the round plan of al-Manṣūriyya outside Qayrawān, the new city had a rectangular shape, but the palace complex followed the model, already established in al-Mahdīyya, of two palaces facing each other across an esplanade: one for the caliph and one for his heir.[60] This kind of referencing, in both the Fatimid and Andalusi Umayyad cases, established continuity and bound the new city with the history of the dynasty's rule.

In al-Andalus, given the different context, the effort to establish a rapport between the two cities could also work the other way, with innovations employed in Madīnat al-Zahrā' translated to Cordoba. Thus, for example, the off-center location of the minaret of the congregational mosque of Madīnat al-Zahrā', constructed around 940, anticipated the situation of 'Abd al-Raḥmān III's tower minaret for Cordoba, and al-Ḥakam II's extension of the Great Mosque of Cordoba visually recalled the space and some of the decorative elements of 'Abd al-Raḥmān III's reception hall.[61]

The caliphs' travel between Madīnat al-Zahrā' and Cordoba and their periodic residence in each affirmed the definition of the new city as twin to the old. Sources refer to the cities as *al-ḥāḍiratān,* the two capitals, and do not indicate that Madīnat al-Zahrā' served as a summer residence, or provide any other logic for the caliph's presence in one site or the other.[62] It is striking to note that when the caliph was in residence in Madīnat al-Zahrā', public ceremony embraced both cities. However, if the caliph were in residence in Cordoba, all ceremony focused on his court there. Cordoba, because it had a long history as a thriving city, still functioned as the hub of the caliphate in many ways, and Madīnat al-Zahrā' depended on it despite its status as a city.

The bonds between the two cities became visible on certain ceremonial occasions, most dramatically in the lining up of men—palace officials, military and guard units, recruits from Cordoba—across the distance between the two cities.[63] The protocol of many of the caliph's ceremonial receptions, whether they took place in Madīnat al-Zahrā' or in Cordoba, symbolically represented the close association between the caliph and Cordoba by giving the prefect of the (*ṣāḥib al-madīna*) of Cordoba pride of place among the official class. He stood to the right of the caliph and personally ministered to him, while the prefect of the City of al-Zahrā' generally stood to the left.[64]

This discussion of Madīnat al-Zahrā' and the Great Mosque

of Cordoba has explored how the Umayyads used monumental construction to express their revival of the true caliphate and argued that the caliphs developed a distinctive ideological relationship between Madīnat al-Zahrā' and Cordoba. Madīnat al-Zahrā' rose as a monument to the caliphate, proclaiming a new stage in the history of the dynasty and the peninsula and demonstrating the power, majesty, and authority of the caliphs. Like all the caliphs' achievements, the new city testified to their divine favor and challenged rival claims. At the same time, the Andalusi Umayyads consciously cultivated Cordoba as the traditional seat of the dynasty. In so doing, the caliphs invested the historical identification of Cordoba with Umayyad rule with new ideological significance.

CEREMONY

Ritual protocol and public ceremonies organized by the caliphal court of al-Andalus helped create and renew Umayyad caliphal authority in a number of ways. Ritual distinguished communication with the caliph from mundane experience and served as a "traditionalizing" device, giving the caliphate a timeless quality.[65] The theatricality of ritual occasions and public ceremonies with their costumes, staging, stylization of action, and sequential organization aroused the emotions of spectators and participants alike as they symbolized and enacted the caliph's professed qualities and functions as Commander of the Faithful and the caliph of God.[66]

The elaboration of court protocol and ceremony had in fact become one of the insignia of dynastic rule in the Islamic world by the tenth century. The Fatimids, employed the same "ceremonial idiom" of gestures, salutes, and acts of homage, developed by the Abbasids, to assert their leadership of the Muslims and express their distinctive claims to legitimacy. This language of symbols and ritual action could be used to express general principles and accommodate them to specific circumstances.[67] The Andalusi Umayyads, staking their claims to the caliphate in competition with the Abbasids and Fatimids, employed the idiom to assert and convey their own legitimacy.

Unfortunately, extant sources do not allow us to trace the introduction and elaboration of court protocol and ceremonial in al-Andalus. Ibn Sa'īd, a thirteenth-century historian born in Granada, notes that the Andalusi Umayyads were able to command the awe (*hayba*) and confidence of their subjects by deed and display and reports that, since the reign of the first Andalusi Umayyad amir, 'Abd al-Raḥmān I (r. 756–788), the Umayyads expressed their authority through the magnificence of their persons and of their courts.[68] Ibn Sa'īd's North African contemporary, Ibn 'Idhārī, however, attributes the introduction of pomp and ceremonial to 'Abd al-Raḥmān II (r. 822–852).[69] Histories of the reigns of the amirs do not give us much of a view of their ceremonial life. Accounts of the reign of the first caliph, 'Abd al-Raḥmān III, are more clearly punctuated by ceremonial occasions, beginning with his accession, even if full descriptions are lacking.[70] Ibn Ḥayyān's chronicle, for example, presents excerpts of panegyric odes or *qaṣā'id* recited before the caliph to commemorate significant victories or events but does not portray the ceremonial context of their recital.

Reports by Ibn Ḥayyān, and later sources, that 'Abd al-Raḥmān III received embassies from abroad and presided over magnificent audiences often do not describe them in enough detail to serve as a basis for analysis.[71] For example, when Ibn 'Idhārī reports on the caliph's reception of envoys from the Byzantine emperor in 949, he declares that the caliph sent a military escort for his distinguished visitors and held an audience of unprecedented pomp and display, but then excuses himself from its description on the grounds that it would be too long to include in his history.[72] His account of the arrival of a prior Byzantine embassy in 945, equally brief, nonetheless helps to fill in the picture a bit further: the caliph sat on his throne with his heir, al-Ḥakam, seated on his right. His other sons sat to his left and right along with the wazirs and chamberlains, according to their ranks. Delegations from all over the country had been invited to attend, so when the envoys entered the caliph's presence with their gifts, Ibn 'Idhārī tells us, they were taken aback by the majesty of the ruler and the size of the assembly.[73]

Al-Maqqarī presents a fuller account of the arrival and reception of the Byzantine embassy in 949 that better conveys how ambassadorial receptions, particularly for representatives of prominent powers, were designed to impress and intimidate not only the guests, but those in attendance. According to the report, 'Abd al-Raḥmān III sent a delegation to Pechina to meet the Byzantine envoys. As they approached the outskirts of the capital, he honored them with a military parade and the escort of two prominent eunuchs from his palace. They were thus led to Munyat Naṣr, where they waited in seclusion for their audience with the caliph some weeks later. The caliph chose to receive the Byzantine messengers in the *bahw* or vestibule of the hall named *al-majlis al-zāhir* in the *qaṣr* of Cordoba, traveling from Madīnat al-Zahrā' to do so. We are told that, for the occasion, the courtyard was covered with carpets and the doorways were shaded by canopies and adorned with curtains. The caliph sat on his throne, flanked by his heir on his right and his other sons seated on both left and right, as well as the ministers according to their ranks. The chamberlains and those invited to attend stood in their designated places. The Byzantine envoys delivered their written message, and the audience concluded, as the caliph commanded, with orations and the recitation of verses in praise of the reception and in encomium of the caliph's rule.

The narrator of this account expressly reports that when the Byzantine envoys entered the caliph's presence they were awestruck by the evidence of the splendor of the kingdom and the greatness of the ruler. The account describes a similar effect on the others present, recounting that the *faqīh* designated to deliver a speech for the occasion was so overwhelmed by the moment and the glory of the caliphate that he could not speak and fell into a swoon. Even the master of language, Abū 'Alī al-Qālī, apparently could not express himself beyond a few words. Finally, another *faqīh,* Mundhir ibn Sa'īd al-Ballūṭī, stepped forward to make an oration, and his rhetoric won the approval of the caliph, who subsequently appointed him chief *qāḍī* of Cordoba.[74] Even if the story of the dumb-stricken orators is apocryphal, it tells us that such receptions were intended to be fearsome in their solemnity.

The preserved text of al-Ballūṭī's speech gives us a compelling view of the reception, and others like it, as an occasion to celebrate the caliph's rule, articulate his legitimacy, and inspire obedience to his authority. In this instance, the orator spoke very much as the mouthpiece of the caliph, exhorting the assembled audience and the Muslims of al-Andalus as a whole to heed the message that the Days of God were on them and to recognize that the agency of their deliverance was the caliphate of the Commander of the Faithful. Much of the speech enumerated how the caliph saved them from all the evils of *fitna* and achieved conditions in al-Andalus that made them the people best off in the world, in terms we are familiar with. In this context, al-Ballūṭī described the arrival of the delegation from Constantinople as evidence of the caliph's accomplishments and of how, through him, God fulfills His promise: "God has promised those of you who believe and do good works to make them masters in the land as He had made their ancestors before them" (sura 24:55). In closing, he reminded the audience that they owed obedience to the caliph, citing the Qur'an further: "Obey God and obey the Apostle and those in authority among you" (sura 4:59). He warned that whoever withdraws his obedience, sows division in the community, and deviates from the religion is "forfeiting this life and the hereafter. That way perdition lies" (sura 22:11). More particularly, the speech suggested that the audience owed allegiance to the caliph for all they enjoyed and admonished them to hold fast to him, given the particular circumstances of al-Andalus, a peninsula surrounded by polytheists and heretics determined to inflame revolt, divide the community, dishonor their women, sap the message of the Prophet, and cause them to forsake the true religion.[75]

It is likely that 'Abd al-Raḥmān III elaborated ceremonial

conventions over the course of his reign, particularly after his adoption of the caliphal title and prerogatives, according to the standards of his rivals.[76] The construction of a new seat for his caliphate in Madīnat al-Zahrā' was integral to this process. Having established his authority over the peninsula and extended his interests abroad, north and south, he no longer personally conducted campaigns but received supplicants for his favor at his court where the strength of his reign and his right to rule were conveyed by his setting and the orchestration of movement toward and away from him. The caliph used ceremony to enhance his prestige and as a means to create or reinforce allegiances. We know that 'Abd al-Raḥmān III often treated those who submitted to him leniently and tried to bring them into his regime by ordering them to Cordoba and enrolling them in his personal standing army (*ḥasham*). It is possible that he used ritual and ceremony to formally incorporate the former rebels into the body politic as al-Ḥakam II did later, as we will see.

Al-Ḥakam II may have developed protocol and ceremony further than his father had. Certainly by his reign the sight of the caliph was a rare and ritually controlled event. The most useful source for investigating ceremonial in al-Andalus, 'Īsā al-Rāzī's (d. 989) account (as transmitted by Ibn Ḥayyān) of four of the last years of the second caliph's reign, suggests a routinization of ceremonial life in the court and the twin capitals of Cordoba and Madīnat al-Zahrā' by 970.[77] The annalistic history includes fairly extensive descriptions of caliphal audiences held as part of the public celebration of the two annual religious festivals—*'Īd al-Fiṭr* (the feast marking the end of the fast of Ramadan) and *'Īd al-Aḍḥā* (the feast of the sacrifice)—and descriptions of ceremonies we may refer to as military triumphs.

Unfortunately, 'Īsā al-Rāzī's descriptions do not provide enough detail and elaboration to enable us to fully appreciate the staging and ritual program of ceremonial occasions.[78] We do not know, for example, the exact words or gestures that constituted the customary salutation (*taslīm*) to the caliph, what he wore or what insignia he presented. Information is insufficient to develop a sophisticated comparison of Andalusi Umayyad protocol and ceremony with that of the other caliphates and allows for only a few observations. For example, in contrast to the Abbasids and the Fatimids, the Andalusi Umayyad caliph does not seem to have been veiled by a curtain and then ceremoniously revealed but only "screened" by his masters of protocol and chamberlains (the *ḥujjāb*), who stood to his right and left in rows that flanked the reception hall.[79] On the whole, existing references suggest that the essential ritual elements were consistent with the "ceremonial idiom" of the other caliphates. The following elements, for example, characterized a visitor's approach to the caliph: dismounting before entering the official sanctum of the palace-city, awaiting permission to enter the caliph's presence, prostrating and kissing the threshold of the audience hall, and kissing the hand of the caliph as an act of homage.[80]

'Īsā al-Rāzī's text does provide a measure of detail that allows us to see how ceremony expressed al-Ḥakam II's legitimacy in broad terms: ceremonial occasions modeled the caliph's claim to be the source of order and stability, the champion of the faith and the glory of the Muslims, and the agent of its unity.

If we think of ceremony as a social construction that conveys meaning (at least in part) through form, it is not surprising that al-Rāzī's descriptions of ceremonies are largely concerned with representing their order and structure. His accounts all remark on the perfection of the organization or the completeness of the formation, before detailing the elements of the composition. Each account of one of the caliph's more public receptions, involving the attendance and participation of more than his ministers and administrators, begins by locating the caliph on his throne (*sarīr*) in the audience hall of either Madīnat al-Zahrā' or the palace of Cordoba. It reports on the sequence of those received into his presence, whether they sat or stood and where, as well as who ministered to him (served as *ḥājib*) and how the palace officials stood in their ranks. The placement of individuals and categories in the hall reflected the palace hierarchy, with the caliph seated in the central position, and any shift in placement would be understood by all to correspond to a shift in rank and status or to be a specific reference to the significance of the occasion. In this way ceremonies made "patent" the caliph's role as the pole around which order is established and his identity as the ultimate authority who determines social standing.[81]

The caliph's professed commitment to the defense and championship of the faith was readily apparent to the populations of the capital in the departure of commanders and their armies to points north, west, and south. They could appreciate how the resources he marshaled over the course of the year were put to service in holy war.[82] Most of al-Rāzī's accounts of departing armies and reinforcements mention that the people, "great and small," came out to watch, and that the sight was impressive in terms of size, order, and equipment.[83] As a public occasion, the departure of armies was governed by formal codes of conduct and organization that reinforced the message of the caliph's authority as supreme commander. The descriptions give us only a glimpse of that formality.

Most intriguing is a unique account for the year 971 of the blessing and tying of the banners that the caliph's chief commander, Ghālib ibn 'Abd al-Raḥmān, would carry on campaign against the *majūs*, or Norsemen, who were reported to be off the western shores of al-Andalus.[84] According to al-Rāzī's somewhat sketchy report, the caliph ordered that three symbolic banners—named *al-'Uqda, al-'Alam,* and *al-Shaṭaranj*—be taken from the storehouses of the palace of Madīnat al-Zahrā' to the *Dār al-Wuzarā',* the seat of his ministers, and there fixed onto lances. This was done according to instructions, while the imams (prayer leaders) and muezzins recited the Qu'ran and, in particular, sura 48 ("Victory").[85] This sura invokes God's favor and victory for those who fight on His behalf and in this context has the quality of a benediction. Recalling the Prophet Muḥammad's campaigns against the unbelievers, the recitation of the sura created a parallel between them and al-Ḥakam II's expeditions, identifying the latter as divine mission and the caliph as God's agent.

Al-Rāzī's report describes how the eunuch Durrī of the treasury and two officers of the caliph's personal army (*ḥasham*) presided over the tying of the banners and marched with them to the Bāb al-Sudda, the main gate of the palace, accompanied by their pages and the muezzins chanting the *takbīr* ("God is Great"). A special military contingent in full dress, bearing arms, then escorted them from the Bāb al-Sudda to the doorway of the home of commander Ghālib, who awaited their arrival. With the transfer of the banners, Ghālib mounted and followed the procession of his men and equipment out of the city.[86]

The reports of Ghālib's departures for two other campaigns in the next few years, the first to North Africa and the second to the northern frontier, also suggest a formal construction to the occasion of departure and a conscious display before the populations of Cordoba and Madīnat al-Zahrā'. In the first account, Ghālib camped for two days on the parade grounds of Faḥṣ al-Surādiq, to the east of Cordoba, with the government troops, as well as the troops he had recruited from the frontier. On the third day, he paraded them to Madīnat al-Zahrā', where the caliph was in residence, and then to Cordoba, where he spent a few days making final preparations. Al-Rāzi notes that the people praised the procession for its perfect order and the magnitude of the army's equipment and that the prospect filled their hearts with pride and joy.[87]

By the next occasion, in April 975, Ghālib had earned his reputation as a great commander and had received two gilded swords from the caliph along with the honorific title of Dhū al-Sayfayn ("Holder of the Two Swords"), as well as the honor of having his seat in the *Dār al-Wuzarā'* set higher than all the others, honors unprecedented in al-Andalus.[88] Al-Rāzī records that Ghālib's grand departure for the north brought great numbers of people out to watch and reports that the commander left his home in military dress girded with the two swords, preceded by squadron after squadron of troops that filled the roads and the horizon. His route took him by the Bāb al-Sudda of the palace of Cordoba and there, on the terrace, appeared the caliph al-Ḥakam II and his designated heir, Hishām. The caliph raised his hands heavenward to implore God's help and victory for the Muslims.[89]

These three accounts of Ghālib's departures for campaign differ in detail and may be incomplete, but each suggests how such an event was structured to present a visual representation of the caliph's ultimate authority and his delegation of responsibility to his commander. In the first, the caliph's banners passed ceremoniously from the palace to the general; in the second, the general paraded from camp to the current residence of the caliph in Madīnat al-Zahrā' and then to the twin capital of Cordoba; and finally, in the third, the general received the benediction of the caliph as he left for another glorious campaign. This last episode, marked by the public appearance of the caliph, suggests how Ghālib's history of success had come to enhance the glory of the reign and the caliph's authority. The caliph honored Ghālib with his actual presence on the Bāb al-Sudda (typically, the gate represented his unseen presence) and took the opportunity to publicly identify himself with the campaign, showing confidence in its success. The sight of the caliph distinguished the occasion from common experience for all—the commander, the army, and the population of the city—who beheld him and for all who heard of the event later.

The departure of armies clearly demonstrated the caliph's execution of his responsibilities as Commander of the Faithful, but success confirmed his authority. Not surprisingly, the arrival of trophies such as the heads of notable enemies or prisoners in chains offered further occasions for public display. For example, when Ghālib's eunuch Qand arrived in Cordoba with the head of the uncle of the last major rebel in North Africa, Ḥasan ibn Qannūn, the caliph ordered a military parade with the head borne aloft on a lance. The grim trophy thus processed from Qand's camp at the *munya* of al-Na'ūra to the Bāb al-Sudda of the palace of Cordoba. Those who saw it pass cursed the dead man and his followers. At the Bāb al-Sudda, the lieutenant of the prefect of the city stationed there ordered that the head be raised on a post opposite.[90] The next year, when the frontier lord of Lerida defeated a Muslim rebel and his Christian allies, he sent to Cordoba the rebel leader and ten of his followers in chains and the heads of seventeen Christians. These trophies too were paraded through the city, and the heads of the deceased were planted before the Bāb al-Sudda.[91]

The arrival of delegations from abroad seeking to establish or renew treaties and alliances reflected the substantive success of the caliph's armies. Their numbers and frequency increased over the course of al-Ḥakam II's reign, including embassies from the Christian kingdoms to the north, the Byzantine empire, and the Ottonian court, as well as from North Africa. Following the precedent of his father's treatment of envoys from Constantinople, al-Ḥakam II arranged for military escorts to direct arriving dignitaries from the frontiers of his domain to the seat of his rule and to emphasize the significance of their entrance into the capital.[92] The regularity of such processions confirmed to the caliph's subjects that he was the center of power and the one who ensured the glory of Islam.

The verses of Aḥmad ibn Ibrāhīm, treasurer of Madīnat al-Zahrā', recited on the occasion of al-Ḥakam II's reception of Christian ambassadors in 971, exemplify how such an event could be translated into evidence of the caliph's distinctive legitimacy: "All of this serves as a warning to the east and the west, like the dazzle of lightning warns of the thunder / All that remains is for [the caliph] to free Mecca and expel those who must be expelled."[93] The poet's allusion to Mecca refers to the caliph's rivalry with the Fatimids and claims to universal leadership of the Muslims, establishing a connection between the caliph's success on the peninsula and his right to (inevitable) rule over the holy city.

In his chronicle of al-Ḥakam II's final years as caliph, al-Rāzī also describes a more distinctive celebration of military success we can see as particularly representative of the caliph's claims to legitimacy. The historian presents fairly full accounts of two instances and intimations of a third, in which the celebration of a military triumph became integrated with the ritual submission of a former enemy in a ceremonial sequence that proclaimed the invincibility of the caliph fighting God's cause and that demonstrated his ability and desire to create a united community of Muslims.[94]

The first account, chronologically, describes Ja'far ibn 'Alī al-Andalusī's arrival in al-Andalus in 971, after destroying Zīrī ibn Manād, a Fatimid governor. Ja'far had governed the city of Masīla in North Africa for the Fatimids until his rivalry with Zīrī, his Ṣanhājī neighbor, caused a rupture in his relationship with the Fatimid overlord in the region. Allying with the Banū Khazar of the Zanāta tribe (who were loyal to the Umayyad caliphate) he renounced his Fatimid allegiance and, along with the Banū Khazar, confronted and killed Zīrī and a number of his men.[95] The second account describes the celebration of Ghālib's return to the capital after achieving the surrender, in 974, of the last rebel stronghold in western North Africa, defeating the Idrisid amir, Ḥasan ibn Qannūn. Ḥasan's family (descendants of the Prophet through the line of his grandson Ḥasan) had betrayed their allegiance to the Umayyad ruler and supported the Fatimid cause, and when Ghālib returned triumphant to the seat of the caliphate, he brought with him the Idrisid shaykh, Aḥmad ibn 'Īsā Ḥannūn, and his brother and cousins, so that they could personally submit before the caliph.[96] In between these two occasions, Ḥasan ibn Qannūn himself arrived at court seeking formal submission to the caliph, and we discuss here the limited details of his experience as well as the fuller accounts.

The arrival, in the capital, of a former rebel seeking to render homage to the caliph made him rather like the trophy of Zīrī's head, to be paraded in a celebration of victory.[97] However, the accounts of the series of ceremonial events that attended Ja'far's, and later the Idrisids', arrival and approach to the caliph suggest how ceremony could usher outsiders into the community. Ceremony provided a context and a formula for their formal recognition of the caliph's legitimacy, their pardon, and their incorporation into the ranks of the faithful. In so doing, ceremony demonstrated to all assembled the caliph's will to reunite the community and his power to forgive, as well as punish. The gifts he subsequently bestowed underscored the principle that obedience to the caliph brought rewards in this life and the next.

Al-Ḥakam II's policy in North Africa, as expressed to his commanders, was to pursue relentlessly all who did not recognize his authority, until they sought submission. Once they did so, he wrote, the commanders should be generous in granting pardon to ensure peace and the welfare of his subjects and to support the role of his government in bringing together those who had fallen away.[98] The commander in the field could accept submission on his own authority, in communication with the caliph, and generally required a written oath of loyalty (*bay'a*) and hostages. Many, if not all, of the submitting chiefs and leaders of North Africa followed up by sending delegations to the caliphal court to express loyalty and obedience to the regime. This is what Ja'far intended originally, until he decided to go to al-Andalus himself.

Ja'far had sent his brother Yaḥyā with the band of notables of the Banū Khazar who were taking the heads of Zīrī and his supporters to the caliph, hoping to seek his support and advice in confronting Zīrī's son.[99] Ja'far's decision to join his brother raised the standard of the event, since he had been a Fatimid governor, and gave it another focus in addition to the military triumph: the return of the stray to the fold.

Yaḥyā and the Banū Khazar preceded Ja'far in al-Andalus by about a month and were greeted at the point of disembarkation by an officer of the treasury and his assistants, who brought tents and lavish furnishings to accommodate them and sixty-eight horses to transport them. They were en route to Cordoba when news of Ja'far's arrival reached the caliph.[100] He sent Muḥammad ibn Abī 'Āmir to meet him with tents and transport (250 horses) and a gift of four horses and a mule from the caliph's stables equipped with decorated saddles and bridles. Special arrangements were made to carry his women in pallaquins, sparing them the gaze of onlookers. Ja'far and his entourage were then escorted up the peninsula, catching up with Yaḥyā and the Banū Khazar outside the city of Cabra; three nights later, all were camped at Faḥṣ al-Surādiq outside Cordoba.[101] The caliph thus honored Ja'far, Yaḥyā, and the Banū Khazar as soon as he had word of their arrival on the peninsula, his domain, providing them with the best accommodations and escort and protecting the privacy of their women (once the cavalcade camped outside the capital, he arranged for the women to be conveyed discreetly into the city to the houses prepared for them). At the same time, by directing their progress through al-Andalus so completely, he asserted his authority over them. They could only submit to the unfolding sequence of ceremonial events: the *burūz* or military parade through Cordoba, the subsequent procession to Madīnat al-Zahrā' and reception by the caliph, and, at the end of the year, the customary caliphal reception for the *'Īd al-Aḍḥā*.

The caliph designated the *ṣāḥib al-shurṭa al-'ulyā*, or chief of police, Aḥmad ibn Sa'd, to organize and lead an escort taking Ja'far, Yaḥyā, and those who were with them from their camp at Faḥṣ al-Surādiq through Cordoba to the *munya* or estate of Ibn 'Abd al-'Azīz, where they were to wait while preparations were made for their reception at Madīnat al-Zahrā'. Ibn Sa'd arranged the ranks of the different classes of the army (*ṭabaqāt al-jund*) and guard and led them from the palace of Madīnat al-Zahrā' to the camp where the heads of Zīrī and about 100 of his followers were arrayed on lances. The horsemen of the guard seized hold of the lances and distributed them in ranks, with the head of Zīrī raised highest and leading the rest. They then led the cavalcade, followed by corps after corps of the army, and then by the entourages of Ja'far, Yaḥyā, and the Banū Khazar, which included the officers who had been sent to escort them from the southern coast, followed by the most prominent men of Cordoba and the provinces.[102] The parade passed by the Bāb al-Sudda of the palace of Cordoba where it was joined by an additional corps from the guard and by the men of Cordoba who had been recruited to participate. All bristled with arms. The police chief, *ṣāḥib al-shurṭa al-'ulyā,* and commander of Valencia and Tortosa, Hishām ibn Muhammad ibn 'Uthmān, acting for his uncle, the prefect of the city, *ṣāḥib al-madīna,* supervised from his station on the gate with his cousin, as the procession continued through the city and the suburbs to the *munya.* There the guests were ordered to wait, and the escort pitched its camp.[103]

This *burūz* can be read in a few ways, from the perspective of different vantage points. Al-Rāzī's observation—that as Ja'far and Yaḥyā were led through the city, their hearts pounded—suggests that the scale of their escort and its military disposition and the crafted and coordinated quality of their progress toward the caliph were designed to intimidate.[104] Everything they experienced spoke of the caliph's power. Passing by the gate of the caliphal palace in Cordoba, they were presented before a tangible symbol of the caliph and a reminder of what still awaited them. They may have been acutely conscious of themselves as supplicants for the caliph's pardon and good will, even though they were ostensibly celebrating their triumph over Zīrī. Ja'far had, after all, only recently sent a letter to the caliph beseeching al-Ḥakam II to accept his return to the fold and to grant him the status of one who recognized the caliph's legitimacy (*ḥaqq*) and submitted to his guidance.[105] Although the caliph had responded favorably, Ja'far had felt uncertain enough of his situation to come to the Bāb al-Sudda himself.

The population of Cordoba and the notables from the provinces must have been equally impressed by the display of caliphal power and appreciated how the honor Ja'far and Yaḥyā received by their escort, their mounts, and the effort expended on their behalf expressed the caliph's grand beneficence. The parade bearing these two supplicants also distinguished Cordoba and the Bāb al-Sudda, the traditional seat of the Andalusi Umayyads, as the center of a great domain that extended beyond the various districts of the peninsula to North Africa. As the local population were not only spectators but were enlisted to participate, they experienced the events of this day and the next as subjects of the caliph and members of the body politic. The display, planning, and incorporation of the city and its population ensured that, as al-Rāzī notes, talk of Ja'far ibn 'Alī's arrival lasted a long time among the inhabitants of Cordoba, who considered it a wonder of the caliph's majesty.[106]

The parade to Madīnat al-Zahrā' the following day, ending with the wait in the *Dār al-Jund* for permission to enter the caliph's presence, defined the next stage in the ceremonial sequence. The parade through Cordoba was only a prologue to this exaggerated staging of caliphal power. Al-Rāzī describes the arrangements made as the guests waited, again emphasizing the caliph's interest and supervision. Al-Ḥakam II delegated responsibility for the organization of the squadrons and regiments that lined the way between the *munya* and the *majlis,* or caliphal reception hall, to two overseers of the household guard who worked over night by torch light to prepare for the grand procession.[107]

Al-Rāzī's text describes the composition of the two human chains that extended from *munya* to *majlis.* Beginning at the *munya* and extending to the Bāb al-Ṣūra, the southern gate of Madīnat al-Zahrā', stood 16,000 men from the suburbs of Cordoba holding lances and shields from the treasury, armored horsemen and slavic eunuchs (*ṣaqāliba*) from the palace service (*ahl al-khidma*), Berber armored horsemen and the various branches of African military slaves, and a variety of military ranks all fully dressed in appropriate arms and finery, including the bearers of the banners (banners emblazoned with images of lions, leopards, eagles, and snakes). From the Bāb al-Ṣūra to the main gate of the palace, the Bāb al-Sudda, the ranks included 100 of the caliph's best horses, wearing decorated saddles and bridles, as well as further ranks of armed military contingents.[108] In fact, Ja'far, Yaḥyā, and the Banū Khazar passed through a carefully constructed passage of the caliph's men and horses from the moment they stepped out of the door of the *munya* until they eventually saluted the caliph.

The *ṣāḥib al-shurṭa al-'ulyā,* Hishām, and other important officials (still including the original escort), conducted the guests through this passageway. The heads of Zīrī and company led the parade, accompanied by military corps carrying banners—including the *Shaṭaranj al-Shāmī* banner ("the Syrian Chess")—which al-Rāzī identifies as a mark of honor.[109] At the Bāb al-Sudda, Muḥammad ibn Abī 'Āmir and his men dismounted with Ja'far, Yaḥyā, and the Banū Khazar and walked to the *Dār al-Jund* to await permission to enter the caliph's *majlis.* Hishām, who enjoyed the privilege of riding into the palace compound, rode to the place of dismount at the *Dār al-Wuzarā',* where he too waited.[110]

The military quality of the procession and its staging, appropriate to the celebration of a triumph, made visible the practical foundation of the state and conveyed a message of strength and order. Al-Rāzī's descriptions suggest that the formal structure of the reception to follow was similar to the receptions associated with the two religious festivals but that now those who regularly participated in the *'īd* receptions witnessed this tremendous, somewhat threatening, display of might.

The audience with the caliph marked the culmination of Ja'far's journey from North Africa and his transition from a state of opposition to obedience. The reception was held in the *majlis al-sharqī,* the eastern hall ("salon rico"), overlooking the upper terrace and gardens, the same hall where the caliph celebrated the *a'yād* (s. *'id*). When the grand eunuchs of the palace brought Ja'far and Yaḥyā and the Banū Khazar to the *majlis,* the stage for their entrance had already been set. Escorted through the rows of notables from the provinces, palace guards, and prominent officials, all in their finery and armor, they found the human chain leading directly to the caliph seated on his throne.[111]

The caliph allowed these guests into his presence after he had already received everyone else who customarily attended his *'īd* receptions, and they were situated in their assigned positions.[112] The caliph sat in the recess of the hall and his three brothers sat to his right and left. The ministers, or *wuzarā'* (s. *wazīr*), sat next to them, separated by a space. The officials serving as the caliph's principal *ḥujjāb* (s. *ḥājib*) on that day stood on his right and left: the prefect of the city (*ṣāḥib al-madīna*) of Cordoba, Ja'far ibn 'Uthmān, the commander of the household troops (*ṣāḥib al-ḥasham*), Muḥammad ibn Qāsim ibn Ṭumlus, and the commander of the household cavalry (*ṣāḥib al-khayl*), Ziyād ibn Aflaḥ. Two rows of the *ahl al-khidma,* or officials of the palace service, followed, arranged according to their ranks, including the chiefs of police, treasurers and quartermasters, secretaries and eunuchs, extending all the way to the end of the hall. The Qurayshis (members of the tribe of the Prophet), the *mawālī* or clients of the dynasty, and the judges, jurisprudents and notaries had all been received and remained standing and waiting.[113]

Al-Rāzī tells us that at the threshold of the *majlis,* the guests, led by Ja'far, kissed the ground a number of times. They were brought forward, one by one, toward the throne and the caliph extended his hand. Each rendered homage and gave the salutation (*taslīm)* and was ordered to sit, as an honor. The caliph then questioned them in turn and expressed his acceptance of Ja'far and Yaḥyā's return to the fold, promising them they would be satisfied.[114] The interview thus affirmed a commitment of obedience on their part and favor and honor on his.

Although Ja'far and Yaḥyā were treated honorably, their audience with the caliph also had a quality of formal humiliation. Before the caliph and the assembled representatives of his realm, Ja'far and Yaḥyā confessed and repented their past association with the Fatimids. According to al-Rāzī, they explicitly renounced the Shi'i cause (*da'wa*) as one of error and unbelief, affirmed their commitment to *al-sunna w-al-jamā'a,* or Sunni Islam, and raised their voices to thank God for inspiring them to seek the sanctuary of the Commander of the Faithful and thus renew their Islam and strengthen their faith.[115] Invoking the role of the caliph as the guardian of the faith and the straight path, they verbally acknowledged the caliph's legitimacy, putting words to their acts of homage. The other participants in the reception, witnessing this moment, were included in it, having just rendered the obligation of *taslīm* themselves. The occasion thus generated a more general affirmation of allegiances.

Qaṣā'id (s. *qaṣīda*), or panegyric odes, that were recited to commemorate the occasion completed the exchange of submission and acceptance that took place in the reception. Explicitly celebrating the unique legitimacy of the caliph, they reinforced the collective experience of allegiance. As the poets recited their panegyrics to the caliph and his audience, their verses also conjured and addressed an audience that extended beyond the physical and temporal bounds of the *majlis.*[116] Such *qaṣā'id,* by objectifying the specific event, translated it into evidence for the caliph's right to rule and propaganda for the regime. Al-Rāzī presents an extensive portion of a *qaṣīda* by Muḥammad ibn Shukhayṣ that used the events of Ja'far and Yaḥyā's victory over Zīrī, and especially their return to obedience to the caliph, to declaim the legitimacy of the Andalusi Umayyad caliph against that of the Fatimid imam and to enjoin the lands of the east to "awaken from their slumber" and hurry to offer obedience to the true caliph if they hoped for intercession at the dawning of the Resurrection.[117]

As an occasion for the affirmation of ties of allegiance, the triumph finally concluded two days later when the caliph held a separate audience for the armies (*ajnād,* s. *jund*) of the provinces and the prominent men of those regions who had all been called on to attend Ja'far's arrival. Al-Rāzī reports that the ranks of the army entered the caliphal presence first, according to a prescribed order, and performed the right and obligation of *taslīm,* followed by the different delegations of civilians who were asked about local conditions and the conduct of the appointed governors. At the end of this reception, all were given permission to return to their homes.[118]

The sequence of ceremonial events just described conveyed Ja'far and Yaḥyā through their formal submission before the caliph and involved widening circles of participants and a range of spectators, in an affirmation of loyalty. The caliph's reception for the *'Īd al-Aḍḥā* two weeks later provided another occasion for the ritual renewal of ties, and Ja'far, Yaḥyā, and the Banū Khazar were commanded to attend.

The regularity and formality of ritual are used to evoke cosmological significance in many cultures;[119] in the caliph's court they evoked God's creation and order of the universe and the caliph's role as God's deputy. The *'īd* receptions, in particular, expressed the idea that the caliph presided over the faith as his ancestors had before him and that he ensured correct belief and practice. In other words, on these occasions the caliph was seen to enact his covenant with God. This meaning is especially vivid when we recall that the *'Īd al-Aḍḥā* commemorated the prophet Abraham's (Ibrāhīm's) covenant with God, the original covenant of "the first Muslim" (the first to surrender—*aslama*—to God's will).[120] The participation of Ja'far, Yaḥyā, and the Banū Khazar in the caliph's reception for the festival would visibly demonstrate their recognition of the caliph's religious as well as political authority and reinforce their "covenant" with him.

The *'īd* receptions were thus an opportunity to bring "strays" into the fold and visibly incorporate them into the body politic, defining their place in the regime. Al-Rāzī's text shows al-Ḥakam II did this with the Tujībīs of the Ebro valley (Upper March), with Ja'far and Yaḥyā, and with Ḥasan ibn Qannūn and the Idrisids.[121] The opportunity provided by a festival was ideal because the two festivals were already regular occasions for the enactment of the state and society's subordination to the caliph and the hierarchy he defined. Each official and notable called to attend awaited permission to enter, performed the ritual acts of greeting and felicitations, and went to a specially assigned place in the *majlis*.[122]

Ja'far and the Banū Khazar participated in the reception for the *'Īd al-Aḍḥā* as instructed, but we are told Yaḥyā was too ill to attend. Ja'far and the Banū Khazar entered the *majlis* with the *mawālī*—after the caliph's brothers, the wazirs, all of the most important *ahl al-khidma,* and the Qurayshis had greeted the caliph and taken their places. Their entrance with the *mawālī* marked their status among the clients of the dynasty, but then the caliph distinguished Ja'far, al-Rāzī tells us, with the honor of standing with the *ḥujjāb* until the end of the audience, apparently binding him more closely to his service.[123] Al-Rāzī's account reveals that for the next *'Īd al-Fiṭr,* the caliph accorded Ja'far a still more privileged position, a seat just below the *wuzarā',* while his brother, Yaḥyā, and his son, Ibrāhīm, stood in the ranks of the *ḥujjāb* just below the treasurers.[124] Ja'far's privilege seems to have continued until he fell into temporary disgrace in 974. His integration into the annual cycle of *'īd* celebrations represented (and imposed) an enduring commitment to Umayyad rule that could confirm others in their commitment.

Ḥasan ibn Qannūn's arrival in Cordoba provides another example of how the ceremonial reception of a former enemy served as an occasion to exemplify Umayyad caliphal legitimacy. The caliph had instructed his commanders in North Africa that he required Ḥasan to come to the Bāb al-Sudda and personally submit to him before he would trust any avowals of allegiance.[125] Thus Ḥasan preceded Ghālib in his arrival on the peninsula and audience with the caliph by a few months.[126] Unfortunately, we do not have an account of these events; as Ibn Hayyān tells us, his version of al-Rāzī's text is incomplete here, but we can reconstruct enough to recognize the pattern presented by Ja'far's experience.[127] It is interesting to see how the ceremonial sequence accommodated the differences in the circumstances of Ḥasan's arrival before the caliph.

Lines from a *qaṣīda* recited on the occasion of the *'Īd al-Fiṭr* of 974 convey a vision of Ḥasan's arrival on the peninsula and his escort to the capital as an impressive sight and intimidating experience. The poet Ibn Shukhayṣ tells us: "When [Ḥasan] came to the peninsula there encircled his retinue squadrons whose anger caused the very earth to tremble. / Every time he traversed the back of the earth its highlands and lowlands countered him with cavalry and infantry. / Until when he drew near the precinct of our heartlands, his heart throbbing and his intestines in commotion, / He found the armies whose march made him imagine the haughty hills were locusts hopping around him."[128] The way the poet describes Ḥasan's emotional state suggests that the orchestration of his journey through al-Andalus to the caliphal court publicly displayed his subjugation to the caliph: "[Ḥasan] kept crying, 'There is no god but God!' out of anguish like that of seafarers on the verge of shipwreck. / Hoping for life, fearing for death, he was in two opposite states: hope and dejection. / Until there appeared the star of good fortune [i.e., the Caliph] that interceded for him." The poet's rendering of Ḥasan's anxiety over his fate and indication of its relief takes us from the *burūz* to the caliphal reception that followed and the final granting of forgiveness.

Following the pattern of Ja'far's example, the caliph must have received Ḥasan on his arrival in the capital and, as the lines quoted above suggest, granted his pardon after Ḥasan rendered homage and renounced his past. Ḥasan subsequently attended the caliph's reception for the next *'īd,* the *'Īd al-Fiṭr,* as he was obliged to, confirming his obedience and subordination. Al-Rāzī provides an account of that occasion, describing it as a celebration that marked the caliph's happiness for the victory over Ḥasan ibn Qannūn and the security of his rule across the straits.[129] The caliph's relentless struggle against Ḥasan had come to symbolize his determination to destroy opposition and reunite the community and to root out heresy and restore the purity of the faith in North Africa. Thus, in al-Rāzī's words, Ḥasan's presence in the caliph's receptions for the *a'yād* became an "adornment" that demonstrated how the insolent were now humble before the caliph's authority. Ḥasan's attendance on the occasion of the *'Īd al-Fiṭr,* in particular, highlighted his recognition of al-Ḥakam II's legitimacy as guardian of the true faith, as he now officially and publicly recognized the end of the fast of Ramadan as determined by Sunni practice—that is, according to the sighting of the new moon.[130]

As al-Rāzī describes, Ḥasan ibn Qannūn, his brother, Yaḥyā,

and sons 'Alī, Manṣūr, and Ḥasan entered the audience hall with the Quraysh, being members of the tribe themselves, after the brothers, the wazirs, and the *ahl al-khidma* (including Ja'far and Yaḥyā) had already taken their places. They greeted the caliph in turn, then waited while the *mawālī*, judges of the provinces, jurisprudents, notaries, and then ranks from the caliph's personal guard were received.[131] The celebration of the *'īd* ended, according to custom, with orations and *qaṣā'id* testifying to the glory of the reign and the legitimacy of the caliph. After suffering the ignominy of defeat, Ḥasan now had to endure the final humiliation as the poets celebrated the caliph's triumph over him. Ibn Shukhayṣ, for example, disparaged the former rebel by declaiming how the "failed fool" learned that the caliph's "resolve was an irrevocable decree, his wrath destruction, and that his destruction and wrath are on God's behalf, / and that even if he fled as far as China, it would not save him from the caliph's sword."[132] His verses even became offensive, in al-Rāzī's view, when he described the barbarity of the Banū Ḥasan, who "grew up with wild beasts in a savage crowd."[133] Having heaped so much scorn, Ibn Shukhayṣ reminded Ḥasan, and all who listened to his words, of the magnanimity of the caliph who held the power of life and death in his hands.

The verses of Ṭāhir ibn Muḥammad al-Baghdādī (al-Muhannad) celebrated this central theme of the reception more generally, describing how the caliph's pardon purified those who sought it and restored the community as a whole: "When he took possession of them [his enemies] they were in error; then he forgave them and God granted their errant [steps] aright. / His beneficence erased their evil deeds; his acts of virtue covered up their sins. . . . / How many a time did he forgive, though able [to punish]?"[134] By including Ḥasan in the reception for the *'īd*, al-Ḥakam II made manifest his mercy and generosity toward even the most notorious reprobate, once he formally acknowledged the caliph's legitimacy.

General Ghālib's return to al-Andalus in September 974 may have occasioned the greatest triumphal ceremony of al-

Ḥakam II's reign: the caliph's most accomplished commander returned home having secured the obedience of all of western North Africa. Al-Rāzī's description reveals how the ceremonial pattern that defined Ja'far's experience again accommodated the differences in Ghālib's status and circumstances. The parade through Cordoba and the next day to Madīnat al-Zahrā' celebrated Ghālib as returning hero. He arrived with a vast army composed of all the North African amirs who had submitted to his authority, as well as the four prominent Idrisids and their families, tributes to his success.[135] Together with a special escort designated by the caliph, they all rode to the bridge of Cordoba, where a military formation extended up to the Bāb al-Sudda of the palace of Cordoba and the station of the chief of police, and then on to the camp of al-Na'ūra to spend the night. The next day, the escort accompanied them through the human passageway, "constructed" over night, that linked al-Na'ūra to the palace-city. Once through the gates of Madīnat al-Zahrā', Ghālib enjoyed the privilege of dismounting at the *Dār al-Wuzarā'*. The Idrisids who accompanied him had been granted a lesser honor and had to dismount sooner at the *Dār al-Jund;* everyone else had dismounted even before this at the Bāb al-Sudda, the threshold of the caliphal domain.[136]

The caliph's reception honored Ghālib and clearly identified him as the deputy of the Commander of the Faithful. Ghālib entered the audience hall with the wazirs according to protocol, for he was a *wazīr-qā'id* (minister-commander). The caliph distinguished him, however, by having him serve as his *ḥājib* and stand in the most privileged position to his right. Next to him stood the commander of the caliph's guard and cavalry (*ṣāḥib al-khayl w-al-ḥasham*), and opposite him stood the prefect of the city of Cordoba, followed by the prefect of the city of Madīnat al-Zahrā'. On this occasion, the caliph clearly celebrated Ghālib as his "right-hand man."[137]

The presence of Aḥmad ibn 'Īsā Ḥannūn and the other Idrisids in both parade and reception reinforced the message of Ghālib's triumph and the caliph's dominance in North Africa.

They had already, while in North Africa, obtained a grant of security (*aman*) and received gifts from the caliphal stores and stables, even before Ḥasan's surrender.[138] However, their participation in the caliphal reception honoring Ghālib ritually reenacted their submission to the caliph's authority and demonstrated their subordination to the hierarchy he defined. As al-Rāzī describes, they waited their turn to enter the *majlis* in the *Dār al-Jund* until the eunuch secretaries arrived to escort them. Their shaykh was the first to offer the formal salutation and received, in turn, the caliph's pardon and respect.[139]

Al-Rāzī tells us the caliph honored the Idrisid shaykh by allowing him to sit on a raised seat. After all the Idrisids were finally seated, he praised them, thanked them for their obedience, and promised them beneficence and satisfaction. The caliph honored them further by granting their oldest sons an audience as well. The boys each gave the salutation and sat in designated places below their fathers.[140] The occasion thus served to reinforce allegiances into the next generation. In fact, al-Ḥakam II had arranged for is son Hishām to hold a simultaneous reception in an adjacent hall so that all who attended the reception of the caliph rendered homage, in turn, to his designated heir. This included the prominent men of the caliphal service and the capital, the Idrisids, as well as the provincial leaders who had been invited to attend.[141]

By now the reader can recognize the significance of Ḥannun's ritual submission at the heart of the ceremony attending Ghālib's triumphant return to the caliphal capital. The surviving portion of al-Rāzī's chronicle of al-Ḥakam II's reign has allowed us to piece together the elements of a ceremonial sequence emblematic of Andalusi Umayyad claims to caliphal legitimacy, particularly in its reports of Ja'far ibn 'Alī's arrival in Cordoba in 971 and Ghālib ibn 'Abd al-Raḥmān's return in 974. We can see how a celebration of military success, combined with a ceremony marking the formal submission of a former enemy, could be used to enact the caliph's claims to legitimacy and affirm allegiances. The ceremonial sequence identified al-Ḥakam II as the military commander dedicated to warfare against enemies of the faith and the community and demonstrated him to be the genuine leader of the Muslims, dedicated to restoring unity and bringing the deviant back to the true path. In this context, the caliph's former enemies, and his most important subjects, all ritually acknowledged his authority through the act of *taslīm.*

Before concluding, we can make a few final observations about what al-Rāzī's text can tell us about the ceremonial life of Cordoba and its representation, and promotion, of caliphal legitimacy. We have discussed how the *'īd* celebrations identified the caliph with the sacred calendar and highlighted his role as guardian of the faith and how the caliphal receptions regularly enacted submission to the caliph's religious and political authority. It is not surprising that al-Ḥakam II chose the occasion of an *'īd* reception to introduce Hishām as his heir. More specifically, he chose the occasion of the *'Īd al-Aḍḥā* of 974.

The caliph formally identified his heir and secured his recognition through the device of a dual reception, similar to the one described above (Ghālib's reception followed the *'īd* by about a month). The caliph received the prominent men of his administration and capital in the eastern *majlis* of Madīnat al-Zahrā, looking over the gardens, and Hishām received them in turn, seated in a western *majlis.*[142] Al-Rāzī informs us that this arrangement recalled al-Ḥakam II's own first public reception during the caliphate of his father, on the occasion of the *'Īd al-Aḍḥā* of the year 921.[143] This may have followed a customary pattern, as the amir 'Abd Allāh also secured recognition of his heir, 'Abd al-Raḥmān III, by incorporating him into festival celebrations.[144]

The *'īd* ceremonies provided a perfect opportunity to establish the next in line for the dynastic inheritance of the caliphate since they already served as a forum for the affirmation of allegiance to the caliph and, by extension, to his dynasty. The regularity of the festival cycle, which distinguished the *'īd* receptions from all other celebrations, allowed the caliph to project his legitimacy backward and forward in time.[145] The Festival of the Sacrifice was particularly apt because it memorialized the willingness of a father (Ibrāhīm) to sacrifice his son (Ismā'īl) for God. The story of Ibrāhīm affirmed patrilineality by acknowledging the father-son bond as the strongest human relationship, and Islamic tradition identified Ibrāhīm as a Muslim patriarch and Ismā'īl as the progenitor of the Arabs.[146]

Extant sources do not inform us much more about *'īd* celebrations in al-Andalus in the tenth century. Al-Rāzī's descriptions suggest that the caliph's reception defined the occasion. Unlike his Fatimid rivals, al-Ḥakam II did not lead the public prayer for the festivals but delegated this to the *khuṭabā'* or preachers of Madīnat al-Zahrā' and Cordoba, who did so in the open-air *muṣallā* outside the walls of both cities.[147] Seated on his throne in his *majlis* overlooking the city and country below, the caliph established the palace as the center and focus of the official celebration of the religious festivals.

Seeing the caliph in the setting of an *'īd* reception, or on extraordinary occasions such as Ghālib's return to al-Andalus, was a privilege accorded to the official and local elite, who came to the caliph's palace by command and entered his *majlis* by permission. Yet the occasional sight of the caliph was important to maintaining and generating feelings of loyalty and solidarity among the local population as well. Since all public ceremony in the capital, as well as the court, referred to the caliph as a symbol of the integrity of the community and the faith, the caliph had to appear, however infrequently, to his subjects to invest the symbol with meaning. Thus we see al-Ḥakam II and Hishām standing on the Bāb al-Sudda to see Ghālib off on his campaign, to review the troops, or to supervise the distribution of alms after the *'Īd al-Fiṭr* of 975.[148] Such appearances, in turn, ensured that the Bāb al-Sudda itself would continue to signify the caliph's authority and presence, even when he was out of sight.

We can appreciate the importance of the visibility of the caliph in accounts of the restiveness of the population of Cordoba after it had not seen Hishām for some years following his accession to the throne. The chamberlain, Muḥammad ibn Abī 'Āmir al-Manṣūr, who had usurped all effective authority from the young caliph, had deliberately kept him hidden from view because he recognized the potential threat of the caliph's symbolic power. However, to allay dangerous rumors that he had killed the caliph, he presented him to the public. Hishām rode slowly through Cordoba in a cavalcade, ornamented with the insignia of the caliphate (the *ṭawīla,* a high turban, and the *qaḍīb,* or staff), while al-Manṣūr led his "master's" horse by the bridle.[149]

Our sources do not provide accounts of regular caliphal processions in al-Andalus but do record frequent travel between the two capitals, or to the *munyas* in the countryside, as well as inspection tours of public works and hunting and fishing expeditions.[150] Such cavalcades, while governed by a certain protocol, had a spontaneous quality that gave the caliph a certain accessibility, an interesting counterpart to the formality of the caliphal audiences.[151] Al-Rāzī does, however, describe one significant ceremonial procession that reinforces the argument for the importance of the caliph's public visibility.

When al-Ḥakam II fell ill in the fall of 974, he withdrew completely for a few months. At the first signs of recovery, he held a private reception for his closest officials, who had not seen him, and then announced his return to health more publicly by granting relief of taxes for all the Muslims of al-Andalus, proclaiming that he had not ceased to look after their needs.[152] As soon as he could, he rode to the congregational mosque of Madīnat al-Zahrā' with Hishām to attend the Friday prayer, and the next day he left the palace city for Cordoba in a grand and formal procession.[153]

As al-Rāzī describes, the procession became an occasion for the affirmation of allegiances, beginning with the highest officials of the caliph's government. Hishām preceded his father to the gate where the official entourage waited to escort them, and there received the formal salutation of the prefects of Cordoba and Madīnat al-Zahrā', who dismounted to greet him, followed by the others. Al-Rāzī tells us that when the caliph appeared, the same officials approached him and kissed the ground before him, then ritually greeted him and invoked blessings on him.[154]

The procession advanced to Cordoba at a stately pace, taking two days. The caliph and his escort spent the night in the *munya* of Arḥā' Nāṣih and proceeded the next day to the *munya* of al-Na'ūra, where they stopped for the noon prayer. Here the entourage was joined by the chiefs of police and officials from Cordoba, who came to participate in escorting the caliph to his palace in the old capital. When they met at the gate of the *munya*, each dismounted to salute the caliph and his son and then remounted and arranged themselves according to ranks.[155]

The formation of the cavalcade recapitulated the formality of the caliph's audiences, with the prefects of the two capitals each serving as *ḥājib* by the caliph's side, along with the great eunuchs. Just outside Cordoba, the cavalcade was met, in turn, by the most important men of the Quraysh and the *mawālī* on horseback. Each dismounted and rendered homage, invoking God's blessings. The growing procession now paraded through the main market of Cordoba, where the caliph "received" the *ṣāḥib al-ṣūq* or market inspector, the wealthy men and merchants, and others, who saluted him and blessed him—with fervor—according to al-Rāzī. As they continued, they were welcomed by people of high and low status alike, until they at last entered the palace.[156] Finally, as for a formal reception, poets commemorated the occasion, celebrating the health of the caliph and his arrival in Cordoba, extolling his virtues as Commander of the Faithful, and invoking God's blessings upon him.[157] In the verses of Malik ibn Ḥasan, "All ask God, with pure intentions, to preserve [the caliph's] vigor, for he defends our worldly interests (*dunyā*) and guards our faith (*dīn*), grants us justice, and destroys the enemy."[158]

· THREE ·

The Caliphate in Captivity[1]

Are we not the sons of Marwān, however our life has changed and the turns of fate overtaken us?

—Attributed to Muḥammad ibn ʿAbd al-Malik ibn ʿAbd al-Raḥmān al-Nāṣir[2]

Al-Ḥakam II made every effort to ensure the succession of his son Hishām, but at his death his heir was a boy of less than twelve years. Hishām's ascent to the caliphate may have been questionable on legal grounds, as he was a minor, and certainly his youth and lack of experience made him susceptible to the ambitions of others.

Immediately after al-Ḥakam II's death, two of the prominent eunuchs of the court plotted to place the defunct caliph's brother, al-Mughīra, on the throne. Muḥammad ibn Abī ʿĀmir, who had recently returned from North Africa where he had served as chief *qāḍī* in the Umayyad territories, and the *ḥājib* Jaʿfar ibn ʿUthmān al-Muṣḥafī ensured Hishām's accession by averting the eunuchs' coup. Thus two days after al-Ḥakam II's death, Ibn Abī ʿĀmir presided over the swearing of the oath of allegiance (*bayʿa*) to the new caliph, Hishām (II) al-Muʿayyad Billāh.[3] Over the next five years, Ibn Abī ʿĀmir took advantage of his close association with the caliph to establish himself as supreme ruler of al-Andalus.

Muḥammad ibn Abī ʿĀmir achieved his rise to the pinnacle of power in al-Andalus with political savvy and the ruthless elimination of all who had shared in al-Ḥakam II's rule and were in a position to challenge him: al-Ḥakam II's intimates at court, his military commanders, his palace guard. Sources report that he then confined the caliph to his palace. In their representation, Hishām became a prisoner within fortified walls, surrounded by guards who kept him isolated from the outside world and by spies who reported on his every movement.[4]

Ibn 'Idhārī and others drew an analogy between 'Amirid rule and domination of the Andalusi Umayyad caliphate and Buyid rule and domination of the Abbasid caliphate. As they put it, Muḥammad ibn Abī 'Āmir became supreme master of all the affairs of the state and the dynasty after he confined the caliph, and then he made his authority hereditary, following the example of the Daylamī (Buyid) amirs.[5] The Buyid amirs did not make the Abbasid caliph disappear entirely from view in the way the sources suggest Hishām disappeared. In fact, they made the caliph an icon and the center of ceremonial life, constructing the illusion that he delegated his authority to them. While we see glimpses of this kind of iconization in the first five years of Hishām's caliphate, the sources insist the caliph was then "completely cut off from the rest of the world" so that "no one feared him, no one wanted anything from him, and he was soon forgotten. . . . In time, nothing was known about him except his name on the money and in the *khuṭba*."[6]

It is difficult to know whether Ibn Abī 'Āmir went as far as the sources suggest to monopolize not only all power but all prestige. Would he not have gained more by cultivating the caliph as a legitimating symbol than by locking him away as a potential rival? In the last twenty years of his reign, was the caliph never shown to exercise his symbolic authority?

Even if the available sources cannot provide us with a full view of Ibn Abī 'Āmir's rule, they provide an interpretation that informs our understanding of Andalusi Umayyad caliphal legitimacy. The following discussion reconstructs and assesses Ibn Abī 'Āmir's career according to the historical reality of the sources. Read at face value, the accounts suggest some of the ways Ibn Abī 'Āmir manipulated the themes and representations the Umayyads used to promote their authority. If we accept the possibility of historiographical distortion, we can still appreciate how the texts demonstrate the enduring significance of these themes and symbols.

As the sources describe, Ibn Abī 'Āmir began his political career in the service of al-Ḥakam II and held a number of positions, including the office of *wakīl* for Hishām. He enjoyed the favor of Hishām's mother, Ṣubḥ, which was instrumental in his early rise to power and put him in a position to present himself as defender of the rights of the legitimate caliph.[7] Ibn 'Idhārī reports that following al-Ḥakam II's death, it was Ibn Abī 'Āmir who counseled Ja'far ibn 'Uthmān to organize a caliphal cavalcade through Cordoba to intimidate any opposition to the boy's succession. He ensured an enthusiastic popular response to the caliph's accession to the throne by persuading Hishām II to abolish a tax on oil and publicly established his connection with the ruler by leading the parade himself.[8]

The sources suggest Ibn Abī 'Āmir exploited the importance of holy war and military success to Andalausi Umayyad caliphal ideology as he pursued his ambitions and promoted his authority. He maintained Hishām II in the *qaṣr* as an emblem of dynastic continuity and parlayed his military prowess into evidence of his right to command. He thus divorced the rhetoric of dynastic legitimacy from that of performance. Over the years of his rise through the highest ranks in the capital (976–981) and of his exclusive rule (981–1002) Ibn Abī 'Āmir led and sponsored over fifty campaigns and raids into the Christian territories, including the sack of Santiago de Campostella in 997, and asserted his authority over western North Africa.[9]

The saga of Ibn Abī 'Āmir's military career began when he volunteered to lead an expedition against the Christians as soon as Hishām II was secure on the throne. His early military adventures inspired his rapid promotion at court from chief of police to prefect of the city to *ḥājib*. Ibn 'Idhārī explains that Ibn Abī 'Āmir's offer to lead a campaign to the north in February 977 was designed to win the allegiance of the army, who profited from a successful raid, and to establish himself as the leader of the *jihād*.[10] Later that spring Ibn Abī 'Āmir joined Ghālib in a second expedition and returned to Cordoba to the honor of a new appointment. On Ghālib's recommendation, he became the new *ṣāḥib al-madīna* for Cordoba, replacing Muḥammad ibn Ja'far ibn 'Uthmān. Ibn Abī 'Āmir must have appreciated the popular appeal of waging successful war, marching into the capital with booty and prisoners, and the venerable Ghālib is said to have advised him to take advantage of the prestige victory would grant him.[11] When Ibn Abī 'Āmir returned from his third expedition, again with captives, booty, and trophy heads, the caliph granted him the title of *Dhū al-Wizāratayn* (holder of the two wazirates) and the same rank and salary as Ghālib.[12] He married Ghālib's daughter, received the title of *ḥājib* shortly afterward, and then successfully moved to displace his rival in the same office, Ja'far ibn 'Uthmān, with Ghālib's support. After the elimination of Ja'far, it was not long before Ibn Abī 'Āmir turned against Ghālib, who was based on the frontier in Medinaceli, as the last obstacle to his supremacy.

Ibn Abī 'Āmir's continued commitment to *jihād* garnered revenues and secured the material and political support of the army, particularly after he replaced the Andalusi *ajnād* with salaried Berber troops in the early 990s. He could also use *jihād* to promote his popularity and maintain a continuity with the policies of his Umayyad predecessors. We do not have texts of his letters and proclamations, but he must have publicized his victories and expressed his authority in terms of his divine support and dedication to holy war and reinforced the message with the ceremonial departures and arrivals of conquering armies.

Ibn Abī 'Āmir appears to have followed the model of the Umayyad caliphs not only in the prosecution of holy war but in monumental construction, the elaboration of protocol, and demonstrative vigilance over the purity of the faith. He established the palace-city of Madīnat al-Zāhira in 979 as a new seat for the rule of al-Andalus, consciously relocating the administration away from the *qaṣr* of Cordoba, Madīnat al-Zahrā', and the caliph but retaining access to the traditional capital. He chose a site to the east of Cordoba and a name that recalled Madīnat al-Zahrā', defining himself as comparable to, yet distinct from, the Umayyad caliphs. Destroyed in the same outbreak of pillage and looting that left the caliphal palace-city in ruins, no traces of Madinat al-Zahira have been found. Nevertheless, textual descriptions record the resources employed in the project and vaunt the vast size of the walled city and its many lavish palaces, residences, and gardens. Like Madīnat al-Zahrā, Ibn Abī 'Āmir constructed al-Zāhira as a city with a great mosque, markets, caravansarais, granaries, and mills. He gave land grants to his courtiers around the city, and they and others who sought proximity to the *ṣāḥib al-dawla* and center of power built homes in newly created suburbs until the region between Madīnat al-Zāhira and Cordoba became completely inhabited.[13]

Ibn Abī 'Āmir began construction just after the arrest of the *ḥājib* Ja'far ibn 'Uthmān. While Ibn 'Idhārī's text attributes his move to fear of assassination, we might also consider the foundation of Madīnat al-Zāhira as a celebration of Ibn Abī 'Āmir's triumph and a testament of his power. The same source reports that with the establishment of the new city, his independence from Hishām became apparent to all. Ibn Abī 'Āmir ordered that all taxes and all correspondence be directed to Madīnat al-Zāhira and not to the Bāb al-Khalīfa, the gate of the caliph. In Ibn 'Idhārī's words, he then closed the door of the *qaṣr* on the caliph completely, relegating him to a state of nonexistence.[14]

The construction of Madīnat al-Zāhira marked a change in Ibn Abī 'Āmir's rule. To explain his assumption of practical authority, he announced that Hishām II had entrusted him with the supervision of the kingdom (*al-naẓar fī amr al-mulk*), in order to devote himself to the worship of the Lord.[15] While Ibn Abī 'Āmir maintained his official identity as the caliph's *ḥājib,* he nonetheless began to style himself in grander terms. In 981, after prevailing over Ghālib, he assumed the *laqab* al-Manṣūr (Victor), a name that recalled the Abbasid and Fatimid caliphs but also derived from the same root (*n-ṣ-r*) as al-Nāṣir and al-Mustanṣir, suggesting continuity with their rule and projecting the same championship of the faith.[16] Respecting, but also exploiting, the prerogatives of the caliphate, he ensured that his name and honorific followed those of the caliph in the *khuṭba* and on the coins of the realm (*sikka*) and on the embroidery of the honorary robes distributed as gifts.[17] The elaboration of court protocol further enhanced Ibn Abī 'Āmir al-Manṣūr's prestige and demonstrated his authority. He required that anyone who entered his presence kiss his hand and address him as *mawlā* (master), and Ibn 'Idhārī reports that the protocol for the *ḥājib* became essentially the same as for the caliph, with the only difference in their names (and formal titles).[18] In 991 al-Manṣūr designated his son, 'Abd al-Malik (al-Muẓaffar), his successor, and bestowed on him the title of *ḥājib* and high commander.[19] Al-Manṣūr no longer used the title of *ḥājib* himself but only his *laqab* until 996, when he announced his exclusive designation as *sayyid,* or lord, and came to be addressed as *al-malik al-karīm,* the honored king.[20]

We do not know more about court-sponsored ceremony during al-Manṣūr's reign, although incidental references suggest military parades departed to and from Madīnat al-Zāhira.[21] Accounts cited above describing Ibn Abī 'Āmir al-Manṣūr's leading the caliph in parade through the capital suggest the *ḥājib*'s savvy about the manipulation of symbols and ceremonies, representing himself as second in command as he, in fact, led the caliph by the bridle. One of the last public ceremonies before Hishām II's sequestration may have been Ibn Abī 'Āmir's wedding to Ghālib's daughter, Asma. Ghālib brought her to Cordoba from Medinaceli, and Ibn 'Idhārī reports the wedding (*zifāf*) took place on the night of Nayruz, the New Year, and that the caliph himself presided over the ceremony. He declares the spectacle was unprecedented in its majesty and fame, and we can imagine it raised the *ḥājib's* profile tremendously.[22]

The caliph's withdrawal from view shortly thereafter was supposedly complete; he was no longer visible to the inhabitants of Cordoba or even to the ministers of the realm. We have no view of the celebration of the *'īd* festivals. Given their importance in the ritual calendar and the caliph's symbolic religious authority it is difficult to imagine that the caliph no longer took part in any fashion after the construction of Madīnat al-Zāhira. Did the *ḥājib* keep the idea of the caliphate alive simply by keeping Hishām's name alive, visible on the coins and heard in the Friday blessing?

Following the model of the Umayyads, al-Manṣūr sponsored a significant addition to the Great Mosque of Cordoba in 987 to 988, adding eight aisles to the east along the entire length of the mosque. Sources report that the expansion was intended to accommodate the growth in Cordoba's population due to the settlement of immigrant Berbers, their immigration strongly associated with al-Manṣūr's reign. However, we can appreciate al-Manṣūr's conscious decision to make his mark on this Umayyad monument, underscoring the continuity of the regime and confirming his commitment to Cordoba as the traditional capital. Perhaps as a consequence of the urban topography al-Manṣūr could expand the prayer hall only by extending it eastward, destroying the symmetry of the mosque and the axial alignment of the *miḥrāb*. If so, the mosque inadvertently represents discontinuity as well as continuity and al-Manṣūr's indirect relationship to the history of Andalusi Umayyad rule.[23]

Al-Manṣūr no doubt recognized, as his Umayyad predecessors had before him, that patronage of the mosque demonstrated his concern for the community and the practice of the religion. Ibn 'Idhārī represents his work on the mosque as one of his greatest acts of piety and merit, along with his commitment to *jihād* (he supposedly carried a Qur'an copied in his own hand and a winding cloth for burial, on every campaign).[24] In the context of continuous *jihād* against the Christians, the expansion also expressed the vitality of the Muslim community and faith under al-Manṣūr's command, particularly if, as Ibn Ḥayyān reports, al-Manṣūr subsequently had the bells of the church of

Santiago de Campostella brought to Cordoba on the backs of Christian prisoners and suspended as lamps in the Great Mosque.

Ibn Abī ʻĀmir al-Manṣūr's public commitment to the purity of the faith is represented in reports of his purge of al-Ḥakam II's library of all books dealing with philosophy and materialism (*al-dahriyya*), in the presence of the most important *'ulamā.'* Ibn 'Idhārī relates that he was hostile to all who were interested in matters of philosophy and religious controversy or treated the prescriptions of the Shari'a lightly.[25] Al-Manṣūr could claim a firm grounding in religious scholarship, and while he rejected al-Ḥakam II's broad patronage of learning and interest in a range of sciences, he must have conformed to the rhetoric of the Andalusi Umayyad caliphs regarding his vigilance over the religion.[26]

Al-Manṣūr's independent rule lasted for two decades until his death in 1002. Much as he promoted his personal cult, he did not reign unchallenged, and over the course of these decades he vigorously suppressed any opposition, executing his own son 'Abd Allāh in 989. Sources reflecting back on al-Manṣūr's reign provide intimations of opposition to the *ḥājib*'s usurpation of the caliph's authority that perhaps reflect politics contemporary with his rule. For example, Ibn Ḥayyān reports that he read that when Muḥammad ibn Abī ʻĀmir removed Hishām from the sight of the populace (*ḥajaba Hishām 'an al-nas*) and proceeded to rule without him, talk circulated in Cordoba inimical to this state of affairs. The historian cites the following verses he attributes to the time, meant to be read in the voice of Hishām: "Isn't it strange that someone like me has the least thing denied him? All the world is ruled in his name, but he has nothing in his hands."[27] Ibn 'Idhārī reports that al-Manṣūr had Muḥammad ibn Abī Jum'a's tongue cut out before he killed and crucified him for holding "detestable opinions" and predicting the end of al-Manṣūr's reign.[28] Another former partisan of the *ḥājib* received fifty lashes, imprisonment, and finally exile for the following verses: "What you want, and not what Destiny wants, prevails—for you are the Vanquisher [al-Qahhār]. It is as if you were the Prophet Muḥammad, and your supporters were the Anṣār."[29] The poet went too far in comparing al-Manṣūr directly to God (the Vanquisher) and to the Prophet, a comparison that could be considered offensive in religious terms and provocative for a caliph's chamberlain. If the story is true, the poet's effrontery went further, for he recited verses to the chamberlain that the renegade Andalusi poet Ibn Hāni' (d. 973) had composed in praise of the "heretical" Fatimid imam al-Mu'izz.[30]

In North Africa, a number of Berber chiefs took advantage of the change in regime to break the treaties they had agreed to during al-Ḥakam II's reign. Notably, Ḥasan ibn Qannūn resumed his rebellion until al-Manṣūr's army forced him to surrender. This time, however, he did not receive the honorable treatment he had experienced under al-Ḥakam II. While the general in the field granted him security (*aman*) and sent him under guard to Cordoba, al-Manṣūr reportedly had him killed on the way.[31] Ḥasan's loyalty to the Umayyad caliphate may not have been very profound, but sources report that at least some of the rebel chiefs broke with Cordoba because of al-Manṣūr's usurpation of the legitimate caliph's authority. Ibn 'Idhārī, for example, recounts that Zīrī ibn 'Aṭiya Maghrāwī broke his oaths of allegiance because the *ḥājib* had made Hishām his puppet and seized his rule.[32] A number of sources cite verses attributed to one of the Idrisid rebels bemoaning the disappearance of the caliph and condemning the government of the chamberlain: "Can it be that an Umayyad is alive and yet this hunchback governs the vast kingdom?"[33]

The assessment of later historians may heavily color the representation of dissent described here, for the Andalusi and North African historiography of the eleventh century and later portrays al-Manṣūr and his reign in ambivalent terms.[34] Ibn 'Idhārī, as has been observed, celebrates him as a great champion of *jihād* and praises his good works—enlarging the mosque, building bridges, suppressing dangerous opinion, maintaining security, enforcing justice—and his personal piety and learning. He also criticizes him for exceeding his mandate, making a mockery of the caliphate, and introducing Berbers in large numbers into the army—Berbers who would ravage Cordoba and reduce Madīnat al-Zahrā' and Madīnat al-Zāhira to rubble. In this ambivalence we can appreciate how al-Manṣūr's successful performance as ruler, with conscious attention to the precedents of 'Abd al-Raḥmān III al-Ḥakam II, went far to mitigate his appropriation of the caliph Hishām II's practical authority.

Al-Manṣūr never violated the formal boundary between himself and the caliph. He did not declare himself Commander of the Faithful, despite the fact that he exercised the functions of government and represented himself as fulfilling the mandate of the caliphate. It is interesting to see that the North African historian and scholar Ibn Khaldūn (d. 1406) attributed the demise of the 'Amirids and the collapse of centralized rule in al-Andalus in part to the eventual violation of that boundary between caliph and *ḥājib*.[35] Al-Manṣūr's second son,'Abd al-Raḥmān, who succeeded his brother 'Abd al-Malik al-Muẓaffar to the office of *ḥājib*, convinced Hishām II to formally designate him as heir to the caliphate in 1008.[36]

It may well be that the nomination of an heir who was not of the Umayyad house or even a Qurayshi highlighted the captivity of the Umayyad caliphate and precipitated the plot to replace Hishām II with another member of the dynasty. A great-, great-grandson of 'Abd al-Raḥmān III, Muḥammad, who styled himself "al-Mahdī," was able to rally enough support in Cordoba on the basis of this outrage to make a bid for the caliphate himself. In the end, Muḥammad al-Mahdī managed to rule Cordoba for nine months but could not survive the opposition of various military groups and political factions eager to protect their own interests and promote their own ambitions, and his "restoration" of the Umayyad caliphate appears to us a farce. Al-Mahdī's coup underscores the currency and limits of Umayyad dynastic legitimacy. Over the ensuing two decades, as competing factions continued to vie with each other for power (often in alliance with Christian armies), they did so while supporting particular Umayyad claimants to the throne. Ultimately, however, the troops employed in the contest destroyed the capital and the palace-cities, especially after the long siege of 1010 to 1013, and the failure of any one faction or pretender to establish and maintain effective authority and a monopoly of power in Cordoba saw the fractionalization of al-Andalus into petty kingdoms (of the *mulūk al-ṭawā'if*). Finally, in 1031 the inhabitants of Cordoba recognized a local notable as their ruler and "abolished" the Umayyad caliphate, banning all Marwanids from the city.

Respect for Umayyad dynastic legitimacy, however, endured even after the end of Umayyad rule of al-Andalus and the banishment of the Marwanids from Cordoba, as *ṭā'ifa* kings seeking to establish their own legitimacy associated their authority with the Andalusi Umayyad caliphate in a number of ways. Seville, for example, maintained a shadow caliph purported to be Hishām II. Other *ṭā'ifa* kings struck coins inscribed with their *alqāb* and the name "Hishām al-Mu'ayyad Billāh, Commander of the Faithful" or their names coupled with "Abd Allāh, Commander of the Faithful," suggesting their authority derived from a caliph who is unnamed except as "Servant of God."[37]

Part II

STAKING THE CLAIM: HISTORIOGRAPHICAL CONSTRUCTIONS OF LEGITIMACY

Introduction

The Andalusi Umayyads developed and consciously promoted a caliphal ideology. They used letters, documents, proclamations, and the propaganda of their poets to declare their right to rule and interpret and justify their actions, making a case for the revival of the Umayyad caliphate. They also used a variety of visible forms to convey and promote their caliphal authority broadly. The words provided a context for understanding the symbols, monuments, and ceremonies that they employed and elaborated, while the symbols, monuments, and ceremonies gave force to the claims expressed in words, tangibly demonstrating the glory of Umayyad rule, inspiring awe, and securing respect.

The caliphs addressed themselves to a number of audiences—the circle of men involved in the government and politics of al-Andalus, the inhabitants of the kingdom, the rulers and populations of the neighboring territories (the Christian north and the Muslims of North Africa), and finally all who might hear of Cordoba, within and outside the Islamic world, now and in the future. The interest in posterity that informed monumental construction motivated the caliphs to sponsor chronicles of their reigns as records of their achievements, and they gave historians such as Aḥmad al-Rāzī (d. 955), ʿĪsā al-Rāzī (d. 989), and ʿArīb ibn Sa'īd (d. 980) access to their archives so they could immortalize their rule, as, indeed, they have.

The Andalusi Umayyads also promoted historical writing as part of a larger effort to cultivate scholarship and *adab* ("manners" and the literature of cultivated men) and make their court and capital centers of learning and sophistication.[1] They strived to make Cordoba a true challenger for the cultural and intellectual leadership of the Islamic world in competition with Baghdad and later with Cairo. Al-Ḥakam II, in particular, became renown for his patronage of scholarship. He made the Great Mosque a famous center for learning and boasted a personal library of four hundred thousand volumes, said to have ranked with the great libraries of the Abbasids and Fatimids.[2]

Some of the historians and men of letters (*udabā'*, s. *adīb*) employed by the court directed themselves to the cultural integration of al-Andalus into the wider Islamic world, composing works of *adab* that largely cited eastern texts, such as Ibn 'Abd Rabbihi's *al-Iqd al-farīd* and al-Qālī's *Kitāb al-amālī,* or integrating western history into the eastern narrative, as 'Arīb ibn Sa'īd did in his summary and continuation of al-Ṭabarī's universal history.[3] Most of the Andalusi historians, however, dedicated themselves to court and local history. Because all the Andalusi historians contemporary with the caliphate had close ties to the dynasty as *mawālī,* or family clients, and were often court appointees, their histories served to interpret and diffuse the concepts and themes disseminated by the caliphs. The historiography thus represents a secondary and complex, sometimes contradictory, medium for the expression of caliphal ideology.[4]

The chroniclers of the reigns of the caliphs promoted Andalusi Umayyad legitimacy by focusing their accounts of the most significant events of each year on caliphal achievements, from military successes to constructions. This perspective, of course, created an exaggerated impression of caliphal authority and the success of caliphal strategies of rule. Historians such as 'Īsā al-Rāzī recorded panegyrics recited to celebrate specific occasions and included caliphal documents in their texts, thus reviving caliphal propaganda and flagging the events in the historical narrative that the caliphs themselves identified as significant. As we have seen, Ibn Ḥayyān's history of al-Andalus built on the foundations provided by the historians of the caliphal court; his account of the reign of 'Abd al-Raḥmān III (*al-Muqtabis V*) presents multiple excerpts of various earlier historians' reports of significant events, such as the conquest of Bobastro, or the suppression of Ibn Masarra's *firqa*, thus further magnifying their importance.

An example of how contemporary historiography tended to interpret or describe significant events in official terms is the representation of 'Umar ibn Ḥafṣūn as an "antihero." His rebellion tests the Commander of the Faithful and ultimately demonstrates the caliph's superiority. The historians of the caliphal era, especially, devoted considerable space to the Banū Ḥafṣūn and the *fitna* they generated. They remarked on 'Umar's inconstancy, recording the vicissitudes of his relations with the Umayyads and his efforts to cultivate ties with the Abbasids and the Fatimids. Their texts, like the caliph's proclamations, associate his political defiance with religious deviance.[5] Often, the historians use the very language of the caliphal texts in their reports of events, referring to 'Umar ibn Ḥafṣūn as the evil one (*al-khabīth*), the dissolute (*al-fāsiq*), the profligate (*al-fājir*), the amir of error (*amīr al-ḍalāla*), and the imam of criminals (*imām al-mujrimīn*). They describe his rebellion as a fire burning out of control and a *fitna*, or crisis.[6] Ibn Ḥayyān's history of the reign of the amir 'Abd Allāh, largely based on 'Īsā al-Rāzī's work, sets the stage for 'Abd al-Raḥmān III's eventual triumph over the Banū Ḥafṣūn by representing 'Umar in this way. The text even prefaces the account of the *fitna* with an explicit foreshadowing of the first caliph's reunification of the community.[7] If the caliph represented himself as the agent of unity, security, and salvation, the historical record represented 'Umar ibn Ḥafṣūn and his sons as sources of disorder, symbols of inconstancy, and the promulgators of soul-threatening deviation.

The extensive discussions of the threat 'Umar ibn Ḥafṣūn posed to the Umayyad regime suggest he actually commanded widespread support and claimed significant authority, and the history of his rebellion might have been written differently had he succeeded in securing his rule over Cordoba. Ibn al-Qūṭiyya's tenth-century account of 'Umar's revolt gives us an intimation of that unwritten history and demonstrates another more subtle way contemporary historiography could promote the heroic achievement of the caliph.

While Ibn al-Qūṭiyya refers to 'Umar as the profligate (*al-fāsiq*), the leader of the criminals (*imām al-mujrimīn*), and the most deviant of deviants (*ashadd al-mukhtalifīn*),[8] his account of the origins of 'Umar's revolt tells the story of a man with a special destiny, as determined by two prophecies.[9] Like many heroic sagas, 'Umar's begins with an exile: we are told that he left his home province of Malaga after having been seized and whipped by the governor for some petty crime. He traveled to Tahart, in Morocco, and there worked in the tailor shop of a countryman. One day, the story continues, an old man walked into the shop and, having been introduced to 'Umar simply as a Malagan, asked him whether he was familiar with Bobastro and whether he knew of any signs of trouble there. When 'Umar responded that he lived at the foot of the mountain of Bobastro and had not observed anything out of the ordinary, the old man replied sagely that a movement would soon take place there. He then asked: Do you know of a man from the region named 'Umar ibn Ḥafṣūn? The question took 'Umar by surprise, and before he could answer, the old man recognized who he was from a chipped front tooth. He urged him to give up sewing and go home, telling him: "You will be master of the Banu Umayya; they will meet ruin by your hands, and you will rule over a great kingdom."

Ibn al-Qūṭiyya's report of the next stage in 'Umar's career describes a detour from the fulfillment of the prediction, perhaps partly as a dramatic device, and its ultimate realization. 'Umar returned to al-Andalus, failed in his first effort to instigate rebellion, and was enlisted in the Umayyad army. He proved successful in his military career, but harsh and unjust treatment by the authorities in Cordoba compelled him to leave the capital and return home, prompted by the words of an unnamed prophetic shaykh: "Return to the fortress from which you descended, for only death can make you come down from it again. You will rule over a large area of al-Andalus and do battle with Cordoba at its very gates."[10]

The stories of the prophecies are apocryphal, perhaps representative of popular traditions that circulated in support of the Banū Ḥafṣūn at the time of the rebellion.[11] The first may reflect the sentiments of a period when it looked like 'Umar might overcome the Umayyads, while the second more closely reflects his ultimate experience. Recounted by the historian, the prophecies served to identify 'Umar as a significant character in the drama of Andalusi history and, in the context of the history of Umayyad rule, enhanced the prestige of the one who thwarted him. The historian in the victor's court thus appropriated the history of the vanquished: if 'Umar's destiny was to lead a great rebellion, 'Abd al-Raḥmān III was destined to defeat him.

The Andalusi historiography of the caliphal period, and to some extent the Andalusi and Maghribi historiography of the postcaliphal period, grew out of and expanded caliphal ideology. Histories elaborated themes such as the continuity of Umayyad legitimacy but in a more complex and variegated way. They also embodied and perpetuated legends that supported Umayyad rule in a number of indirect and interrelated ways—for example, conveying the divine scheme behind Umayyad rule and the destiny of al-Andalus. If 'Abd al-Raḥmān III promoted an official ideology, the historiography represents the diffusion of his efforts by and among men of culture associated with his regime.

The Abbasids and the Fatimids promoted official histories of their reigns especially in the period of consolidation following their rise to power. They used historical narratives to confer authenticity on their claims to legitimacy. For example, early historical texts established the transmission of their authority, presaged their political ascendancy, or denounced their predecessors and rivals. Andalusi historiography functioned in the same way but not to the same degree of systematic elaboration.

The Andalusi histories read less as ideological propaganda than as products and contributions to the political culture of the caliphate. They were written by men whose families were clients of the Umayyads for generations with the presumption of Umayyad legitimacy and from an enduring appreciation of Umayyad rule. The texts mark the elevated status of the Umayyad caliphate but in contrast to the Abbasid and Fatimid cases did not need to justify a revolution or the foundation of an entirely new state.

Although all the historians we discuss here were partisans of the dynasty, each historian crafted his own historical interpretation. This was true even in the case of narratives constructed entirely from collected reports (whether *aḥādīth* or *akhbār*). All the texts were very much part of the larger Arabic-Islamic historical tradition, but as a group Andalusi histories generated their own local tradition.

The analysis of the histories is directly informed by what we have seen in other representations of Umayyad rule. We focus on how accounts of the distant past of the peninsula, the period of the Muslim conquest, supported caliphal arguments for legitimacy and how Andalusi historiography as a whole reflected and celebrated the strength of Umayyad rule in the tenth century and validated caliphal claims. The reader will observe through the course of the discussion that the meaning of history changes over time and among authors, giving us a range of perspectives on the Umayyad past. Ibn Ḥabīb's universal history (chapter 5), for example, written in the ninth century, presents a view of history as prophecy. First, the text relates the history of prophecy from the first prophet, Adam, to the last, Muḥammad. Second, the text records the unfolding of the last stage of history as the fulfillment of prophecy. Third, the text itself is prophecy in the Islamic sense—that is, it predicts the end of the world and warns members of the community that they should return to God and the true faith. In this perspective, the history of the conquest of al-Andalus and Umayyad rule are part of the divine plan and directly related to the fate of the Muslims. To some extent, all accounts of the conquest support this view and, written from the remove of centuries, have a legendary (and sometimes fabulous) quality. However, what we read in Ibn Ḥabīb's history is quite different from what we find, for example, in Ibn al-Qūṭiyya's history (chapters 4 and 5). The tenth-century *akhbār* about the conquest of al-Andalus present a proprietary approach to the past. They commemorate the deeds of heroic figures and weave ties between the foundations of Islamic rule and the tenth-century present. They read as collections of common lore rather than Qur'anic truth and shape collective memory. The quality of these texts, in turn, contrasts vividly with that of the annalistic histories of reigns discussed above, which present a truth based on documents and citations. All these forms of history and representations of the past contributed to Umayyad legitimacy in a number of ways, each text individually and in discourse with others as part of a corpus.

· FOUR ·

The Conquest Histories: The Foundations of the Umayyad Caliphate in al-Andalus

The legitimacy of the Andalusi Umayyad caliphate rested on complex historical foundations, both pan-Islamic and peninsular. ʻAbd al-Raḥmān III staked his claim to the leadership of the Muslims on his dynastic legitimacy, recalling the caliphate of his Syrian ancestors. At the same time, he justified his assumption of caliphal status and insignia by the success of his rule of the Iberian peninsula and his demonstrated commitment to the mandate of the caliphate.

An investigation of two tenth-century Andalusi histories of the Muslim conquest of al-Andalus and the establishment of the independent Umayyad amirate shows how historians of the caliphal period represented these two seminal "moments" of the past in ways that supported Andalusi Umayyad arguments of caliphal legitimacy. The anonymous *Akhbār majmūʻa fī fath al-Andalus* (Collected Reports on the Conquest of al-Andalus) and Ibn al-Qūṭiyya's (d. 977) *Ta'rīkh iftitāḥ al-Andalus* (History of the Conquest of al-Andalus), portray Umayyad rule in al-Andalus as divinely guided and part of the fulfillment of a special destiny for the dynasty and the peninsula, thus providing a historical buttress for the caliph's reign and setting up his role as the great renewer.[1]

While both texts are contemporary and similar in form, they are quite different in perspective.[2] Both present a compilation of accounts, without attribution, in rough chronological order, and combine a history of the conquest with a dynastic history of the Umayyad amirs up to, and partially including, the reign of 'Abd al-Raḥmān III. *Akhbār majmū'a* is dynastic or *dawla*-oriented. Its treatment of the conquest is subordinate to its focus on the story of 'Abd al-Raḥmān I, the young Umayyad amir who survived the Abbasid revolution that brought an end to Umayyad rule in the east, "reconquered" al-Andalus, and made Cordoba the new seat for his dynasty. The reader will recognize parallels between this representation of 'Abd al-Raḥmān I and 'Abd al-Raḥmān III's own representations of his rule. Ibn al-Qūṭiyya's history is oriented on his homeland or *watan*, and he roots Umayyad legitimacy in local politics and the fate of the peninsula. While many of the anecdotes relayed in *Akhbār majmū'a* and Ibn al-Qūṭiyya's history appear in a number of geographies and histories of al-Andalus, the coherent and distinctive perspectives of these two texts makes their discussion particularly instructive and interesting.[3]

AKHBĀR MAJMŪ'A

Akhbār majmū'a represents 'Abd al-Raḥmān I's arrival on the Iberian peninsula as a pivotal event, best understood in relation to the history of Islamic rule that preceded him. In order to elucidate that relationship and provide a basis for comparison with Ibn al-Qūṭiyya's text, I present in some detail *Akhbār majmū'a*'s basic narrative of the two "events" of the initial Muslim conquest and 'Abd al-Raḥmān I's establishment of the amirate, along with an analysis of their significance to the Umayyad conception of legitimacy.

The portion of *Akhbār majmū'a* devoted to the conquest of al-Andalus includes the history of the actual conquest and a brief description of the history of the early governors under supreme Syrian Umayyad sovereignty, before the Abbasid revolution around 750. While the Syrian Umayyad caliphs do not figure prominently as characters in the narrative of either period, the history affirms their authority over the conquered territories. The account of the conquest represents the caliphs in Damascus as the ultimate source of power and influence and as the final arbiters in disputes among the conquerors about the disposition of the captured spoils, land, and populations. In the account of the turbulent period of the early governors they are the guardians of stability and community.

The history of the conquest establishes al-Andalus as part of the Umayyad caliphal heritage and thus affirms the legitimacy of the dynasty's subsequent rule there. The text begins with the Umayyad caliph in Syria, al-Walīd, appointing Mūsā ibn Nuṣayr as governor of Ifriqiyya and the lands beyond.[4] This act of appointment underscored the Umayyads' determination to exert their authority over the North African frontier. As the text explains, the Umayyads had intended the conquest of Ifriqiyya for some time, but their ambitions had been suspended by political turmoil at the heart of the empire. After the resolution of the second civil war and the recovery of territory lost to the Byzantines, Persians, and Kurds, al-Walīd was finally free to address Ifriqiyya.[5]

As the narrative describes, Mūsā had to make good his title of governor by conquest. He advanced westward from Egypt, conquering towns and their dependencies from hostile Berber tribes along the way, before taking Tangiers, the major fortification of the region. Having secured Tangiers, he marched toward the nearby coastal region of Ceuta, which was under the administration of Julian, a governor appointed by the kings of Spain.[6] Julian and his men repelled Mūsā's attacks and the Muslim commander had no alternative but to acknowledge this territory as the limit of his expansion.

Circumstances beyond the battlefield soon changed the situation dramatically, however. According to the text, the Visigoth king, Witiza, died, leaving at least two sons. The population favored a military commander as king over Witiza's sons. This commander, Roderick, was not of royal descent. Sometime after he assumed power, Roderick raped Julian's daughter, who, the text tells us, had been living in the royal palace like other children of noble families. When Julian learned of this, he swore "by the religion of the Messiah (Christ)" to get his revenge. He surrendered his province on the North African side of the straits to Mūsā and urged him to cross into al-Andalus and attack. He offered to serve as guide on the peninsula and the support of his men.[7]

The text indicates that Mūsā sought the approval of the caliph before acting, thus intimating that the caliph was ultimately responsible for the conquest. Mūsā wrote to al-Walīd about Julian's proposal, and the caliph, as protector of the Muslims, cautiously ordered a reconnaissance mission, urging his commander not to expose the Muslims to the perils of the open sea. Mūsā wrote back to allay his fears: one can see land across the straits. Again, the caliph urged caution and reiterated his order for an exploratory mission. Following this order, Mūsā sent his *mawlā,* or freedman, Ṭarīf, with four hundred men to determine the lay of the land. This brief expedition, which took place in Ramadan of the year 710, yielded great booty with minimal effort and stimulated further interest. Mūsā followed up by sending a larger force of seven thousand men under the command of another *mawlā,* Ṭāriq.

As the account describes, Roderick learned of the incursions from North Africa and set out to confront this second wave of invaders with an army of "one hundred thousand men." Ṭāriq's forces were vastly outnumbered, despite some reinforcements. However, Roderick's forces were divided; many of the Visigoth nobles, including Witiza's sons, resented Roderick's authority over them because of his inferior lineage. They plotted to abandon him in the field of battle, expecting the Muslims to destroy him, plunder the countryside, but then return to Africa. In the execution of their plan, the Muslim army slaughtered

Roderick's forces, although his own fate was unknown. The Muslims found only his white horse, abandoned in a ditch, his saddle of gold, emeralds, and rubies, and his magnificent cloak, embroidered with gold thread and bordered in pearls and rubies. To the surprise and chagrin of Roderick's noble enemies, the Muslims then proceeded to conquer the peninsula and establish themselves there.[8]

Ṭāriq's forces, spurred on by Julian, launched a three-pronged series of attacks, taking one town after another.[9] The Muslims' conquests were both advanced and complicated by Mūsā's apparent jealousy of Ṭāriq's victories. Mūsā crossed the straits himself in Ramadan 712 with some eighteen thousand men and, guided by some of Julian's men, made his own series of conquests while heading toward Toledo, the Visigoth capital, recently fallen to Ṭāriq. Just outside the city the two met. Ṭāriq dismounted to offer his respect to his commander, and Mūsā struck him with his whip, admonishing him for going against orders.

Mūsā continued to treat his subordinate officers badly. As the story goes, on entering Toledo he required Ṭāriq to turn over all the booty he had collected, including a table that had purportedly belonged to King Solomon. Later, he tried to wrest a royal captive from another of his generals. In relaying these stories, the text suggests Mūsā was anxious to claim all the glory of the conquests for himself and hoped to impress the caliph with the prizes others had won. The narrative of Mūsā's role in the conquest eventually concludes with his own chastisement and humiliation. In the year 713 or 714, an envoy from al-Walīd arrived ordering Mūsā, Ṭāriq, and another general, Mughīth, back to Damascus. Mūsā arranged to leave his son, 'Abd al-'Azīz, in charge of al-Andalus and another son, 'Abd Allāh, in command in Ifriqiyya.[10] Ṭāriq and Mughīth reached Damascus before Mūsā. Since al-Walīd had died while they were en route, they presented themselves to his successor, Sulaymān, and complained bitterly of Mūsā's treatment. When Mūsā finally arrived in the capital himself, the caliph compelled him to account for his actions. Later we learn how Ṭāriq exposed Mūsā for lying about finding King Solomon's table and how the caliph reprimanded and fined Mūsā severely for his misconduct.[11]

While the main actors in this history are Roderick, Julian, Ṭāriq, and Mūsā, the Umayyad caliphs' jurisdiction over the conquerors' actions is clear, and the text contains fortuitous events within a framework of (or insistence on) caliphal control.[12] The narrative of the subsequent period of the first governors, preceding 'Abd al-Raḥmān I's arrival in al-Andalus, is similarly constructed, beginning and ending with the affirmation of caliphal interest in the region. While giving an impression of control from above, the body of the narrative describes a period of warfare and devastation that suggests that the Umayyad hold on al-Andalus and North Africa was tenuous, at best.

The section on the governors opens with the caliph Sulaymān's appointment of a successor for 'Abd al-'Azīz, Mūsā's son, who had been murdered. Sulaymān ordered an investigation of the murder and the punishment of its perpetrators but died before this command yielded any results.[13] His successor, 'Umar ibn 'Abd al-'Azīz, also undertook to participate actively in the affairs of al-Andalus and also personally named its new governor. The text suggests that 'Umar was particularly concerned to integrate this distant province into the empire. He ordered a cadastral survey and geographical description of the conquered territories and kept in close contact with his governor, who consulted him about the reconstruction of Cordoba.[14] The narrator suggests that the caliph's efforts to inform himself of conditions in al-Andalus reflected an anxiety over the isolation of the Muslims there.[15]

The narrative continues to describe the succession of governors in al-Andalus, most of whom were appointed by the governors of Ifriqiyya or Egypt (acting in their capacity as delegates of the caliph), and their conquest of much of the peninsula.[16] When Berber rebellions broke out in North Africa and later in al-Andalus, the text describes the caliph Hishām's determination to prevail over them at all costs. However, although Syrian troops helped defeat the Berbers in al-Andalus, warfare once again rent the peninsula, this time between the Syrian forces and local factions.[17] The section ends with the eminent men of al-Andalus sending a desperate appeal to the governor of Ifriqiyya for a governor whom all could respect and willingly obey, "as they would the caliph." He complied, sending a Syrian of good family from Damascus. The latter indeed managed to restore order.[18] The account of the first governors thus closes with an artificial sense of unity and a temporary reaffirmation of Umayyad authority before the outbreak of the Abbasid revolution and collapse of order in al-Andalus.[19] As the narrator remarks: the chaos that followed the revolution "made one fear for the loss of Islam in al-Andalus."[20]

Akhbār majmū'a's history of the conquest of al-Andalus describes the incorporation of the region into the Islamic world under Umayyad aegis but treats 'Abd al-Raḥmān I as the real founder of Muslim rule on the peninsula. In this representation he provided the dynastic stability that would allow Islam to flourish, and in this way his story accentuates the previous fragility of Islam in al-Andalus. The text presents 'Abd al-Raḥmān I's story as an act of creation: he founded a new civilization and brought order and religion to a wild wasteland. The historical account supports the boast attributed to him: "No one has done as I have. Inspired by noble indignation, baring a double-edged sword, I crossed the desert and traversed the sea, undeterred by the harshness of the land or the depths of the ocean. I conquered a kingdom and established an independent minbar for prayer. I organized an army out of ruins, and populated cities that had been deserted."[21]

As the text goes on to suggest, this creation of a new civilization was bound up with the regeneration of his dynasty. 'Abd al-Raḥmān I provided the basis for Umayyad salvation: "Then I called my family to a place where they could live as at home. I came fleeing from hunger, the sword, and death, attained security and prosperity, and gathered together a people."[22]

The narration of 'Abd al-Raḥmān I's story shifts focus to dramatic effect. The story of his flight from Syria begins with scenes of Abbasid persecution of members of the Umayyad family.[23] As the text relates, the Abbasids, having declared themselves the new leaders of the Muslim community, undertook to humiliate the members of the previous ruling dynasty. Al-Saffāḥ, for example, ordered that Abān ibn Mu'āwiya's hand and foot be cut off and that he be paraded throughout Syria with a crier shouting: "This is Abān ibn Mu'āwiya, the best horseman of the Banū Umayya." The unfortunate captive did not survive the experience.[24] The text goes on to record examples of Abbasid ruthlessness and treachery.[25] The Abbasids' efforts to root out and kill all surviving members of the Umayyad family culminated in an elaborate plan. The new rulers lured the Umayyads out of hiding with promises of reconciliation and assurances of safety, but those who returned from their refuges in Iraq, Egypt, and Medina were brutally murdered. The account of the massacre conforms to a literary topos, here used as a shorthand way to convey "great betrayal." As the story goes, the victims innocently gathered in the tent of their enemy, who purported to be their host, and were favorably received. Suddenly, the reception turned into a bloodbath, the host into an executioner, and the bodyguard into the agent of death.[26]

'Abd al-Raḥmān I first appears in the text in the description of the Abbasid roundups and assassinations. The narrator mentions that 'Abd al-Raḥmān's brother, with whom he lived, was killed but that 'Abd al-Raḥmān happened to be out hunting when the Abbasid horsemen arrived at their home.[27] Soon the narrative shifts from the fate of the Umayyads generally to 'Abd al-Raḥmān specifically. We are told that most of the Umayyads who managed to escape the Abbasids headed for Ifriqiyya because they heard from seers that their refuge would one day be in the west.[28] This vague reference to some apparently well-known prediction works as the beginning of a literary tease that builds suspense and serves to emphasize the foundation act. This is the first indication of a prophetic destiny for the dynasty; with each subsequent elaboration, 'Abd al-Raḥmān I emerges more clearly as the one marked to save the dynasty from the catastrophe that has befallen it.

'Abd al-Raḥmān I's story moves to the foreground with the Umayyads' gathering in Ifriqiyya. After a brief introduction explaining that 'Abd al-Raḥmān was a youth of seventeen at the time of the revolution and lived with his brothers and other members of the family at Dayr Ḥanna in Qinnasrīn, the narrator presents what is purported to be the hero's own account of some of the details of his flight. 'Abd al-Raḥmān tells two stories: the first is an elaboration of a portent like that of the seers mentioned above, and the second describes his close escape from the Abbasid assassins. Together they link his experience with the tragedy and revival of his family.

'Abd al-Raḥmān I presents the portent of the Umayyad fall as an explanation for his escape westward, as such predictions seem to have linked the fate of the dynasty with refuge in the west, but the story he tells is really about the caliph Hishām's recognition of 'Abd al-Raḥmān's special identity as savior of the dynasty. Briefly, the story runs as follows: when 'Abd al-Raḥmān was about ten years old, his father died, and he and his brothers were taken to see their grandfather, the caliph Hishām, at Ruṣāfa, his country estate. When the boys arrived, they were greeted at the gate by Hishām's brother, Maslama, who welcomed each in turn. When he came to 'Abd al-Raḥmān, he held him close and kissed him, weeping. Forgetting all about the others, he asked that the boy be lifted up to his mount and placed before him on the saddle. At this point, the caliph appeared and wondered at the sight. Maslama explained, somewhat cryptically: "The event draws near; this is he." At the caliph's bewilderment, he added, "I have seen the distinctive signs on his face and neck." From that day, until his death, the caliph favored 'Abd al-Raḥmān with gifts and brought him to Ruṣāfa once a month. 'Abd al-Raḥmān assures us that this experience made a lasting impression on him.[29]

'Abd al-Raḥmān's second story, about his escape from death

at the hands of the Abbasids, also sets him apart from his less fortunate kin and marks the beginning of his special destiny. The personal narration of the story lends it a peculiarly tragic quality. The story begins with the Abbasids' arrival at the family estate. In this account, 'Abd al-Raḥmān and his family were forewarned by his son's fright and his brother's glimpse of the advancing horsemen. The family scattered, so when the horsemen arrived, the place was deserted. 'Abd al-Raḥmān and his younger brother headed toward the Euphrates, but before they could negotiate for provisions and horses, a servant betrayed them, directing the enemy toward them. They fled, managing to keep ahead of their pursuers until they reached the bank of the river, where they had no recourse but to throw themselves in. The Abbasid horsemen pulled up and shouted from the shore to the men struggling in the water: "Come back! You have nothing to fear!" 'Abd al-Raḥmān kept swimming, but seeing his brother's energy flag, he swam back to the middle of the river to encourage and assist him. The boy, however, seduced by the soldiers' words, turned around and started swimming back toward them. "Come toward me, my beloved," cried 'Abd al-Raḥmān, but his words were lost, and the two thus headed to opposite banks. The horsemen on the shore, who had dismounted and stripped in order to jump in the river and pursue 'Abd al-Raḥmān, instead hauled up his brother and decapitated him before his eyes. While his brother succumbed to Abbasid false promises and met his death by Abbasid sword, 'Abd al-Raḥmān persevered and survived. Crossing the river was the first step to crossing the desert and then crossing the sea to al-Andalus, the new seat of the dynasty.[30]

The final version of the prophecy of 'Abd al-Raḥmān I's role in Umayyad and Andalusi history follows closely after his personal narrative, expanding quite naturally on the earlier references. In this story, we are told that a Jew used to prophesy to the governor of Ifriqiyya, 'Abd al-Raḥmān ibn Ḥabīb, that a man of royal lineage (*min abnā' al-mulūk*) by the name of 'Abd al-Raḥmān, who had curls over his forehead, would one day make himself master of al-Andalus. Ibn Ḥabīb, hoping that the prophecy might apply to himself, grew his curls long in front. However, the Jew pointed out that he was not of royal descent (and so the prophecy could not pertain to him). When 'Abd al-Raḥmān I arrived in Ifriqiyya, the governor recognized him at once and called the Jew for confirmation. As he presented 'Abd al-Raḥmān to him he remarked: "This is he, but I intend to kill him." The Jew replied, concluding the story, "If you kill him, then he is not the one predestined to conquer al-Andalus. If you leave him alone, he may be." The reader, knowing how the story unfolds, is left to puzzle over the certainty of fate.[31]

Once the text establishes the importance of 'Abd al-Raḥmān I's mission through such narrative devices as prophecies, it goes on to relate how 'Abd al-Raḥmān I actually managed to penetrate the peninsula and establish himself as ruler. This involved a heavy reliance on Umayyad supporters and some careful political maneuvering. A bloody power struggle between two tribal confederations, the Yemenis and the Qaysis, had divided the community of al-Andalus in the wake of the Abbasid revolution.[32]

While still in Ifriqiyya, 'Abd al-Raḥmān contacted his Umayyad *mawālī,* or clients, on the peninsula, explained his situation, and appealed to their loyalties, making clear his intention to rule al-Andalus.[33] With their guidance and support, he crossed the straits and negotiated alliances with members of the competing factions that, with success on the battlefield, eventually brought him to power. Victorious, 'Abd al-Raḥmān I established order, essential to the preservation of religion and civilization.[34]

'Abd al-Raḥmān's own boast of how he imposed order on chaos and established a kingdom in what he describes as a hostile and depopulated country has a legendary quality. His escape from the massacre of his family and his travails in the river, desert, and sea mark him as the survivor who will restore the dynasty after its collapse, just as the prophecies and the signs inscribed on his body said he would.

'Abd al-Raḥmān I's story describes dynastic renewal and defines the beginning of a new epoch in what may viewed as a cyclical pattern in Umayyad history.[35] This conception of cyclical dynastic history is conveyed in an amusing anecdote in which the Abbasid caliph al-Manṣūr expresses his admiration for his rival, the Umayyad amir.

> One day, the caliph al-Manṣūr asked some of his companions, "Who is the hawk (*saqr*) of the Quraysh?"
>
> "The Commander of the Faithful [al-Manṣūr]," they replied, "Because he quelled the disturbances, pacified the kingdom, and purged it of malignancies."
>
> "No, you haven't guessed correctly," prodded the caliph.
>
> "Mu'āwiya, then."
>
> "No."
>
> "'Abd al-Malik ibn Marwān?"
>
> "No."
>
> "Then who could it be, O Commander of the Muslims?"
>
> "It is 'Abd al-Raḥmān, who escaped unharmed, by virtue of his cunning, from the lances and swords. He crossed the desert, traversed the sea, entered the land of the infidels, founded cities, recruited armies, and organized a kingdom where previously there had been anarchy, thanks to his sound direction and firm character. Mu'āwiya mounted a horse whose saddle had already been prepared by 'Umar and 'Uthmān. 'Abd al-Malik took the caliphal oath before his predecessor died. The Commander of the Faithful (al-Manṣūr himself) counted on the support of his family and partisans. But 'Abd al-Raḥmān was alone, without any help but that of his wits, and without any companionship but his firm will."[36]

The anecdote clearly represents 'Abd al-Raḥmān I as following the model of two eminent ancestors, Mu'āwiya and 'Abd al-Malik, both of whom were founders in the history of the dynasty and also had to triumph over civil war. Mu'āwiya, the first Umayyad caliph in Damascus, established Umayyad dynastic rule on the basis of his right to avenge the murder of the third caliph, his kinsman 'Uthmān. 'Abd al-Malik ibn Marwān, of another branch of the Umayyad clan, reestablished Umayyad authority in the wake of another serious crisis or civil war.[37] This evocation of a recurring pattern affirms the important continuity of Umayyad authority in a new context, while the magnitude of ʿAbd al-Raḥmān's achievements offers the expectation of an even more significant renewal. This last point is driven home by the fact that it is the Abbasid caliph himself who recognizes the Umayyad's heroic qualities.

Akhbār majmūʿa's representation of ʿAbd al-Raḥmān I coincides in many ways with ʿAbd al-Raḥmān III's self-representation. Both ʿAbd al-Raḥmān I and ʿAbd al-Raḥmān III created community in a region rent by factionalism and thus provided the basis for the regeneration of Islam. The appearance of each was presaged by signs and predictions, and both were physically marked as bearers of a special destiny. Both radiated with the promise of the fulfillment of some greater design.[38]

The identification of a periodic quality to Umayyad history, expressed in the anecdote quoted above, promoted the idea that ʿAbd al-Raḥmān III, like ʿAbd al-Raḥmān I, introduced another revolution in the experience of the dynasty. *Akhbār majmūʿa*'s reflection of ʿAbd al-Raḥmān III in its representation of ʿAbd al-Raḥmān I magnified the special attributes of both, making one a legendary ancestor and giving the other a messianic future, ultimately reinforcing the claims and expectations of the caliphate. ʿAbd al-Raḥmān III, it is suggested, was destined to retrace the footsteps of his eponym and reclaim his Umayyad inheritance, directing a new conquest from west to east.[39]

Ibn al-Qūṭiyya's representation of ʿAbd al-Raḥmān I, while less mythic in tone, also contributes to this sense of recurring pattern and the inevitability of ultimate success. In his account, when ʿAbd al-Raḥmān I prepared to confront Yūsuf al-Fihrī, who had established himself as governor of al-Andalus, he recalled the memory of a significant day in Umayyad history, drawing parallels based on the date and family names of the participants. ʿAbd al-Raḥmān's plans called for battle on a Friday, during *ʿĪd al-Aḍḥā*, and he expressed his hope that the day would turn out to resemble that of the battle of Marj Rāhiṭ, which also occurred on the *'id*. Ibn al-Qūṭiyya reminds us that at Marj Rāhiṭ the Umayyad caliph Marwān ibn al-Ḥakam confronted another al-Fihrī, al-Ḍaḥḥāk ibn Qays al-Fihrī, one of the commanders of the pretender Ibn al-Zubayr. The reader knows fortune favored the Umayyads on that occasion and is made to anticipate the outcome of 'Abd al-Raḥmān's battle. Through the association with the famous early battle, 'Abd al-Raḥmān's success achieves significance as a portentous watershed event, while the progress of the consolidation of his rule in al-Andalus bears the imprint of past traditions.[40]

Akhbār majmū'a and Ibn al-Qūṭiyya shared a strong appreciation of Umayyad legitimacy and presented common themes in their representations of the conquests of al-Andalus, and yet the emphases of their accounts differ. Both substantiate the Umayyads historical claims to authority but in distinct terms; both represent Umayyad rule as the realization of God's design but conceive the design differently. Compatible with each other, together they complement the Andalusi Umayyad caliphs' representation of their legitimacy.

TA'RĪKH IFTITĀḤ AL-ANDALUS

Abū Bakr Muḥammad ibn 'Umar ibn al-Qūṭiyya (d. 977), as his name suggests, traced his lineage from the Visigoths (*al-Qūt*). He presented himself as a direct descendant of Witiza's grand daughter, Sara. A renowned grammarian, noted poet, and somewhat controversial hadith scholar, Ibn al-Qūṭiyya was born, and died, in Cordoba, although his family had long been established in Seville.[41] He was a contemporary of the caliphs 'Abd al-Raḥmān III and al-Ḥakam II, and of the historians Aḥmad and 'Īsā al-Rāzī. His history generally shares the Rāzīs' favorable treatment of the dynasty; as his work makes clear, his family became clients of the Umayyads from the period of the conquest.[42]

Ibn al-Qūṭiyya's *Ta'rīkh iftitāh al-Andalus* is, like *Akhbār majmū'a*, both an account of the conquest of the peninsula and a dynastic history that extends into 'Abd al-Raḥmān III's reign, ending with the caliph's defeat of the Banū Ḥafṣūn.[43] His pride in his own genealogy suggests the orientation of his interpretation of the conquests, with its focus on the alliance between the house of Umayya and the house of Witiza.

The chronicle opens with a summary of the rise of Roderick. Witiza's three sons were still boys at his death, and so his widow ruled as regent in Toledo. Roderick, a general in Witiza's army, left the court and, with the support of his men, established himself in Cordoba. By the time Ṭāriq entered al-Andalus, the Witizan princes had reached maturity and deeply resented Roderick's position. In deciding to betray him, according to Ibn al-Qūṭiyya, these men were the "cause" of the conquest.[44] The conspiracy described in *Akhbār majmū'a* between Witiza's sons and Ṭāriq here becomes central to the conquest story; the royal Visigoths' outrage at Roderick is more significant than Julian's, and their alliance with the Muslims more critical to the history of Muslim success than Julian's. As the story goes, when Ṭāriq's forces entered the peninsula, Roderick appealed to Witiza's sons to join him in combating the invaders. The youths sent a message to Ṭāriq expressing their hatred for this military upstart and offered to desert his army in exchange for security of persons and property. Ṭāriq came to terms with them first and then sent them on to Mūsā in Ifriqiyya, who referred them to the caliph al-Walīd. Al-Walīd formally confirmed the agreement, and the story thus establishes its first connection between Witiza's family and the Umayyads.[45]

As we have seen, *Akhbār majmū'a* describes the destiny of Islam in al-Andalus as dependent on the Umayyads, particularly on 'Abd al-Raḥmān I. In Ibn al-Qūṭiyya's text, however, while 'Abd al-Raḥmān's arrival was an important development, Ṭāriq emerges as the more fully developed heroic figure. In Ibn al-Qūṭiyya's account, Ṭāriq had a vision of the Prophet and his companions as he crossed the straits from Ifriqiyya to al-Andalus. As these visionary figures encouraged him in his endeavor, he took the dream to be a good augury. The anecdote conveys the impression that Ṭāriq's boats were actually conveying Islam to Iberia.[46]

Ṭāriq's role in this version of the conquests noticeably outshines Mūsā's. Although Mūsā appears to be one of the prominent agents of the conquest in *Akhbār majmū'a,* here he remains largely in the background, and his representation is largely negative. His jealousy of Ṭāriq's achievements is not counterbalanced by his own achievements. Mūsā's reception in Damascus is even more dire in this than in the other version: the caliph Sulaymān imprisoned him and actually ordered the assassination of his son, 'Abd al-'Azīz. The same caliph who seemed eager to investigate 'Abd al-'Azīz's murder in one text now appears to be responsible for it in a story that clearly disavows Mūsā's association with the Umayyads.[47] The editor and translator of Ibn al-Qūṭiyya's text, Julian Ribera, offers an interesting suggestion about this twist: Mūsā and his son became allies of Roderick's family, and Ibn al-Qūṭiyya, as a partisan of Witiza's family, naturally disparaged this association.[48]

Ibn al-Qūṭiyya establishes the alliance between Witiza's sons and the Umayyad caliph al-Walīd, forged through Ṭāriq's agency, as a direct cause for the success of the Muslim expedition into al-Andalus, and he gives meaning to their achievement through two anecdotes. These stories represent the change in power on the peninsula as part of the inexorable progress of God's justice: the usurper of the Visigoth crown is brought down by the scion of a dynasty that has itself suffered from ignominious usurpation.[49]

Ibn al-Qūṭiyya presents the following story of the augury of the Muslim conquest as a legend, but he relays it because it clearly advances his presentation of Roderick as an intruder in the Visigoth succession and a violator of Visigoth political and religious traditions:

> It is said that the Visigoth kings had a house in Toledo with a special chest in it which contained the four gospels. This house

> was greatly revered, never opened except when a king died and his name was inscribed in it. When Roderick assumed the royal authority and took the crown for himself (an act of which the Christians did not approve), he opened the house and the chest, defying the Christians. Inside, he found images of the Arabs with bows on their shoulders and turbans on their heads, along with this warning: "if this house is opened and these figures are taken out [of the chest], a people resembling them will enter al-Andalus and conquer it."[50]

Ibn al-Qūṭiyya's version of Julian's story provides a further elaboration of Roderick's violation of social norms, emphasizing his character as a scoundrel. In this story, Julian was a merchant who procured horses and hunting birds from North Africa. One day, Roderick required him to go to Africa, but Julian excused himself, as his wife had recently died and he did not want to leave his young daughter alone. Roderick ordered him to send the girl to the palace and to go ahead with his trip. Roderick then yielded to temptation and raped the girl, betraying Julian's trust.[51] When Julian learned what happened, he told Roderick that he had left some horses and falcons in North Africa, the likes of which had never been seen. Roderick, unaware of what Julian had in mind, authorized him to return for them. Julian took his money and sought Ṭāriq, enticing him to conquer the peninsula.[52] Together, this story and the story of the sacred chest express a certain satisfaction with Roderick's defeat at the hands of the Muslims. He is an obvious villain and his demise is a proper retribution for his arrogance and hubris.

Ibn al-Qūṭiyya's account of the conquest introduces Islam to the peninsula, establishes Umayyad authority in al-Andalus, and demonstrates how the Muslims, led by Ṭāriq, served as the agents of the collapse of an illegitimate Visigothic rule. 'Abd al-Raḥmān I's specific foundation of an independent Umayyad amirate on the peninsula appears secondary, but his story is nonetheless important in the elaboration of Ibn al-Qūṭiyya's drama, leading to the restitution of justice for both the Witizan and Umayyad dynasties. Ibn al-Qūṭiyya's account affirms an alliance between the two "royal" houses through strong personal connections: between Sara and 'Abd al-Raḥmān I and between Artabus (one of Witiza's sons) and 'Abd al-Raḥmān I.

As we have seen, *Akhbār majmū'a* establishes 'Abd al-Raḥmān I's legitimacy as heir to Hishām's rule in a very powerful prophetic anecdote. In contrast, Ibn al-Qūṭiyya presents 'Abd al-Raḥmān's association with Hishām in a story that demonstrates the Witizan association with both caliph and heir. By his account, Ibn al-Qūṭiyya's ancestor, Sara, traveled to Damascus to present grievances against her uncle, Artabus, who hoped to dispossess her of her estates. Hishām promised to guarantee the agreements made between Ṭāriq and all three of Witiza's sons and formally took responsibility for Sara, arranging for her marriage. Ibn al-Qūṭiyya establishes the connection between Sara and 'Abd al-Raḥmān I in this context: when Sara is presented to Hishām's audience, she finds 'Abd al-Raḥmān, as a boy, with him. 'Abd al-Raḥmān, according to the text, later remembered this meeting and made clear that Sara was always welcome in his palace in Cordoba. On the death of Sara's husband, 'Abd al-Raḥmān himself arranged for her remarriage.[53] The report of this act, in this context, demonstrates how 'Abd al-Raḥmān I had clearly taken Hishām's place and how the locus of power had shifted from Damascus to Cordoba.

Ibn al-Qūṭiyya's text suggests Sara's close affiliation with Hishām and 'Abd al-Raḥmān I enhanced her prestige but also that 'Abd al-Raḥmān's position was similarly strengthened by his association with the royal Visigoths. In a brief section following his account of 'Abd al-Raḥmān I's rule, Ibn al-Qūṭiyya includes a few stories about Artabus. In one, Artabus and 'Abd al-Raḥmān appear to be rivals: two men with claims to authority who have been deprived of their birthrights, facing each other in disputed territory. Ultimately, however, they recognize the similarity of their situations and a kind of mutual dependence.

As the story goes, 'Abd al-Raḥmān envied Artabus's popularity in the realm and seized his estates. Artabus's material situation quickly deteriorated, and he went to Cordoba to ask for an audience with the amir in order, he said, to bid him farewell. When 'Abd al-Raḥmān received him, he inquired about the reason for his visit, noting his shabby attire. Artabus responded that he had been brought to this by the amir's unjust treatment: "It was you who brought me here. You separated me from my estates and diverged from the agreements made by your forefathers. I did nothing to deserve this." 'Abd al-Raḥmān asked Artabus about his apparent plans to leave al-Andalus, remarking, "I believe you want to go to Rome (Rūma)!" Artabus denied this, adding, "But I heard you want to go to Syria!" 'Abd al-Raḥmān responded, acknowledging the difficulty of his circumstances, "And who would let me return there? I fled for my life." In the denouement, Artabus offered to help 'Abd al-Raḥmān secure al-Andalus for his children, and in return, 'Abd al-Raḥmān rewarded him with the restoration of his property and the investment of special honors.[54]

By this account 'Abd al-Raḥmān I and Artabus acknowledged the limitations of their circumstances and the Umayyad-Witizan alliance has been reconfirmed three times: al-Walīd confirmed the original alliance made with Ṭāriq, Hishām reconfirmed it with Sara, and 'Abd al-Raḥmān with Artabus.

Ibn al-Qūṭiyya does not present 'Abd al-Raḥmān as a legendary figure in the manner of *Akhbār majmū'a.* He does not describe the gruesome massacres or the heroic flight. 'Abd al-Raḥmān does not singlehandedly create civilization out of chaos but depends very much on the assistance of local Umayyad clients. His advent is not anticipated by signs and portents. He is not the prefiguration of the *mahdi*-like representation of 'Abd al-Raḥmān III. His heroism is human. He successfully established himself as ruler in al-Andalus on the basis of his inherited authority as an Umayyad prince and became heir to the mantle of Visigothic legitimacy as a representative of the Umayyad dynasty.[55]

As histories of the conquest, *Akhbār majmū'a* and *Ta'rīkh iftitāh al-Andalus* root the legitimacy of the Umayyad dynasty in the past. Not surprisingly, they feature the Umayyad rivalry with the Abbasids as a prominent theme. The Abbasids were obvious villains in the eyes of Umayyad partisans, as the usurpers of Umayyad authority in the east and in the tenth century as rivals to be demolished by Andalusi Umayyad assertions of their right to the caliphate.

Akhbār majmū'a preserves (or revives) the memory of the Abbasid usurpation as a violent wrong that demands to be righted. The text emphatically contrasts their illegitimacy with the legitimacy of the Umayyads. The story of the massacres and 'Abd al-Raḥmān's escape drives the narrative of his reign. As the text asserts, only after 'Abd al-Raḥmān extinguished a rebellion in Beja launched under the black banners of the Abbasids did he finally abolish the practical Abbasid threat to his life and rulership. The final moment of this account represents the enduring rivalry of the two dynasties and the (renewed) Umayyad challenge to Abbasid rule: 'Abd al-Raḥmān sent the heads of the leaders of the rebellion to Qayrawān as a message to the Abbasid caliph al-Manṣūr.[56]

Ibn al-Qūṭiyya provides a more dramatic version of this rebellion in Beja that emphasizes the personal rivalry between 'Abd al-Raḥmān I and al-Manṣūr. In this account, al-Manṣūr clearly instigated the rebellion, sending a standard and a deed of investiture to its leader, along with a message urging him to attack. The rebel proclaimed himself ruler and gathered a great deal of popular support. When 'Abd al-Raḥmān I finally managed to defeat and kill him, he had his head dressed in salt and camphor and sent, along with the banner and the deed of investiture, to al-Manṣūr in Mecca, where the caliph had gone on pilgrimage. When al-Manṣūr saw what had become of his protégé he exclaimed: "Thank God for putting a sea between us and this kind of an enemy!"[57]

Both versions of this anecdote read as assertions of Umayyad independence and help define 'Abd al-Raḥmān I's role in the past as the founder of the dynastic amirate. The story identifies a boundary between Umayyad and Abbasid spheres of power:

Abd al-Raḥmān I sent the rebel's head as a warning not to interfere in his domain, and the Abbasid caliph heeded it. Ibn al-Qūṭiyya's text elsewhere refers to such a demarcation between the two spheres of authority. In his account of the caliph Hishām's efforts to suppress the Berber rebellion in Ifriqiyya, Ibn al-Qūṭiyya notes that the Arab and *mawālī* armies sent to confront the Berbers had heard predictions of the downfall of the Umayyads and the rise of the Abbasids and that Abbasid rule would not extend beyond the Zab river. They understood this to mean the Zab in Egypt, but in fact, it was the Zab in Ifriqiyya.[58]

Read with 'Abd al-Raḥmān III's caliphate in mind, however, we can also see 'Abd al-Raḥmān I's sending of the severed heads as the throwing down of a gauntlet, a counterchallenge to Abbasid rule in Qayrawān or in Mecca, particularly as both cities were in the arena of contest in the tenth century. In this light, al-Manṣūr's relief that a sea lay between him and the Umayyad ruler of al-Andalus reflects a tenth-century appreciation of Abbasid weakness and Umayyad strength.

The early Abbasids, represented in the person of al-Manṣūr, were both the enemy and the standard by which the Andalusi Umayyads could model and gauge their dignity, as manifest in the story about al-Manṣūr's esteem for 'Abd al-Raḥmān I, where al-Manṣūr is the source of highest praise. In the tenth century, partisans of the Andalusi Umayyads confidently asserted the qualities of their rulers against this standard. A panegyric dedicated to 'Abd al-Raḥmān III and recorded in *Akhbār majmū'a* describes the Umayyad caliph as following the perfect model of 'Abd al-Malik but also as measuring up to, and surpassing, Abbasid standards: "You made the caliphates of al-Manṣūr and al-Rashīd forgettable and put to shame the caliphates of al-Mahdī and al-Wāthiq."[59]

The tenth-century conquest histories participate in a kind of revisionism. They assert continuity, establishing a solid chain of command from Mu'awiya and 'Abd al-Malik and Hishām to 'Abd al-Raḥmān I and 'Abd al-Raḥmān III, in a history that was actually characterized by revolution and flux.[60] In their accounts of the defeat of Roderick and the arrival of 'Abd al-Raḥmān I, they envisage the success of the dynasty as the enactment of God's justice; in fact, this scenario depends on hindsight. The rebellions, which constantly plagued Umayyad rule and might have brought an end to the regime, appear in the historical narrative as showcases of strong rule, described in ways that bolstered the authority of the one who suppressed them. Although neither devotes much space to 'Abd al-Raḥmān III's reign, both the conquest histories anticipate his rule. Ibn al-Qūṭiyya and *Akhbār majmū'a*'s interpretations of the conquests support 'Abd al-Raḥmān III's historical claims to the caliphate and also create a certain tension, an expectation of the full realization of a promise dating back to the early history of the peninsula, especially if we read them with 'Abd al-Raḥmān III's self-representation in mind. *Akhbār majmū'a*'s conquest history, in particular, contributes to the expectation of a divinely heralded agent of God's will and justice.

· FIVE ·

Al-Andalus: Land of the Umayyads

The tenth-century conquest histories of al-Andalus confirmed the Andalusi Umayyad caliphs' dynastic claims to the Iberian peninsula, as well as North Africa and the Mashriq, by recording the transmission of 'Abd al-Raḥmān I's authority from the caliph Hishām and the historical recognition of his legitimacy. The contemporary historiography also supported the claim that the Andalusi Umayyad caliphs fulfilled the responsibilities of their divine mandate by recording the evidence of their achievements but also indirectly in the way historical writing expressed a confidence in Umayyad rule. One way we can explore this dimension of the historiography is to look at the treatment of the "landscape" of al-Andalus in historical texts of different periods and consider how the different representations may reflect the impact of Umayyad rule.

The landscape in historical texts often escapes notice. Serving as background to the drama of history, the "landscape" is the setting where events unfold. However, the set of a drama does contribute to its mood and tone. Descriptions of place, where they exist in historical texts, can be charged with personal, political, or cultural meaning. In this case, the representation of the cities and countryside of al-Andalus by Andalusi historians heightens our appreciation of Umayyad authority and power. Just as narratives of events presume to report "what happened" but are often telling in their subjectivity, so literary landscapes situate us in places with recognizable names and features but control what we see and interpret "what is (or was) actually out there." The historians who recounted the stories or presented the descriptions of place need not have been conscious of this level of their manipulation.

The changing literary landscape of Andalusi historiography provides an interpretation of Umayyad rule as critical to the introduction and success of Islam on the peninsula and to the prestige and prosperity of al-Andalus. The historical texts demonstrate how the Umayyads transformed an alien and hostile land into an Islamic domain that resembled their homeland. The descriptions of al-Andalus read as evidence of God's favor for the Umayyads and the peninsula, highlighting the caliphs' mastery of a land that resisted the authority of the pre-Islamic rulers before them. The literary landscape reinforces the representation of the reign of the caliphs as the dawn of a new age: they created a new civilization.

The examination of the literary landscape begins with Ibn Ḥabīb's ninth-century representation of al-Andalus as a forbidding place, portending danger. The landscape changes in the tenth-century histories of Ibn al-Qūṭiyya and *Akhbār majmūʿa,* as these texts name, mark, and map specific places and demonstrate how the movement of armies, the destruction and construction of fortresses, and the definition of boundaries staked a claim to the peninsula. The texts express pride in Muslim domination of the once infidel peninsula and confidence in Umayyad rule. Ibn Ḥayyān's *Muqtabis,* drawing heavily on tenth-century histories and governed by respect for the Andalusi Umayyad caliphate, depicts ʿAbd al-Raḥmān III as an engineer of change and a master of the physical geography of al-Andalus. The accounts of the caliph's construction of Madīnat al-Zahrāʾ, in particular, powerfully express his authority over the land and its social, political, economic, and cultural life.

The analysis of these texts from three different generations of historians must take into account developments in Arabic Islamic historical writing over the same period, and the discussion here situates the texts in this larger historiographical context.

LANDSCAPE OF FEAR

Ibn Ḥabīb's *Kitāb al-Ta'rīkh,* or universal history, is one of the oldest extant histories in Arabic and is representative of early historical writing.[1] In the ninth century, compilers of historical traditions (*akhbār*) were religious scholars, collectors of hadiths (traditions of the Prophet and his companions), or philologists. They appreciated history as an aid to the study and implementation of the Qur'an and hadith and as a dimension of the larger quest to understand God's plan for humankind. However, their histories could also reflect, among other things, a pride of place and an interest in recording the heritage and significance of a region, whether Egypt or al-Andalus.[2]

Ibn Ḥabīb (c. 790–853) was born and grew up in al-Andalus, studied hadith and law in Cordoba, and then traveled east for three years to the Hijaz, Egypt, and Jerusalem in further pursuit of his studies. Sometime after his return to al-Andalus, the amir 'Abd al-Raḥmān II appointed him a *faqīh mushāwar,* member of a council in service to the *qāḍī* of Cordoba and occasionally to the amir as well. He held this position until his death in the early years of the amir Muḥammad's reign.[3] Ibn Ḥabīb earned his reputation as a jurist and is perhaps best known for his adherence to, and promulgation of, the teachings of Mālik ibn Anas. His history reflects his training as a hadith scholar and a pietistic concern to recount the history of Islam and to warn believers of the Day of Judgment.

The text begins with the creation of the world and continues with a concise treatment of the history of the prophets, the life of Muḥammad, the history of the first four caliphs and the Umayyad dynasty, and the history of the Umayyad rulers of al-Andalus. The narrative is based on the Qur'an and composed of hadiths and historical traditions arranged sequentially, ending with apocalyptic predictions. The reader can recognize from this outline that Ibn Ḥabīb defined the portion of his "universal" history devoted to the age of Islam by the history of the Umayyad dynasty, shifting his focus from east to west with the conquest of the peninsula and the foundation of Umayyad rule. This text binds the fate of Islam inextricably with the fate of the Umayyads and of al-Andalus.

Ibn Habīb locates the apocalypse in al-Andalus, and the overarching message of the text is that the end of the world is nigh, as is evident in the deterioration of the moral and even the natural order. In the introduction to his history, he explicitly states that he will describe the destruction of al-Andalus and the events preceding the Final Hour, according to the reports and signs (*riwāyat* and *'alāmāt*).[4] In the body of the text, he inserts two chapters that specifically refer to the Final Judgment—one presents estimates about the duration of the universe, and the other presents hadiths about how men will be judged—but the text as a whole is replete with admonitions.[5]

The portion of the history devoted to the conquest of al-Andalus itself only alludes to the expectation of Divine Judgment, but this is because it serves, in part, as an encomium to Mūsā ibn Nuṣayr, one of the few of the "successors," or members of the second generation of the community of the Prophet, to come to the peninsula.[6] Embedded in the reports of the conquest, however, is a general warning about the consequences of greed. The conquest of al-Andalus was like the raiding of a treasure chest, full of immeasurable wealth for the taking. Such tremendous booty, while a great boon for the Muslims, was also a source of temptation and corruption. Anecdotes such as the following provided moral instruction to Ibn Ḥabīb's audience. Immediately after the victory over Roderick, Ṭāriq's men looted silver, gold, and innumerable priceless objects and hoarded them. They set sail for Tangiers, and in the middle of the sea, they heard a voice cry: "Drown them, for they have hoarded." In fear, the men rushed for their Qu'rans and hung them around their necks, praying to God for mercy, but the boat they were in capsized.[7]

Ibn Ḥabīb delivers his message about corruption and pending punishment more emphatically over the course of his *Kitāb al-Ta'rīkh* through the repetition of anecdotes that serve as historical examples and through admonitory hadiths and Qu'ranic verses. His history of the pre-Islamic prophets, based largely on Qu'ran and hadith, presents a cycle of moral decay followed by warnings, destruction, and renewal, as in the stories of Noah and Moses. Great men such as Alexander the Great and King Solomon, who commanded incredible wealth and power, are shown to be humbled before God.[8]

Ibn Ḥabīb's rendition of the history of the caliphs is rather telegraphic, only briefly mentioning the important events of each reign, if any. However, the report on the last caliph he treats, Hishām (r. 724–743), is relatively long and conveys a reminder of the hubris of the wealthy and powerful, a message perhaps directed at the Umayyad amirs of Cordoba, who traced their descent from Hishām. The report concerns Hishām's construction and enjoyment of his country estate, al-Ruṣāfa. It begins with a description of the magnificence of the site and the caliph's appreciation of "what God had extended to him" but closes with a message that the things of this world are but transitory.[9] The next report tells a similar story: the caliph is approached by a man who warns him that on the Day of the Herald the oppressors will be cursed, insinuating that the caliph will be among them. On inquiry, the man explains that Hishām's agent had appropriated his land and added it to the caliphal domains. Hishām immediately orders the agent to relinquish all of the caliph's land, gardens, residences, servants, slaves, and cattle, "so God will forgive me and not consider me one of the oppressors."[10]

Ibn Ḥabīb's consistent admonitory tone is greatly reinforced by his complaints about his own times and the prognostications he presents about the future.[11] Remarks about the depravity of his own society punctuate the history of the creation and the prophets. In the first such comment, Ibn Ḥabīb tells his audience that all the despicable things "in this time of ours, which is the end of the world," had already occurred in the time of Adam.[12] As mentioned above, he represents the history of humanity as a cycle of corruption, punishment, and renewal through the divine guidance of the prophets. Ibn Ḥabīb can compare the vices of his society with those of past societies, but as Muḥammad was the last of the prophets, the moral disintegration of these times would seem to presage the end of the world.

Ibn Ḥabīb suggests that the Final Hour is imminent in his remarks about the evil he sees around him, but these suggestions are given more substance in a series of stories and hadiths predicting collapse, destruction, and the end of time. The portion of the text dedicated to the history of the conquest presents two predictions that foretell the collapse of Muslim rule in al-Andalus and the destruction of Cordoba. Ibn Ḥabīb himself says that when Mūsā first rode into Cordoba on his mule Kawkab, he exclaimed over the city's wonders and anticipated its damnation within two hundred years.[13] The second prediction, on the authority of al-Layth ibn Sa'd, describes how when Mūsā conquered Toledo, the city of the kings, he found a structure called the house of kings. Inside were twenty-five crowns adorned with sapphires and pearls, one for each of the twenty-five infidel kings who had ruled the peninsula. It is said, remarks the source, that the number of Muslim rulers of al-Andalus from the time of its conquest until the days of its destruction will equal the number of non-Muslim kings: twenty-five.[14]

Immediately after his account of the conquest, Ibn Ḥabīb lists the names of the governors of al-Andalus from the conquest until the arrival of 'Abd al-Raḥmān I. Their number totals eighteen. If we count the number of Umayyad amirs that follow in the account, we have seven. 'Abd Allāh is the twenty-fifth Muslim ruler, and of his reign the text tells us that his rule was weak and all kinds of grievances ensued. Children and possessions were captured, the markets collapsed, and prices rose. Switching tenses, the narrator tells us that the fall of the reign will be harsh and describes Cordoba as fat, fleshy, weak, and contemptible. The Berbers will seek refuge there at the end of time, spoiling both the civilized and unpopulated regions.[15]

This prediction of the end of Muslim rule is followed by a series of anonymous reports ("It is said . . . ") predicting the destruction of Cordoba and other cities in al-Andalus. The demise of al-Andalus is implicitly associated with the Final Hour through a sequence of hadiths that follow, describing the general state of corruption that will precede the apocalypse. People will be clever at pursuing the things of this world but neglect the Qu'ran. Any acts of faith they perform will lack conviction. They will become greedy and stingy, without shame or compassion, indulging in music and wine, committing adultery or seeking satisfaction with members of their own sex. Religious knowledge will dwindle away, replaced by confusion and murder, in a topsy-turvy world torn by rebellion and earthquake.[16]

The *Kitāb al-Ta'rīkh*'s fixation on the end of time, while part of a tradition or genre of apocalyptic writing current in the Islamic world of the ninth century, may also express a real anxiety about the fate of Islam in al-Andalus.[17] The redactor of his text, as we have seen, identified the signs of the end times with the reign of the amir 'Abd Allāh. The text presents the landscape of al-Andalus through the prism of this anxiety. In a few instances, it situates the reader in a specific time and place: "Oh people of Cordoba, take charge of your women and children. Do not let them live near the gathering place at the *bayt al-ẓulm* [house of injustice] nor near the congregational mosque, for the massacre will have no mercy for child nor woman. It will occur on Thursday, between the noon and afternoon prayers, until the setting of the sun. The safest spot during the massacre will be the place called kadiyat Abī 'Abda, at the site of the church."[18]

Otherwise, the text does not present many views of landscape except for the vivid landscape described in the accounts of Mūsā ibn Nuṣayr's conquest of the peninsula. Here, Mūsā's exploits have little to do with the conquest of actual cities. In a series of accounts, he moves through an alien and uncivilized landscape where the land shakes or the sea is solid or all is shrouded in darkness.[19] Rivers, the sea, desert, and mountains all loom large. It is a landscape of fear and wonder.

Moving through this eerie land, Mūsā and his men encountered strange idols or statues, jinn, and devils. The stories conform to types and gradually assume a repetitive quality. For example, in two different anecdotes, Mūsā and his men tried to capture a strange copper fortress in the middle of nowhere. In one story, each time one of the men managed to peer over the walls of the fortress, he fell into a fit of laughing and threw himself over the parapets.[20] In the other, the men who climbed up disappeared over the other side and later had no memory of their experience.[21] In the first story, Mūsā surmised that the fortress was the work of the devil; in the second he discovered jinn and withdrew. Another type of story is the discovery, in some remote spot, of sealed jars or bottles or copper domes. One is opened, and a devil or a jinn emerges, revealing himself to be one of the many King Solomon had locked away; the rest of the containers are then left intact and in place.[22] A third type is the encounter with idols, usually by a river (in one case, by an aqueduct), who either indicate direction or frighten Mūsā's men into turning back.[23]

The strangeness of this landscape enhances Mūsā's prestige as the hero of the story. However, the stories with the most surreal landscape and inhabitants are not necessarily the ones that most explicitly demonstrate his bravery and resolve or the magnitude of the booty he secured. The more important point is that this mythic landscape sets the conquest of al-Andalus apart from familiar experience and poses a contrast between the land as discovered and the land Ibn Ḥabīb and his audience know—the land that has become Islamic and been transformed.

This conquest history describes the extension of the boundaries of civilization. Indeed, the strange idols and fortresses all mark the edges of Mūsā's exploration; his encounters with them always send him and his troops back in the direction from which they came. Beyond them lie lands outside the bounds of human habitation and of human knowledge.

Reinhardt Dozy has suggested that Ibn Ḥabīb's account of the conquest draws on popular legends, reflecting early perceptions of the peninsula and encounters with the unknown.[24] Indeed, some of the earliest Arabic geographies that treat al-Andalus present a similar representation. Ibn Khurdadhbeh (mid-ninth century), Ibn al-Faqīh al-Hamadhānī, and Ibn Rusta (early tenth century) share some anecdotes with Ibn Ḥabīb's text and must have drawn on some of the same sources.[25] It is not difficult to imagine tales about gesturing idols to have spun out of actual encounters with the many statues that decorated the buildings and landscape of Visigothic and Roman Spain. Ibn Ḥayyān reports, for example, that the walls of Ecija were graced with white marble statues that appeared from a distance to be human guards.[26] Al-Maqqarī describes a statue in Italica of a woman with a boy that was so realistic that it appeared to be alive.[27] The magical landscape could very well derive from the real.[28]

Some of these stories may also have derived from the Greek and Latin texts that informed the Arabic geographies. Julia Hernández Juberías supports the view that the legend of the "city of copper" originated with the adventures of Alexander the Great. José Alemany-Bolufer argued that the story of Mūsā's siege of "a city in the desert of al-Andalus with walls of copper that shone like fire" is really an appropriation and adaptation of Plato's description of a city on the island of Atlantis.[29] It seems that some of the Greek geographers also described Iberia as a rich land on the fringes of civilization, a place of Homeric adventure.[30]

Dozy wondered at Ibn Ḥabīb's recounting of fables that surely must have clashed with the collective knowledge of his countrymen, if not with his own reason.[31] However, Ibn Ḥabīb's reports of the conquest should be understood in the context of his preoccupation with the apocalypse. "Accuracy" or specificity would not necessarily be important to this grand scheme. The representation of the land as strange and forbidding suggests its primeval state before its transformation by Islam and also underscores the peninsula's distance and isolation from the heartlands of Islamic civilization, a possible concern for the jurist-historian in his own day. Ibn Ḥabīb's text depicts the conquering Muslims at sea, farther than the flight of a bird can reach, or marching to the ends of the world.[32]

LANDSCAPE OF CONFIDENCE

By the tenth century, historical writing in the Islamic world had become more widespread and more diverse and had taken on new forms.[33] This period saw a proliferation of biographical dictionaries, geographical treatises and gazetteers, encyclopedic works, and local and dynastic histories, often written by secretaries and clients of the court.[34] Ibn al-Qūṭiyya and *Akhbār majmū'a* present a view of al-Andalus very different from Ibn Ḥabīb's. Their texts reflect a different perspective on history generally but also express a confidence in the state of Islam in the peninsula at the time of writing. Their conquest histories describe the possession of al-Andalus and its incorporation into the *dār al-Islām,* the abode of Islam, in a manner that suggests and reinforces a sense of security and stability.

Both texts describe the conquest routes Ṭāriq and Mūsā took as a kind of encirclement of the peninsula. Each conqueror marked his progress through the capture and garrisoning of cities, his passage commemorated by the naming of natural landmarks. Thus al-Andalus itself, as described by the text, was defined and inscribed with a new history and rendered culturally significant to its Muslim inhabitants.[35]

Ibn al-Qūṭiyya describes Ṭāriq's advance from Carteya to his confrontation with Roderick on the banks of the Beca River and then his progress to Ecija, Cordoba, and Toledo. From Toledo, he went through what became known as "Ṭāriq's pass" into Galicia and onward to Astorga. Mūsā's route began at the harbor that thereafter bore his name, proceeded along the coast of Sidonia to Seville, and then continued through one pass and then another, each called "Mūsā's pass," into Galicia and on to Astorga, where he met up with Ṭāriq and received word that the two were ordered to return to Damascus.[36]

Akhbār majmū'a also describes this kind of staking out of the territory, locating battle sites and identifying specific landmarks that indicate the progression of the conquest, but it presents variations in the routes and different etiological examples. Ṭarīf landed on an island that took his name: Ṭarīfa. Ṭāriq's battle with Roderick occurred on the shores of the lake of Janda near Algeciras, and from there he marched to Ecija, where he set up camp by a spring that subsequently bore the name "Ṭāriq's spring." Ṭāriq then divided his army, and each detachment pursued its own lines of conquest.[37] The text delineates the extremes of Ṭāriq's advance: he found King Solomon's table in a town that takes the name of al-Mā'ida (the table), pressed on to Amaya, and then returned to Toledo, where he awaited Mūsā.[38] Mūsā, meanwhile, landed at Algeciras and proceeded to Medina Sidonia, Carmona, Seville, and Merida before meeting up with Ṭāriq in Toledo. He then set out for the region of Zaragoza, where he conquered a number of towns.[39]

The two texts describe different boundaries to the northern limits of the conquered territory—Astorga in the west and Zaragoza in the east. Together they include most of the peninsula. *Akhbār majmū'a* makes clear, however, that the borders fluctuated and that the most extensive delineation of the boundaries of Islamic al-Andalus came later, under the governor 'Uqba ibn al-Ḥajjāj (who assumed office in 728). At that time the Muslim conquest extended over all the peninsula up to Narbonne in the east and all of Galicia in the west, except for a mountain stronghold in Asturias where Pelayo and a small band of thirty men and ten women, survivors of an extended siege, were left as no longer worth pursuing. As the narrator remarks, the Muslims underestimated these hardy souls, who turned out to be quite a "serious matter."[40]

Although the Christians to the north challenged the definition of the territory under Muslim sway over the course of Umayyad rule, the conquest histories establish a claim to the entire peninsula when they identify the outermost bounds of the Muslim advance as Galicia and Narbonne. They provide a map of al-Andalus that may or may not have corresponded to its actual configuration at any time and a charter for the caliphate.

The texts record the generation of a number of new cognitive maps of the peninsula. At the behest of the caliph 'Umar, the governor al-Samḥ (718–721) provided a description of the shape of the land and its rivers and conducted a cadastral survey that identified which cities and regions succumbed to the Muslims by force and which surrendered by treaty.[41] This is one of a series of "maps" that became relevant to the Muslim rulers and their historians. Another cognitive map discernible in the historical texts details demographic patterns: the distribution of Arabs and Berbers, tribal and clan confederations, or military divisions.

Akhbār majmū'a presents its own survey of the conquest, recording the Muslim appropriation of specific cities and even buildings.[42] In this way, it provides a striking contrast to Ibn Ḥabīb's history of the conquest. Stories about the conquest of particular places also have the ring of legend but with a very different effect: these legends impress on the reader the possession of major cities and monuments and their incorporation into a new regime.

Akhbār majmū'a's conquest stories of the important cities of Cordoba, Tudmir, Carmona, Seville, and Merida describe a transition from Visigothic to Muslim rule, from one era to another. The narrator calls on the reader to observe this change—for example, in the way he introduces his accounts of the conquest of Cordoba and Seville. He tells his audience that when Ṭāriq divided his army, he sent Mughīth with a division to Cordoba, "which was one of the greatest cities in those days and is currently the citadel (*qaṣaba*) of al-Andalus . . . and the capital of the kingdom."[43] Recounting Mūsā's advance on Seville, the narrator explains that the city was the most important city of al-Andalus, renowned for its buildings and monuments, and that it had been a capital of the kingdom that preceded that of the Goths. He recounts that although the Goths established their capital in Toledo, the best of the Romans—the most worthy men in law, religion, and secular matters—stayed in Seville. After some months of siege, Mūsā conquered Seville with the help of God, and the Christians fled to Beja.[44]

The incorporation of the conquered cities into the new kingdom depended in part on the terms of conquest: capitulation by force or negotiated surrender. The stories of the capture of the above-mentioned cities each describe a different variation of these terms. Conquest by force could mean an extended siege (as in the case of Seville), the penetration of the city walls through advance knowledge of the weaknesses of its defenses (as in the conquest of Cordoba), or through ruse (as in the conquest of Carmona).[45] Conquest through negotiation could involve cunning on the side of the Christians, as in the story of Tudmir, or alternatively, their naive response to the Muslim besiegers, as in the story of Merida.[46] In this sense, the tales of the conquest of particular cities present a canonical typology for modes of submission. Of course, the terms of surrender, whether by force or by treaty, affected the treatment of the inhabitants and their property, and the conquest history records their status.

In their details, the stories describe the transfer of authority from Christian to Muslim and the actual possession, through occupation and appropriation, of the cities of the peninsula and their histories. The stories have a legendary quality that gives them a remoteness in time, suggesting the success of the conquest.[47] The stories of the conquests of Cordoba, the Umayyad capital to be, and Merida, are discussed here in some detail to demonstrate how such accounts underscored the stability of the Muslim (Umayyad) kingdom in the tenth century.

As mentioned above, after Ṭāriq defeated Roderick, he divided his army on Julian's advice. One division headed for Rayya, and another for Granada; he himself headed for Toledo, and his commander Mughīth set out for Cordoba. Mughīth established his camp in the woods of Secunda, not far from Cordoba. Some of his spies came across a shepherd and his flock and brought him back to be interrogated. The shepherd divulged that all the prominent inhabitants of the city had left for Toledo, leaving the governor with four hundred defenders and the common population. When Mughīth asked about fortifications, the shepherd replied that while the walls of the city were quite strong, there was a breach in the gate of the statue, which the narrator specifically identifies as the gate opposite the bridge.[48] Under cover of a rainy night, Mughīth's men crossed the Guadalquivir and examined the gate but could not find the breach that had been described to them. They sent for the shepherd, who revealed it to them; its location had been obscured by a fig tree. One of the Muslims then scaled the wall, and Mughīth threw his turban up to him to serve as a rope for others to follow. He then mounted his horse and waited before the gate for those who had climbed over the wall to surprise the guard and let him, and the rest of his men, in. Once again, the narrator specifies that the gate in question is the gate of the bridge, also known as the gate of the statue, or the gate of Algeciras (although, he adds, in those days the bridge had been destroyed and so there was no bridge in Cordoba). Resuming his tale, he recounts that the Muslims surprised the guard and opened the gate to Mughīth, who hurried to the palace of the ruler. The prince, however, having learned of the Muslims' entry, had fled with four or five hundred soldiers and others via the western gate of the city, or the gate of Seville, taking refuge in the nearby church of San Aiello. Mughīth occupied the palace of Cordoba and the next day began his siege of the church, writing to Ṭāriq with news of the conquest.[49]

This is the first of three anecdotes, recounted in a sequence broken up by other stories, that describe the conquest of Cordoba; the reader is brought back to this important city again and again. In this first part, the narrator is very careful to orient his audience, translating the landmarks of the story into terms familiar to the tenth century. The gate that features so prominently in the story has three names, which describe it in different ways.

It is the gate of the statue because of the statue that graced it, the gate of the bridge because it faced the site of the old Roman bridge that the Muslims soon rebuilt, and the gate of Algeciras because it faced the road in that direction. The three names are all significant in terms of the Muslims' experience and express the city's Muslim identity.

In the next installment of the story, we learn that Mughīth besieged the Christians in the church of Cordoba for three months until he heard that the governing prince had fled, leaving his soldiers in the church. Mughīth understood that the fugitive was making his way toward the mountains of Cordoba, intending to join his compatriots in Toledo, and decided to pursue him alone. Outside the village of Catalavera, Mughīth spied his rival up ahead and spurred his horse. The Visigoth turned around and, seeing the Muslim commander hard on his heels, became distraught and left the road, only to plunge into a ravine and lose his mount. Mughīth found him thus, sitting on his shield, and took him prisoner. As the narrator recounts, he was the only Christian prince to be taken prisoner; the others either negotiated a surrender and were granted their freedom or fled to Galicia.[50]

Mughīth returned to Cordoba, compelled the Christians holed up in the church to come out, and ordered that their heads be cut off. From then on, the narrator informs the reader, the church has been called "the church of the prisoners." The account ends reporting that Mughīth assembled the Jews of Cordoba and put them in charge of guarding the city, posted his own soldiers in different locations, and moved into the governor's palace.[51]

This story identifies the church as a specific landmark and gives it a name that recalls a particular incident in the new history of the city. This is another instance of how naming asserts possession and jurisdiction. In this context, it commemorates an act of appropriation that transforms a specifically Christian building into a monument to the Islamic conquest.

More broadly, the story of Mughīth's chase of the Visigoth

governor echoes the story of Ṭāriq's confrontation with Roderick, the Visigoth ruler. According to that account, Roderick disappeared in the midst of battle. Only his horse was found, mired in the mud of a ditch. Mughīth's confrontation with the Visigoth prince who has been unhorsed is like a modified version of Ṭāriq's story; this time the enemy is actually captured (to be conveyed to the caliph). The conquest of Cordoba is complete, but it has yet to be established as the capital of Muslim al-Andalus.

The next installment of the story of Cordoba centers on the location of the new seat of power. The context for the recounting of this anecdote is Ayyūb ibn Ḥabīb's assumption of the office of governor of al-Andalus in the summer of 716 (after the murder of Mūsā's son, 'Abd al-'Azīz) and his transfer of the capital from Seville to Cordoba. The narrator reports that when Ibn Ḥabīb moved to Cordoba, he took up residence in the palace that Mughīth had chosen as his home, the subject of the following anecdote. When Mūsā learned that the caliph al-Walīd had recalled him to Damascus, he decided to return to the coast (where he would find a boat to cross the Straits) along Ṭāriq's route of conquest so he could acquaint himself with the region. When he reached Cordoba, he reprimanded Mughīth for inappropriately residing in the former Visigoth governor's palace. Mughīth obligingly moved, and Mūsā himself settled into the palace for the duration of his stay. We are told that Mughīth's new residence was a magnificent estate with abundant water and olive and date trees, located near the gate of Algeciras, or the bridge, facing the breach that his men had used to penetrate the city. The estate had been called al-Yuṣṣāna and had belonged to the prince Mughīth had taken captive; it had a splendid palace that henceforth took the name "Mughīth's palace."[52]

In this story, the transfer of authority from Visigoth to Muslim and from the family of Mūsā and 'Abd al-'Aziz to a new set of governors is represented in a move from one palace to another. Mughīth, as conqueror of Cordoba, appropriated the official residence of its former governor and the symbol of his command. When he was forced to move, his new residence became the site of the new seat of power on the peninsula, for this was where Ibn Ḥabīb subsequently chose to reside as governor. The aura of authority associated with the administrative center of the former regime became superseded (after the demise of the Banū Nuṣayr) by the prestige of Mughīth's name and the historically significant location of his palace, opposite the famous breach that brought about the fall of the city.[53]

In retrospect, the conquest of Cordoba was an important element of the foundation history of the new Islamic rule, for the city became the heart of the kingdom. *Akhbār majmūʿa* presents a simplified account of events that outlines the essential drama and highlights the symbolic details. We have the betrayal of the city by an unnamed shepherd, a chase in which the main protagonist pursues his counterpart, and a massacre that proclaims his triumph. The church and the palace, as we have seen, become symbols of the new authority. The deliberate featuring of Mughīth's turban in the scaling of the wall suggests that the turban signifies the specifically Muslim identity of the conquerors. The story of the turban finds echo in the story of ʿAbd al-Raḥmān I's banner, which was fashioned from a turban; the two stories reinforce the identification of the turban as a symbol of Muslim conquest.[54]

The city of Merida was less central to the subsequent history of al-Andalus than Cordoba, and so its conquest was not charged with the same obvious import. Nevertheless, imparting the story of the conquest of Merida suggests how all of *Akhbār majmūʿa*'s accounts of conquests of the cities of al-Andalus promote a legendary past and convey a confident appreciation of the Muslim domination of the peninsula.

Merida was a major commercial city on the Guadiana river until ʿAbd al-Raḥmān II destroyed much of it in the suppression of a seven-year revolt.[55] As the narrator of *Akhbār majmūʿa* describes it, Merida was home to some of the great lords of Visigothic al-Andalus and the site of many monuments, a bridge, castles, and churches—too many to be described.[56]

Mūsā and his men encircled the city and became embroiled in bloody combat with a detachment sent forth from the city to engage them, one mile outside the city walls. After the battle, the Muslim infantry and cavalry spent the night in a rock quarry Mūsā had discovered. The next morning, when another force from the city came out to meet them, the Muslims ambushed them from their hideout in the quarry and massacred a great many. Those who managed to escape with their lives sought refuge behind the walls of the city, which, we are informed, were stronger than any others built by man.[57]

The Muslims continued their siege for some months. Under cover of a siege engine used to approach the walls, a group of sappers began to dig at the foundations of one of the towers. However, the mortar proved resistant to their picks and shovels, the infidels (*al-'ulūj*) on the walls above bombarded them, the engine collapsed, and the Muslims were crushed. That is why, recounts the narrator, the tower is called the "tower of the martyrs."[58]

The city was finally conquered at the end of Ramadan (June 713) on *'Īd al-Fiṭr,* the feast day breaking the fast, in the following manner. When the Muslims under the tower were killed, the infidels said to themselves: "We have just broken the forces of the enemy. If there was ever a day to negotiate a truce, today is the day." Hoping to secure favorable terms, a delegation left the city to meet with Mūsā, whom, they found, was a fairly old man with a white beard. They tried to impress certain conditions of surrender on him, but he rejected them, and the delegation returned home. The next day, the evening of which marked the beginning of the feast, the delegation made another attempt. They came out to see Mūsā, and this time his beard was red because of the henna he applied to it in honor of the holiday. The infidels said to one another: "I believe he must be one of those who eats human flesh, or he is not the man we saw yesterday." Negotiations seemed to be inconclusive, for the next day, the day of the feast, the delegation came out again, and this time found Mūsā with a black beard (the effect of further application of the henna). The delegation returned to the city and warned its inhabitants: "Fools! You are fighting against prophets who transform themselves at will and rejuvenate themselves. Their king, who was an old man, has become young again. Go and give them whatever they want."[59]

After this, peace was indeed arranged with the following conditions: the property of the Christians who were killed in the ambush at the quarry and of those who fled the city for Galicia would belong to the Muslims (the rest of the inhabitants could retain their property), while the jewels and property of the churches would go to Mūsā. The gates of the city were opened to the Muslims on the day of the feast of *'Īd al-Fiṭr.*[60]

This drama is composed of three acts: the story of the ambush, the story of the martyrdom, and the story of the beard. Although we know the scene is the city of Merida, we do not have the kind of landmarks that the story of the conquest of Cordoba presents, apart, perhaps, from "the tower of the martyrs." This reads as a generic legend of the conquest of an important city.

The representation of the transfer of authority from Christian to Muslim hands centers on the story of the beard. The occasion of the Christian surrender is clear: *'Īd al-Fiṭr,* one of the most important Muslim holidays. The changing color of Mūsā's beard was a coincidence of this timing, on which the submission of the city turned. The tale highlights these fortuitous circumstances and delights in the Christians' ignorance and naiveté, sharing the joke with an audience well familiar with the effects of henna.

The story most certainly conforms to a type. The message that the Christians think the Muslims are cannibals or prophets conveys an obvious sense of superiority and self-satisfaction. Ibn al-Qūṭiyya tells an anecdote (which recurs in various forms elsewhere) about the conquest of Carteya, the first city conquered in al-Andalus, that conveys the same message in a similar manner. On conquest, Ṭāriq ordered his men to cook up the bodies of some of the prisoners he had taken and killed. He then released the rest of the prisoners who, thinking the Muslims were cannibals, spread the word to all they encountered, "and God filled their hearts with terror."[61]

These stories juxtapose illusion with reality in a way that sets the reader apart, as being in the know, from some of the (Christian) characters. They provide an interesting contrast to Ibn Ḥabīb's fantastical tales; the Muslims are in control where they were once confounded and bedazzled. This kind of storytelling reflects a distance from the moment of conquest and a confidence in possession.

The tenth-century conquest histories describe the incorporation of al-Andalus into a new history. We can see this in the elaboration of geographical etiologies and in the way *Akhbār majmū'a*'s accounts of the conquest of individual cities assert Muslim domination through narrative style. The reports of the conquests read as legends, where history turns on the actions of a few personalities and the subtle hand of divine fate. In each case, the story line is simple, with only a few telling details. The stories name cities and perhaps identify them by landmarks, but for the most part, they objectify the conquests as types and the cities as symbols. In the context of the tenth century, such stories conferred the cities of the peninsula with a past that affirmed Muslim hegemony in the present.

How do these texts represent the landscape of 'Abd al-Raḥmān I's "conquest"? 'Abd al-Raḥmān I's conquest of the peninsula nearly fifty years later was not about the Muslim appropriation of Christian lands, cities, and palaces but the assertion of specifically Umayyad authority over al-Andalus. In these circumstances, the texts define the peninsula in terms of allies and enemies.

Ibn al-Qūṭiyya's text, as we have seen, established the alliance between the Banū Umayya and the royal Visigoth family. The text is generally concerned to identify and record who became involved in both the original conquest and in each stage of 'Abd al-Raḥmān I's progress and to locate their descendants geographically.[62] For example, the text informs us of who participated in the swearing of the first oath of loyalty to ʻAbd al-Raḥmān I, who participated in the raising of his banner, and who were the first of his men to cross the river into Cordoba.[63]

Akhbār majmūʻa's more detailed account of ʻAbd al-Raḥmān I's political alliances and advance through al-Andalus provides a more comprehensive document of who joined the amir's cause and when. The text reports who received ʻAbd al-Raḥmān I's initial appeal for help, how they responded, who traveled across the straits to escort him to the peninsula, who met him when he touched land, who received him at Torrox at the home of one of his most important supporters, who joined him in the battle against Yūsuf al-Fihrī, and who commanded his victorious forces.[64]

The landscape of the narrative of ʻAbd al-Raḥmān I's arrival in al-Andalus and his establishment of Umayyad rule in 756 is thus largely subsumed beneath the roster of supporters: individuals and tribes. For example, when ʻAbd al-Raḥmān, preparing for his final confrontation with al-Fihrī, wrote to all the districts of al-Andalus and to the Berbers for support, the narrator records who responded: all the Yemenis, three Qaysīs (names cited), and three men from the tribe of Thaqīf (names cited), rather than men from the regions involved.[65]

From this perspective, ʻAbd al-Raḥmān I's drive to establish his authority on the peninsula was a call to allegiance: the land was legitimately his to claim, and the "conquest" a realization of that claim. Al-Ṣumayl, Yūsuf al-Fihrī's general, expressed the idea of Umayyad domination of al-Andalus most crudely when he explained to ʻAbd al-Raḥmān's partisans why he decided to reject the amir's cause: "I realized that he comes from such a people that if one of them peed on this peninsula, all of us, and all of you, would drown in his urine."[66]

ʻAbd al-Raḥmān I reclaimed al-Andalus for the Umayyads and inaugurated a new epoch in Umayyad and Andalusi history. The representation of the amir as founder conjures its own landscape, one that shares some of the mythical quality of the landscapes of Ibn Ḥabīb's account of the Muslim conquest. In the amir's boasts of his achievements, al-Andalus appears to be an untamed, hostile environment, its cities in ruins, their populations dispersed. By his account, 'Abd al-Raḥmān traveled a great distance, crossing river, desert, and sea, and then conquered this place, bringing security (organized an army) and civilization (populated cities).[67] The landscape depicted in this interpretation of 'Abd al-Raḥmān I's story dramatizes his achievements. The general topographical description of the obstacles he encountered, without mention of names or other specific details, removes them from the level of everyday experience. The amir is a heroic founder of a new kingdom and a new civilization.

The two landscapes of 'Abd al-Raḥmān I's adventures described here complement two themes of the amir's representation: the continuity of Umayyad authority and a new beginning in the history of the dynasty and the peninsula.

Turning from the age of the conquests to the era of Umayyad rule, historical accounts of Umayyad rule dating from the tenth century, or based on tenth-century accounts such as Ibn Ḥayyān's history of the reigns of 'Abd al-Raḥmān III and al-Ḥakam II, contrast dramatically with Ibn Ḥabīb's *Kitāb al-Ta'rikh* in the way they treat the rebellions that denied and threatened Umayyad rule. As *Akhbār majmū'a* and Ibn al-Qūṭiyya relate, after 'Abd al-Raḥmān I prevailed over Yūsuf al-Fihrī and established his rule, he continued to face opposition to his authority; over the course of his reign he suppressed revolts in Beja, Niebla, Seville, Merida, Tudmir, Algeciras, and Zaragoza. His successors all faced similar challenges or worse; uprisings even took place in Cordoba during the rule of al-Ḥakam I, and 'Abd Allāh nearly lost control of the peninsula altogether. In spite of this history of rebellion, the historiography of the caliphal period presents a textual landscape that clearly is possessed and dominated by the Umayyads; this representation reflects the security wrought by 'Abd al-Raḥmān III.

THE CALIPH'S DOMAIN

In previous chapters we have seen how 'Abd al-Raḥmān III had to reassert Umayyad authority over a land rife with sedition. Here we consider more closely the representation of the caliph's domination of the land he ruled over. In recording 'Abd al-Raḥmān III's efforts to reestablish central control over the peninsula, contemporary narrative accounts like 'Arīb Ibn Sa'īd's, describe a reconquest, for the eighth Umayyad ruler followed an itinerary that covered most of the peninsula. For over a decade and a half, he concentrated on the fortresses and cities in the central region, with occasional forays to the frontiers. Once the central provinces were more or less secure after the capture of Bobastro in 928, the newly proclaimed caliph systematically conquered fortresses and towns in first the eastern and then the western provinces. His reconquest of the rebellious regions culminated in the capture of Toledo in 932. Ibn Ḥayyān makes the association with the original conquest explicit, pointing out that Ecija, the first city 'Abd al-Raḥmān III conquered, was first taken by Ṭāriq.[68] The representation of 'Abd al-Raḥmān III's battles to assert his authority as a reconquest suggests both a new beginning and a continuity with the past. 'Abd al-Raḥmān III reasserted his dynasty's authority on the peninsula, recreated the community, and revived the religion.

Ibn Ḥayyān's history makes clear that the caliph's achievements far surpassed those of the original conquerors, his eponymous ancestor, 'Abd al-Raḥmān I, or any of the Umayyad amirs. In his account of 'Abd al-Raḥmān III's victory over Toledo, the historian represents the caliph's power and authority as unprecedented in the history of the peninsula. He alone put an end to the cycle of conquest, rebellion, reconquest, and rebellion that had plagued rulers for centuries.

Ibn Ḥayyān's account of 'Abd al-Raḥmān III's reconquest of Toledo includes reports from a variety of sources. He begins with an overview of the history of the city, presenting 'Īsā ibn

Aḥmad al-Rāzī's report on its early pagan history and Isḥāq ibn Maslama's summary of Gothic rule and account of the history of the city under Muslim rule, as well as a brief description of the city itself.[69] He then reports on the start of the siege that would last two and a half years. He presents the final account of Toledo's surrender, and the celebrations that ensued, some pages later, as the first entry for the year 932.

The first two accounts of the pre-Islamic history of Toledo set the stage for 'Abd al-Raḥmān III's triumph: Toledo was the great fortress and city, renowned in ancient times, that successfully frustrated the ambitions of kings of many nations.[70] As Ibn Ḥayyān exclaims: "Oh, how she thwarted the great kings and resisted the most skilled armies! The most well-recruited campaigns withdrew without any success until God granted that the caliph, lord of the kingdom (*rabb al-dawla*), broke her. God distinguished the caliph from all previous commanders with His great victory."[71]

The interpretations of pre-Islamic history Ibn Ḥayyān provides fit together in a continuous narrative and serve to make sense of the Muslim experience of rule in al-Andalus. The Muslim historians, drawing on unnamed sources, appropriated the pre-Islamic past in order to represent the Muslim domination of the contemporary "present" and enhance the caliph's prestige. Because these accounts are important to our understanding of the representation of the caliph and his authority over the land he ruled and are in themselves interesting tenth-century interpretations of an ancient history, they are presented in abbreviated form below.

'Īsā al-Rāzī begins by reporting that the city of Toledo was founded by a pagan king named Diyūsuqiyūs (the Roman praetor Digitius?), some five thousand years after the era of Adam, and goes on to describe its history under the Romans. When the Romans conquered al-Andalus, they chose Toledo as their capital and made it the grandest of all the cities of the peninsula. After some time, however, the provinces of al-Andalus rebelled against Roman rule. A rebel leader named Viriathus from

Lusitania overthrew the Roman governor and expelled the Romans from Toledo. As the historian reports, this was the first revolt (*thawra*) of many in the history of Toledo. After this they became common for the Toledans.[72]

'Īsā al-Rāzī goes on to describe the Romans' persistent efforts to regain control of the city. Year after year, for seven years, they launched campaigns against Toledo, but their attacks were always repelled. When one of Viriathus's companions betrayed and murdered him, another of his men took his place and continued the struggle. Frustrated by the brave resistance of the Toledans, the Romans tried to seduce them with gifts and grand promises and eventually succeeded in dividing the population. The rebel leader was killed, and his head was sent to the Roman general with an invitation to enter the city. The Romans arrived under cover of night and, once in possession of Toledo, found themselves in a position to dominate al-Andalus once again.[73]

Continuing his narrative, 'Īsā al-Rāzī reveals that the history of the city remained tumultuous, despite peaceful interludes. Toledo had suffered during the period of rebellion but prospered under the Romans for a while. According to Roman chronicles, al-Rāzī recounts, Roman rule flourished for a hundred years. Eventually, however, the city again rebelled and expelled the Roman general, and al-Andalus became engulfed in discord and schism, war and violence; the population diminished, and starvation loomed for those who survived. Then the Toledan Antonius came to power and subdued the city, tended to its buildings, and constructed its great wall and remarkable bridge.[74]

The situation remained far from secure, as 'Īsā al-Rāzī's account goes on to demonstrate. The supreme ruler of Rome, Julius, first of the Caesars (whose name became a title for all generals who succeeded him), decided to attack Toledo. Julius gathered together a grand army in Rome and marched to al-Andalus, which he found on the verge of ruin, its people ravaged by misery. He marched straight to Toledo, surrounded, and besieged it. The city proved strong enough to endure the siege; the besiegers ran out of food first. Unable to provision themselves, they returned to Rome without a single victory. According to al-Rāzī, the Romans attributed the failure of this expedition to weakness and lack of courage. Toledo continued to be a problem for the caesars that succeeded Julius, rarely submitting to Roman rule until it was finally extinguished in al-Andalus.[75]

Ibn Ḥayyān continues the narrative with Isḥāq ibn Maslama's account of Visigothic rule. According to Ibn Maslama, the first Gothic ruler in al-Andalus was Suinthila, who conquered it from, and defended it against, the Romans one year before the Hijra. He launched a campaign against Rome itself, conquering some cities there. On the Iberian peninsula, the Basques resisted him but were forced to flee from the plains to the mountains. He ruled seven years and died in Toledo, succeeded by the Goth Sisenand, whose reign lasted six years but was not notable. After him ruled Chintila, who waged war successfully in Africa and returned to Toledo, where he died.[76]

Ibn Maslama continues his account of the reign of the Visigoths, devoting more attention to the rulers whose history touched on that of the Muslims. The next ruler in the account is Wamba, whose reign, Ibn Maslama reports, was magnificent. Wamba was the one who decorated the churches of Toledo, perfected its buildings, and had the marble over the city gates engraved. When news of the Prophet and his victories over all he met in combat reached him, he gathered the bishops and notables of al-Andalus and informed them. Julian, one of the most prominent men, told him: "I believe his nation will conquer the people of al-Andalus." When asked how he knew, he replied: "Because this is in the verses of Maṭrayūs, the wise man, according to Daniel." Wamba ruled for eight years, after which Ervig ruled. His reign coincided with a terrible famine in al-Andalus during which the inhabitants considered emigration. His rule lasted seven years, followed by that of his son, who was of a bad disposition and mistreated his subjects, oppressing them with heavy taxes. His rule lasted sixteen years.[77]

Ibn Maslama's account continues to approach the intersection of Visigoth and Muslim history. The next ruler, he reports, was Witiza, whose reign began in the year 77 of the Hijra. He was a man of good conduct and behavior, loved by his subjects; he ruled for twelve years and died. After him ruled Roderick, who was the last to rule the Goths, Ibn Maslama recounts, because the Arabs invaded the peninsula after he opened the forbidden house in Toledo, according to the well-known account; in this way was inaugurated the reign of Islam.[78]

Returning to the history of Toledo, in particular, Ibn Maslama reports that the city continued in its excesses and unruliness until God sent Islam and extended the authority of the Arabs into al-Andalus. One of the first to enter the country, Ṭāriq ibn Ziyād, hurried to conquer Toledo at the first opportunity, bringing an end to Visigoth rule and the triumph of Islam, glorifying the true religion. The conquest was easy because the people of the city had been demoralized by discord, and their numbers reduced.[79]

Muslim rule did not bring an end to Toledo's rebellious history, as Ibn Maslama goes on to recount. During the reign of the governors of the Islamic state, the city continued in its disobedience. The situation continued during the reign of the Umayyad caliphs (amirs), to whom power had passed in al-Andalus. The struggle with Toledo greatly tired the first caliph (amir), 'Abd al-Raḥmān (I) ibn Mu'āwiya ibn Hishām, founder of the dynasty in al-Andalus to whom the whole country submitted. Toledo resisted for seven years; he could not conquer it except after the most arduous war, and then the city rebelled against his son, the imam Hishām ibn 'Abd al-Raḥmān, whom all the rest of al-Andalus accepted. Hishām brought the city into submission, only to have it rebel against his son, the caliph al-Ḥakam. Al-Ḥakam, "that flintstone whom no one could make spark," conquered the city time after time and trampled on it as on pebbles, making it suffer with every attack. But Toledo again rebelled under his son, the imam 'Abd al-Raḥmān ibn al-Ḥakam, a gentle man, much loved for his mild character. The rebellion caused him grief for a while until his temperament changed, and he forced the city to submit in such a way that it remained submissive for the rest of his reign. But after his death, Toledo rose up against his son, the caliph (amir) Muḥammad. Muḥammad confronted it immediately and sent campaign after campaign, year after year, until the city finally asked for truce, which meant paying the tribute, accepting governors, and exchanging hostages. When Muḥammad died and sedition (*fitna*) spread through al-Andalus, Toledo broke its truce and rebelled in the most extreme manner. As the rulers of the time, first al-Mundhir and then ʻAbd Allāh, were occupied with the rebels closest at hand, Toledo remained in rebellion.[80]

As Ibn Maslama describes, God put an end to the *fitna* with the reign of the imam al-Nāṣir li-Dīn Allāh: his reign dispelled the darkness and provided a light to guide those who were lost; those who were in rebellion submitted. But the Toledans continued in their error and deviance, thinking that he was like his predecessors, until they experienced the strength of his strong arm. He surrounded the city with armies and raised fortresses against it. The city was in a stranglehold until he became its master. Al-Nāṣir forced the Toledans into obedience and brought them into the community by violent means.[81]

Using these extracts from the histories of ʻĪsā al-Rāzī and Ibn Maslama, Ibn Ḥayyān describes a history of a rebellious Toledo that began early under Roman rule in Iberia and extended through the Visigothic and Muslim periods up until the reign of ʻAbd al-Raḥmān III. The city had a "custom" of rebellion. Thus represented, rebellion seems less threatening, almost a test each ruler must pass. Unlike the Roman governors, each of the Umayyad amirs managed to subdue the city for the period of his reign, until the collapse of central authority after Muḥammad's death. ʻAbd al-Raḥmān III, however, more than passed the test; we understand that he finally put an end to the custom. An exemplar of his achievements, the account of ʻAbd al-Raḥmān III's domination of Toledo, once a capital of great kingdoms, defines his reign as an apogee in both the history of the dynasty and in that of the peninsula.

Ibn Ḥayyān's representation of the reconquest of Toledo underscores the adage that history is written by the victors, confirming the message of the text itself. He caps the accounts of 'Īsā al-Rāzī and Ibn Maslama, which serve as a historical preface to his own account of 'Abd al-Raḥmān III's siege and conquest of the city, with the *qāḍī* Sa'īd ibn Sa'īd's description of the city he adjudicated in, as if the claims made on the city's history must be balanced by claims to its physical features.[82]

Ibn Ḥayyān's accounts of the siege and conquest of Toledo express the caliph's domination of the land most bluntly in terms of force—the power to strangle an invincible city. The siege began in the spring and summer of 930, executed with the caliph's personal participation. As the text demonstrates, as soon as he entered the region, he assumed physical control over it. On the way to besiege Toledo, the caliph easily dominated the city's rebel outposts, occupied strategic river ports, and asserted his authority over the plains, ensuring control over the crops. The Toledans were forced into their city and cut off from their resources. By the account, the caliph himself surveyed the city's situation and determined the best location in which to set up camp and harass the inhabitants, choosing the site of the cemetery at the city gates. He then ordered the construction of a permanent fortress for the besiegers, a city called Madīnat al-Fatḥ, the City of Conquest, on the peak of the mountain overlooking the city's port. He arranged for the provisioning of the new city with the establishment of markets and populated it with workmen who could maintain it. With these arrangements, after sixty-one days on campaign, the caliph entrusted the siege to his capable commander. The narrator assures us he departed with circumstances secure: the Toledans were trapped in their hole, unable to raise a head, let alone enter and leave the city. Their means of livelihood destroyed, it was only a matter of time before they surrendered.[83]

Two years later, the narration continues, after the Toledans' appeal to their Christian neighbors resulted in the defeat of the infidel forces and the supplication of the Toledans, the caliph rode into the city to take possession. Circulating through the streets and passageways, he marveled at the impregnability of the city's defenses, the richness of its resources, and the size of its population despite the decline due to the siege. Again, on surveying the situation, he took the city in hand, supervising the repairs of the damages caused by the war and the reorganization of its defenses. The historian exclaims over the caliph's creative ideas in ensuring his permanent control: 'Abd al-Raḥmān III rebuilt the bridge and ordered the construction of a fortress between the bridge and the city wall, which would serve as a residence for the governor and his men. This fortress would ensure that he would have exclusive control over access to the city. After initiating construction and arranging for the provisioning of his garrison, the caliph left the city to the charge of his commander and *mawlā* (client), Durrī ibn 'Abd al-Raḥmān. Toledo remained tranquil, the markets opened, and people returned to their economic and religious duties.[84]

This account of the siege and surrender represents 'Abd al-Raḥmān III's power through his ability to command the construction of a city such as Madīnat al-Fatḥ or the refortification of Toledo and to maintain a firm hold over the activities of a region so that no one could come or go without his authority. He personally surveyed the land that he claimed as his own and determined how best to make his presence felt. This representation of the caliph's authority echoes, in its general features, 'Abd al-Raḥmān III's own representation of his conquest of Bobastro. In the two circulars he sent out to be read in the great mosques of all the provinces, 'Abd al-Raḥmān III described his systematic destruction of the countryside around Bobastro, his securing of the neighboring rebel outposts, and his stranglehold on the fortress-city that finally forced the Banū Ḥafṣūn into submission. He recounted how he rode into the conquered city and marveled at its defenses, before ordering its destruction (except for a few select fortresses to house his governor and troops). He described with relish his reduction of Bobastro to a bare mountain top, listing specific acts of destruction: he razed walls and palaces, mosques and churches, houses and shops to the ground; he unearthed tombs.[85]

Such representations of 'Abd al-Raḥmān III's conquests demonstrated his ability to create and destroy and defined him as an agent of God whose power extended from His power. Not surprisingly, the accounts of the conquests also feature the caliph's ability to punish and forgive. Abd al-Raḥmān III began his campaign against Toledo with letters and a delegation exhorting the population to return to obedience and rejoin the community.[86] When the Toledans failed to comply, he resolved to punish them and began his siege. After the defeat of the Christian troops from Galicia who came to relieve Toledo, the Toledans begged 'Abd al-Raḥmān for forgiveness. The caliph pardoned and granted amnesty to all, and the people rejoiced at the lifting of the siege.[87] The narration emphasizes that although 'Abd al-Raḥmān had a strong arm, he was generous in his treatment of rebels. As we have seen, the Andalusi Umayyads represented themselves as committed to the restoration of the community and the integration of strays into the fold.

Ibn Ḥayyān's account of 'Abd al-Raḥmān III's conquest of Toledo concludes with an extract from Aḥmad al-Rāzī's work that confirms the caliph's benevolence and the success of his efforts to bring the city back into the community. The extract presents an old man's experience of the siege of Toledo: he recalls the starvation of the city and the besieging commander's offer of safe-conduct to all the poor people who had nothing to live on. As the siege continued, more and more people took advantage of this offer, including soldiers and cavalrymen. Finally, seeing death at hand, the Toledans sued for peace and security. Despite the fact that the city had no choice but to surrender, 'Abd al-Raḥmān III agreed to the terms they sought, responding to their disobedience with indulgence. He made arrangements for the benefit of the people and the region and separated the population from the governor's fortress with a high wall; spirits quieted and adhered to the true path.[88]

The old man's words describe the caliph's absolute possession of the land and control over its inhabitants. Like a reprobate child, Toledo (al-Andalus) was made to submit and obey, for its own good. The caliph reasserted authority and reestablished order and stability in a land that was clearly his responsibility. The representation of the reconquest assumes 'Abd al-Raḥmān III's claim to the domain and demonstrates his mastery over it. This mastery involved the construction of a new landscape.

As we have seen, Ibn Ḥayyān reports that after 'Abd al-Raḥmān III's experience at the battle of Al-Khandaq (Alhandega), the caliph devoted himself to his passion for construction. Al-Maqqarī's seventeenth-century text *Nafḥ al-ṭīb min ghuṣn al-Andalus al-raṭīb* preserves attributed excerpts from texts that reveal something about this passion, drawn from the works of Aḥmad al-Rāzī, Ibn Ḥayyān, Ibn Bashkuwāl, and Ibn Sa'īd.[89] Later historians must have depended on the work of "historians who lived in the prosperous times of the caliphate," at least to some extent, in their descriptions of the monuments and cities of Cordoba and Madīnat al-Zahrā', since so much was destroyed in the *fitna* that marked the collapse of Umayyad rule. While the later historians certainly had their own interests in the lost Umayyad capital that likely colored their representations, it is also likely that their concern to demonstrate the magnificence of Cordoba and the prosperity of the region was shared by (if not derived from) contemporary historians. By paying careful attention to the excerpts al-Maqqarī provides us with, we can glimpse the textual representation of the landscape of Cordoba of the late tenth century. Later, we consider the nostalgic view of historians writing after the demise of Umayyad rule.

The architecture of power such as palaces, congregational mosques, recreational estates, gardens, bridges, aqueducts, and public works figured prominently in the textual landscape of Cordoba in the caliphal period. We know, for example, that the tenth-century historian Aḥmad al-Rāzī (d. 955) wrote, in addition to his history of the rulers of al-Andalus, an account of the roads and harbors of al-Andalus, its greatest cities, and the most important features of each region.[90] This work included, or was supplemented by, "a description of Cordoba, its quarters, and the residences of its principal inhabitants, composed in the style of 'Īsā Abī Ṭāhir's history of Baghdad, in which he described the residences of the courtiers of Abū Ja'far al-Manṣūr."[91] This brief report of al-Rāzī's work suggests that descriptions of the city and the peninsula became another display of power in the caliphal period. The representation of the city in terms of its prominent and prestigious residences and public buildings became a testament to the glory of the regime, rivaling that of the Abbasids in their heyday.[92]

Al-Maqqarī's citations of al-Rāzī and Ibn Ḥayyān in the section of his work devoted to the description of Cordoba, while brief, give us a sense of the range of interest and detail of the original works. Again, we see the appropriation pre-Islamic history as a way to enhance the current rule of the Umayyads: "Al-Rāzī says: Cordoba is the mother of cities, the navel of al-Andalus, the heart of the kingdom in ancient times and the present, in the pre-Islamic (*jāhiliyya*) and Islamic eras."[93] Al-Rāzī and Ibn Ḥayyān both say that the city "was built by Octavian, the second caesar of Rome, who ruled most of the world."[94]

Al-Maqqarī's citations of al-Rāzī's description of the natural environment of al-Andalus present a pleasant vision of a land enjoying a moderate climate (with some regional variation) where fruit can be harvested all year long. The historian recorded for his caliphal patron the boundaries of the peninsula, the distances between cities, and the major products or harvests of each province, providing a survey of his dominions.[95] The surviving fragment of his description of Cordoba, however, is quite limited and simply highlights the city's most characteristic features: "the river is the greatest river in al-Andalus, her bridge is one of the wonders of the world in its construction and design, and her mosque is the largest in al-Andalus and the Islamic world."[96]

The interest of the historians of the caliphal period in the details of the city's monuments is suggested by the ensuing description of the bridge. Ibn Ḥayyān reports that the bridge had seventeen arches and was originally constructed some two hundred years before the invasion of the Arabs. When Cordoba was conquered, the bridge had fallen into terrible disrepair but the Muslim governor al-Samḥ ordered the construction of a new bridge on the ancient foundations in 719 or 720.[97]

In their representations of Cordoba, the historical texts devote considerable attention to three important Umayyad constructions: the Great Mosque of Cordoba, the garden-palace of al-Ruṣāfa, and the palace-city of Madīnat al-Zahrā'. Based as much as possible on al-Maqqarī's citations of al-Rāzī and Ibn Ḥayyān and occasionally supplemented by al-Maqqarī's summaries of the information available to him, the analysis suggests that even the descriptions of the monuments of Umayyad rule expressed the dynasty's exceptional power and authority. The historians' contextualization of the constructions, in fact, added dimensions to their significance.

The histories of the Great Mosque of Cordoba and Madīnat al-Zahrā' begin with 'Abd al-Raḥmān I and his construction of the original mosque and first truly Umayyad palace, the palace-estate of al-Ruṣāfa. 'Abd al-Raḥmān I set about defining Cordoba as his capital through the construction of significant original monuments and set a precedent in the representation of authority for his successors. Mosque and palace become insignia of rulership from the beginning of the dynasty's reign: "Some of the historians say that once 'Abd al-Raḥmān al-Dākhil established his rule, he built the palace in Cordoba, built the Great Mosque, on which he spent eighty thousand dinars, and built al-Ruṣāfa [just outside of] Cordoba to resemble the Ruṣāfa of his grandfather, Hishām, in Damascus."[98] The close association between the historiographical representation of the founding amir and that of the first caliph, discussed in chapter 4 is here transcribed into the history of building: the model achievements of 'Abd al-Raḥmān I are repeated and surpassed by 'Abd al-Raḥmān III.

The historical texts treat the Great Mosque of Cordoba as an icon of Umayyad rule. Allegedly built on the site of a Christian church, the new mosque asserted Muslim hegemony.[99] In addition, 'Abd al-Raḥmān I, as the first ruler to construct a congregational mosque in the city, made a statement about his and the Umayyads' responsibility for and leadership of the growing Muslim population. This iconology became meaningful with the passage of decades. Al-Maqqarī reports that the mosque begun by 'Abd al-Raḥmān I was finished by his son Hishām but that the subsequent eight Umayyad rulers of al-Andalus each added to the original structure. He notes that adding to the mosque became expected; it became a customary means of articulating legitimate authority.[100] The building and its representation expressed the continuity of Umayyad rule and its successful guidance and protection of the community.[101]

As we know, the regular expansion and elaboration of the mosque reflected the continuous growth and prosperity of the community and reached a climax in the caliphal period with the additions built under 'Abd al-Raḥmān III and, especially, under al-Ḥakam II and al-Manṣūr. Not surprisingly, al-Maqqarī devotes a great deal of attention to these additions, quoting extensively from Ibn Ḥayyān, Ibn Bashkuwāl, and Ibn Sa'īd.

While the mosque was a monument to the Umayyads' leadership of the Muslims, the palace was the real showcase for power. Nowhere is this more vividly portrayed than in the accounts of Abd al-Raḥmān III's construction of Madīnat al-Zahrā'. Yet the representation of this caliphal monument also begins with 'Abd al-Raḥmān I.

From the inauguration of Umayyad rule, the landscape of Cordoba began to change. After 'Abd al-Raḥmān I secured his rule, he not only ordered construction on the palace of Cordoba and built the Great Mosque and al-Ruṣāfa but also set about the general improvement and enlargement of the city. As al-Maqqarī reports, on the authority of "some historians," 'Abd al-Raḥmān I restored villas and ordered new constructions and surrounded the city with a wall.[102] The Umayyad passion for building became even more manifest in 'Abd al-Raḥmān I's descendants.

The process by which the Umayyads reshaped the landscape of Cordoba and of al-Andalus more generally and made the peninsula their own is symbolically represented in the account of 'Abd al-Raḥmān I's construction of his garden-palace of Ruṣāfa. Al-Maqqarī cites Ibn Sa'īd, who reports on the authority of his father, that one of the first things 'Abd al-Raḥmān ibn Mu'āwiya built in the early days of his reign was the *munya* of al-Ruṣāfa, where he planned to reside most of the time. He built a beautiful palace surrounded by extensive gardens in which he planted exotic seeds and trees imported from all over, some brought back by special emissaries he sent to the east to procure them. Many of these plants flourished in the soil and climate of al-Andalus and soon they were growing throughout the country.[103]

This account asserts the inauguration of a new regime and its historical legitimacy in material terms. 'Abd al-Raḥmān I moved his residence from that of the previous governors into a new palace estate outside Cordoba he had constructed, as Ibn Sa'īd's report expressly mentions, in the image of Hishām's estate outside Damascus.[104] This deliberately described reproduction of the place where 'Abd al-Raḥmān I spent his childhood affirms the special relationship between grandfather (caliph) and grandson (amir) and commemorates the transfer of authority from one to the other, recalling the anecdote in *Akhbār majmū'a* in which 'Abd al-Raḥmān I paid a visit to Hishām's Ruṣāfa and was there recognized to be the salvation of the Umayyad dynasty.[105] Finally, the parallelism between the Ruṣāfa outside Damascus and the Ruṣāfa outside Cordoba suggests that "Ruṣāfa" became a marker for the capital of the Umayyad empire, first in Syria and now in the west.[106]

The account of 'Abd al-Raḥmān I's construction of al-Ruṣāfa, a palace filled with luxuries and a garden replete with exotic fruit and flowers, demonstrates the ruler's ability to command great resources and even recreate what has been lost. The new Ruṣāfa, with its garden of imported vegetation, symbolizes the creation of a new homeland in al-Andalus, reflecting the image of the old. In fact, the text also describes the Umayyad amir's active sponsorship of the transformation of the Andalusi ecology. The seeds and plants he purportedly brought from "Syria and other countries" were cultivated in the royal gardens and then disseminated throughout the land.[107]

The textual representation of al-Ruṣāfa associates the transplanting of the Umayyad dynasty from Syria to al-Andalus with literal transplantation. This is expressly articulated in four verses, cited from Ibn Ḥayyān, that 'Abd al-Raḥmān I reportedly declaimed at the sight of a lone palm tree in the middle of his garden:

> A single palm tree spreads before us in the middle of al-Ruṣāfa, far removed from the east and the land of palm trees;
>
> I remarked that it resembled me in having emigrated a great distance westward and in my melancholy at being far from my small son and my people:
>
> You grow in a land to which you are a stranger, we are alike in our great distance [from home];
>
> May the rainclouds water you and nourish you in your exile.[108]

In this identification between dynasty and garden, the cyclical renewal of the land may be seen as a metaphor for the experience of the dynasty: the death of each ruler was followed by the emergence, glory, and decline of the next. Finally, over time, the seedlings imported from abroad and carefully nurtured in the garden became naturalized and came to define the environment.

The creative power of the Umayyads represented in 'Abd al-Raḥmān I's construction of al-Ruṣāfa is glorified in 'Abd al-Raḥmān III's construction of Madīnat al-Zahrā'. The apocryphal story of his decision to build describes the satisfaction of a whim: 'Abd al-Raḥmān III originally founded the palace at the behest of his beloved concubine, al-Zahra, who asked him to build her a city that would take her name. When al-Zahra sat in the great hall of the palace for the first time, she expressed dismay at the contrast between the beautiful white city and the black mountain it nestled in. 'Abd al-Raḥmān III ordered the removal of the mountain but was then persuaded by one of his counselors that the task was impossible. Instead, he ordered that all the trees on the mountain be cut down and replaced with fig and almond trees. The narrator reports: there was no more beautiful sight, nor better fragrance, than that of the trees in blossom.[109]

The story represents the decision to build a caliphal palace complex as a casual undertaking. The implication, of course, is that the caliph's resources were unlimited. In fact, the story explains that the funds for the palace came from the estate of another one of 'Abd al-Raḥmān III's concubines, who had bequeathed her great wealth to the redemption of captives. As there were no Muslim captives anywhere in the land of the Franks, the money could be used at the caliph's discretion.[110] We are given to understand that money was so abundant that even a concubine had the wherewithal to fund or command the building of a vast palace; the kingdom was so secure that not a single Muslim captive needed to be redeemed.

The caliph's power seemed to be limited only by the bounds of human capability; his desire simply to remove the offending mountain was checked by his counselor's reminder that only its Creator could destroy the mountain. The story of his transformation (rather than destruction) of the mountain still provides a startling demonstration of power that echoes the images of the razing of Bobastro and the accounts of 'Abd al-Raḥmān I's recultivation of the land.

The message of power conveyed in the anecdote is given weight and substance by subsequent accounts of the specific resources expended in the construction of Madīnat al-Zahrā'. Ibn Ḥayyān's account is full of minute detail, a way of conveying the vastness of the enterprise. He draws on the writings of the *faqīh*, Ibn Dahhūn, who cited Maslama ibn 'Abd Allāh, the architect (*al-'arīf al-muhandis*). By this account, during every day of construction, six thousand blocks of stone were used, exclusive of the stone used for paving, which were brought in by at least fourteen hundred pack animals, including four hundred belonging to al-Nāṣir li-Dīn Allāh, and one thousand mules hired at the rate of three *mithqals* a month each. Eleven hundred loads of lime and gypsum were carried out every third day; the site had two baths, one for the palace and one for the rest of the populace.[111]

Ibn Ḥayyān also recounts that the buildings of Madīnat al-Zahrā' employed four thousand columns of all sizes; some were brought from Rome (Madīnat Rūma), some were a gift from the ruler of Constantinople. The buildings had over fifteen thousand doors, each covered with iron and brass.[112] Marble was brought from Carthage, Ifriqiyya, and Tunis.[113]

Ibn Ḥayyān reports, on the authority of some of the people employed in al-Zahrā', that 'Abd al-Raḥmān III spent three hundred thousand dinars a year on the city's construction for twenty-five years—that is, until he died.[114] In his estimation, Madīnat al-Zahrā' was one of the most awesome constructions ever built by man, great in both substance and conception.[115]

This description has its counterparts in the accounts of the enlargement of the Great Mosque, with Ibn Ḥayyān as the authority on total expenditures. The historians of the period and those that followed were concerned to capture the scale and dimensions of these monuments. In this way the reader is made to appreciate how far the caliph's influence was felt—materials were brought from all over—and how strong and prosperous the community was, most of the funds coming from the spoils of war against the infidel. Al-Maqqarī includes many (later) accounts of the marvels of the palace, some perhaps embellished or apocryphal, and verses extolling its wonders.

The texts represent al-Zahra' as unique on the peninsula, outclassing the monuments of previous dynasties and kingdoms there, as well as in the Muslim world. As al-Maqqarī's text recounts, when al-Nāṣir built the palace of al-Zahra', all the people agreed that absolutely nothing like it had been built anywhere in Islam. Every visiting king, ambassadorial delegation, or intelligent merchant—people who were astute and worldly—swore that they had never seen or even heard of anything like it, nor could they even imagine its existence.[116] The implication is that the Andalusi Umayyad caliph's palace-city surpassed the palaces of his Abbasid and Fatimid rivals.

If 'Abd al-Raḥmān I planted a garden that came to represent the land of al-Andalus, 'Abd al-Raḥmān III built a city that represented the civilization of the peninsula. The caliph built his own world, from the ground up. We have seen 'Abd al-Raḥmān III's power to create and destroy before, but the descriptions of Madinat al-Zahra' reflect the achievements and ambitions of the dynasty beyond the battlefield and assert a strength and authority that came from stability.

The landscape of 'Īsā ibn Aḥmad al-Rāzī's tenth-century history of the reign of al-Ḥakam II, as recorded in Ibn Ḥayyān's *Muqtabis,* reflects the same confidence in Andalusi Umayyad rule. That text locates the caliphal reception hall and palace and the twinned cities of Madīnat al-Zahrā' and Cordoba at the center of a world extending beyond the formal boundaries of Umayyad al-Andalus. Far from a forbidding place of danger, the scale of the peninsula seems reduced by the accounts of al-Ḥakam II's exercise of authority. Descriptions of the caliph's military escorts, for example, render al-Andalus the threshold of the caliph's residence, while reports of the departure of armies portray it as the platform of his ambitions.

In this chapter, I have tried to suggest how the representation of the peninsula in historical texts reflected the tenor of their narratives and, after the period of *fitna* that preceded 'Abd al-Raḥmān III's reign, expressed an appreciation of al-Andalus as a land conquered, transformed, and glorified by the Umayyad dynasty. The Umayyads introduced and cultivated Islam in this alien region and brought it into the heart of the Islamic cultural world.

We can conclude by considering a final interesting expression of the impact the Umayyads had on al-Andalus. The texts under discussion sometimes represent the transformation of the peninsula as a "Syrianization" or "orientalization."[117] In some instances, historians record real phenomena suggestive of a broader transformation, as in the example of 'Abd al-Raḥmān I's construction of a new Ruṣāfa and promotion of botanical culture, transplanting date and pomegranate trees, among other eastern plants. Another example is how, early in its history, al-Andalus acquired a nomenclature that specifically associated some of its regions with those of the Levant. The Syrian divisions that arrived to help subdue the Berber revolts during the caliphate of Hishām were subsequently settled in various Andalusi provinces. These divisions bore the names of their geographic origins, and the places they settled in al-Andalus soon acquired these as secondary names or designations: the Damascus jund or division located in Elvira or Granada, that of Jordan in Rayya, Palestine in Sidonia, Emessa in Seville, Qinnasrīn in Jaen, and Egypt in Beja and Tudmir.[118] Centuries later, al-Shaqundī could still refer to Granada as "the Damascus of al-Andalus."[119]

In other instances, the historical texts cultivate an association between al-Andalus and the Umayyad east, as in their identification of various popular legends about King Solomon with al-Andalus. Ibn Ḥabīb's reports include Mūsā's discovery of devils Solomon had sealed up in jars. Accounts of Ṭāriq's discovery of a marvelous jeweled table belonging to Solomon can be found in texts ranging from the earliest histories of the conquest of al-Andalus, such as Ibn Ḥabīb's, to the latest.[120] Al-Maqqarī and Ibn 'Idhārī relate a story that explains how the table from Jerusalem happened to be found in al-Andalus: Ishbān ibn Ṭīṭūs, the Roman conqueror of al-Andalus, brought the table back from his sack of Jerusalem, along with other treasures.[121] These stories bridged the Levant (Jerusalem) with the west and gave al-Andalus a past and a status comparable to that of Syria- Palestine.

We have seen how the Great Mosque of Cordoba recalled important Umayyad monuments in Damascus, Jerusalem, and Medina, representing visually the historical and dynastic links between Umayyad al-Andalus and the domains of the first Umayyad caliphate. Stories about the foundation of the mosque articulate and reinforce the connection between the two seats of Umayyad rule. Al-Maqqarī cites al-Rāzī's report that the conquerors of al-Andalus wanted to follow the caliph 'Umar's opinion concerning the treatment of churches in territories that capitulated to the Muslims by treaty and mentions, in particular, the case of the church of Damascus. In consequence, according to al-Rāzī, the Muslims and Christians of Cordoba divided the great church of Saint Vincent between them; the Muslims used their half to create a congregational mosque, while the Christians used theirs as a church. This situation continued, with the mosque growing ever more crowded, until 'Abd al-Raḥmān I bought the rest of the structure and built a new mosque.[122] The parallel this tenth-century account invokes between the foundation of the Great Mosque of Cordoba and that of Damascus links the two cities together, suggesting that Damascus was a model for Cordoba.

Another legend about Solomon confers prestige on the mosque, while similarly defining the experience of al-Andalus in terms of the historical traditions of the east. In this case, the story of the mosque's foundation associates it with the Temple Mount in Jerusalem. Al-Maqqarī cites Ibn Bashkuwāl's report that the site of the Great Mosque of Cordoba was a large hole where the inhabitants of the city used to throw their garbage. When Solomon, son of David, came to Cordoba, he told the jinn to fill the hole and clear the area, for it would be the location for a temple for the worship of God. Later the Great Mosque was indeed constructed on this ground.[123] Ibn Bashkuwāl's account is reminiscent of accounts of both the foundation of the temple of Jerusalem and of the Dome of the Rock. Again, a story expresses and complements the mosque of Cordoba's architectural and decorative references.[124]

The Andalusi historical texts record the transformation of the Iberian peninsula under Umayyad rule in physical, political, economic, social, and cultural terms. Looking at the "landscape" of the accounts of the caliphal age (and later) reminds us that their interpretation of the past was profoundly shaped by the Umayyads' self-representations and claims, and hopes and ambitions. Thus Cordoba is explicitly upheld as the rival of Baghdad, and al-Andalus may resemble Syria. These texts do not simply describe the Umayyads' influence on the peninsula; they render the landscape Umayyad.

· CONCLUSION ·

The Andalusi Umayyad Caliphate in Retrospect

In life they graced the earth; in death they grace the books and the histories
—al-Shaqundī.[1]

Although the reign of the Umayyads ended ignobly, the legitimacy and prestige of their rule became a legacy to be claimed and fought over, and the caliphs and their courts a model for emulation. Andalusi and North African histories written after the demise of Umayyad rule immortalized the power and grandeur of their caliphate and expressed a certain nostalgia for a golden age passed that increased over time.

Descriptions of the great achievements of the Umayyad rulers, their patronage of learning and culture, their palaces and gardens, their generosity and justice, presented in the later historiography, derived from contemporary sources but also reflected a pride of place characteristic of the *ṭā'ifa* (petty kingdom) and later periods in the history of al-Andalus. The expansion of the arts and sciences promoted by the caliphate increased in the eleventh century under the patronage of the *ṭā'ifa* rulers. With this developed a certain defensive pride in the status and progress of knowledge and culture in al-Andalus. One manifestation of this pride was the production of anthologies devoted exclusively to the work of Andalusi prose and poetry, such as Ibn Bassām's *al-Dhakhīra* (c. 1106–1109) and Ibn Khāqān's (d. 1137) *Qālā'id*. Ibn Ḥazm (d. 1064) reportedly composed a treatise in response to a Berber remark that al-Andalus did not seem to have many notable men, or if it did, their achievements were not recorded.[2] In his treatise he describes the virtues of al-Andalus and the talents of its inhabitants and lists the most prominent works and authors in all the major disciplines, pointing out how they rivaled well-known examples in the east. This form of praise for Andalusi achievements became fairly standard, taken up by later writers who sought to commemorate an al-Andalus now perceived to be in decline—for example, al-Shaqundī (d. 1231) and Ibn Sa'īd (d. 1287).[3] Al-Maqqarī's seventeenth-century *Nafḥ al-ṭīb* may be seen as the beneficiary, as well as culmination, of this development; al-Maqqarī presents extensive extracts of the work of all three of these apologists and draws on other *faḍā'il* (virtues) literature, poetry, and historical, biographical, and geographical sources to present a compendium of the history of al-Andalus and all its virtues.[4]

A survey of al-Maqqarī's *Nafḥ al-ṭīb* suggests that historians looking back on the caliphate from a later vantage point were struck by, and emphasized, the strength and prestige of the Umayyad regime and the harmony and prosperity of the Andalusis in this period. Al-Maqqarī's text describes the tremendous wealth of the Andalusi caliphate: such was the success of 'Abd al-Raḥmān III's reign that state revenues from direct and indirect taxation were estimated at 6,245,000 dinars, while the treasury's share of the booty from his campaigns against the infidels was deemed inestimable. 'Abd al-Raḥmān III used one-third of his revenues to pay his troops, one-third for his own expenses, and one-third on building. It is said that when he died, he left a surplus of five million dinars in the treasury.[5]

The historian provides reports of the military campaigns of the caliphal period as well as descriptions of court life and caliphal patronage of the arts and sciences, particularly during the reign of al-Ḥakam II, and detailed accounts of caliphal expenditures. According to Ibn Khaldūn, the gifts and monuments of a dynasty are proportionate to its importance and power.[6] Al-Maqqarī's text is replete with elaborate descriptions of both. As one example demonstrates, a particular gift given to or by the caliphs might include gold, perfumes, clothing and cloth, carpets and cushions, weapons and horses, slaves, or villas.[7] He also devotes an entire volume of *Nafḥ al-ṭīb* to reports on Cordoba, Madīnat al-Zahrā', and Madīnat al-Zāhira and descriptions of their marvels, including a hall in the *qaṣr* of Madīnat al-Zahrā' that housed the unique pearl sent by the Byzantine emperor. The hall boasted eight ornately decorated arched entrances supported by colored marble columns, a ceiling tiled with silver and gold, and a pool of mercury in the center.

Histories of al-Andalus written from the eleventh century onward associate the Andalusi Umayyad caliphate with the glory of Cordoba. As Ibn Sa'īd relates, Cordoba grew and flourished from its conquest by the Muslims until the year 400 A.H. (1009–1010 C.E.), when it was ravaged by *fitna;* it was conquered by the Christians in 633 A.H. (1236 C.E.). In his view, Cordoba's unsurpassed greatness was due to and depended on the dynastic reign of the Umayyads.[8] Again and again, sources cited by al-Maqqarī describe the city as the seat of the Umayyads, the center of the kingdom, the dome of Islam, the gathering place of poets and scholars.[9] All the verses and descriptions dedicated to the city and its buildings, palaces, gardens, and recreational estates (*munyas*) are thus celebrations of Umayyad rule.

With the passage of time, the decline of the caliphate, of Cordoba, and of Muslim rule in al-Andalus, the Umayyads joined the legendary ranks of the pre-Islamic dynasties that once ruled the peninsula. The ruins of their rule remained for the contemplation of future generations, inspiring nostalgia as well as respect for God's decree, while their histories perhaps provided comfort or a touchstone for generations of displaced Andalusis who could recall that Muslims once dominated the peninsula and Christian kings were supplicants before the caliphs and that the caliphate of the west once rivaled that of the east.[10]

A THIRTEENTH-CENTURY ASSESSMENT

The man with discernment mourns the consequences of matters that make fools laugh[11]

—*Ibn Sa'īd.*

The thirteenth-century historian Ibn Sa'īd developed a theory of rulership based on the Umayyad example in an extract from his *al-Mughrib* preserved in al-Maqqarī's *Nafḥ al-ṭīb.*[12] In this text, Ibn Sa'īd idealizes Umayyad rule and recognizes the importance of their dynastic legitimacy and their ability to command the respect and trust of their subjects.

Ibn Sa'īd's identification of the Umayyads as a model for good government emerged from his analysis of why the Muslims had lost so much of the peninsula to the Christians at the time of his writing. He attributes this to a lack of unity—or worse, a rivalry among the Muslims—that rendered them incapable of defending their fortresses and ultimately, their cities.[13] Surveying the history of the peninsula, he observes that only under the Umayyads was al-Andalus secure, its population united under one ruler. He endeavors to explain why this was so and why it ceased to be so.

Ibn Sa'īd's interpretation of Andalusi history ignores the difficulties the Umayyads had in maintaining control of the peninsula; for him they represent the only stability al-Andalus has ever known. The following is a summary of Ibn Sa'īd's more discursive account of the history of al-Andalus. Al-Andalus was conquered in the year 92 of the Hijra and administered as a province of the Syrian caliphate by governors who were either dismissed shortly on being named or deposed by rebels. In this confusion, Muslim power could not be consolidated. Only when 'Abd al-Raḥmān I conquered the peninsula and established an independent kingdom for his dynasty was Islam set on a solid foundation. Under Umayyad rule, al-Andalus reached the height of strength and prosperity. Then civil war broke out among the

Muslims and they became prey to the Christians, until the latter came to control most of the peninsula.[14]

Ibn Sa'īd suggests that dynastic continuity was one of the most important features of Umayyad rule, contributing to the individual ruler's ability to command authority. After 'Abd al-Raḥmān I, each ruler inherited his reign. Considering the political fragmentation of his own times, Ibn Sa'īd remarks that now, in the west, changes in dynastic rule occur frequently, while in the east people are more concerned to protect a system of orderly succession and preserve the authority of the ruling dynasty, fearing the threat of discord and its tendency to undermine the foundations of the state and introduce corruption into the community.[15]

In addition, the Umayyads were able to gain confidence of their subjects by protecting their rule with rigor, governing wisely, pursuing impartial justice, ensuring respect for the law, and seeking and heeding the counsel of the learned. In addition, they commanded awe (*hayba*) in the ways they displayed their authority in the magnificence of their persons and courts and later in the adoption of the caliphal titles.

We can discern from the construction of his discussion that Ibn Sa'īd approved of the Umayyad rulers' self-conscious display of power because it was supported by their ability to govern. In this context, the trappings of rule enhanced their prestige because it reflected their successes.[16] In contrast, he shows contempt for the petty rulers who subsequently adopted the trappings but were unable to exercise true leadership.[17]

Describing circumstances corresponding to the late 'Amirid period, Ibn Sa'īd ascribes the demise of the Umayyads to their inability to maintain order, the corruption of their justice, and the loss of their subjects' awe and affection. In the circumstances of their ineffective rule, he observes that the magnificence of their courts and the pomp of their appearances no longer inspired respect and love but disdain.[18] In his view, the competition among those of lowly status and minimal talents for the office of the caliphate was both a symptom and a consequence of this change of attitude. Meanwhile, as he relates, the governors of the provinces seized independent control of their districts, pronouncing the names of the Umayyad caliphs who no longer ruled in the *khuṭba* or else acknowledging the nominal authority of the Abbasid caliph in a similar manner. In the confusion and disorder of the period, these petty rulers themselves began to assume the titles and honorifics of former caliphs, imitating them in everything.[19]

Ibn Sa'īd's analysis of Andalusi history and the model of Umayyad rule underscores the importance of dynastic legitimacy wedded to the effective exercise of power. We can appreciate the conclusion he draws from the example of the Andalusi Umayyads in their heyday: the key to successful rule is military strength joined with dynastic authority, diligent administration, and the cultivation of awe and affection.

A MODERN ASSESSMENT

The descendants of Marwan reclaimed their dynastic right to the leadership of the Muslims in the tenth century, with Cordoba serving as the seat of the restored Umayyad caliphate. They assumed the symbolic prerogatives and insignia of the caliphate: the title of Commander of the Faithful and the right to have their names and title pronounced in the *khuṭba* and inscribed on the coins minted in the realm. They proclaimed, demonstrated, and elaborated their authority and legitimacy to multiple audiences, both within and beyond the boundaries of al-Andalus. As they did so, the Andalusi Umayyad caliphs referred to the past: to the inheritance of their Umayyad ancestors, to the legacy of the *rashīdūn* caliphs, and to the model of the Prophet. They also addressed the present—the circumstances of their rule in al-Andalus and their rivalry with the Abbasid and Fatimid claimants to the command of the faithful—and invoked the future and the promise of a final Umayyad redemption and vindication. Whether they expressed their legitimacy in words, in construction, or in ceremony, they did so with this multivalent appeal.

The study of how the Andalusi Umayyads staked their claims to the caliphate underscores the importance of historical dynastic claims to the leadership of the Muslims as a way to establish universal authority. The Abbasids and Fatimids based their legitimacy on the lineage of the Prophet, yet each of these dynasties also elaborated its own complex history of designations to establish a continuous transmission of authority and overcome the gap of centuries between the origins of Islam and their rise to power. The Andalusi Umayyads, as contenders in this context, could identify themselves as *ahl al-bayt* and assert a familial association with the Prophet but more easily asserted the historical continuity of their authority through the person of ʿAbd al-Raḥmān I, whose story bridged al-Andalus and Syria and whose lineage linked them back to Ḥishām, the caliphs before him, and ultimately ʿUthmān, the third of the *rashīdūn* caliphs. The real challenge for the Umayyads was to overcome the fact of the Abbasid revolution and its implications for the legitimacy of the dynasty.

The Andalusi Umayyads' argument for their right to lead the Muslims depended on the evidence of their rule. They demonstrated their commitment to the defense of the unity of the community and the integrity of the faith, defining their mandate in terms of holy war against deviants at home and abroad and against polytheists who failed to acknowledge their sovereignty and in terms of the promotion of the true path defined by the Qur'an and the early community, identified with the Maliki *madhhab*.

In their emphasis on holy war, the Andalusi Umayyads could develop an identification with their Syrian ancestors. The original Umayyad *dawla* has been characterized as an expansionary state inspired by *jihād* ideology, and the same could be said for the Andalusi Umayyad caliphate.[20] When not expanding or defending the frontiers of the first Islamic empire against external enemies, the Syrian caliphs defended their rule against internal enemies in campaigns also described in terms of holy war. They represented the rebels to their rule as dangers to both the community and the faith and referred to them as deviants and evildoers, sowers of discord, and proponents of innovation, while they presented themselves as defenders of the security, prosperity, piety, and unity of the community and as guarantors of the mission of the Prophet.[21] Court poets in Syria in the eighth century celebrated the caliph as God's rope, or sword, or refuge, as the tent peg of the religion and a guide, or light, to salvation, and as a *mahdī* or rightly guided imam.[22] It is easy to see striking similarities between the way the Andalusi Umayyads defined and promoted their caliphal authority and the way their ancestors did. Both Andalusis and Syrians affirmed that the Umayyad caliphs were God's agents on earth, chosen to champion the true religion and guide the believers to salvation.[23] We have seen how the Andalusi Umayyads visibly invoked this association by applying mosaic decoration to the Great Mosque of Cordoba, recalling 'Abd al-Malik's Dome of the Rock and al-Walīd's congregational mosques.

At the same time, the Andalusi Umayyads' commitment to their righteous cause directly addressed the Fatimids' expansionary ambitions. Their rivalry with the Fatimids fueled their self-promotion as defenders of the faith and guardians of the community as they sent magnificent armies southward and then received repentant rebels in their capital. The Fatimid threat galvanized the Andalusi Umayyads and mediated the way they defined their commitment to the purity of the faith. In opposition to the Fatimids, they denounced esoteric interpretations of the Qur'an and dedicated themselves to uphold the sunna of the Prophet and the legal precedents of the *rashīdūn*. In symbolic terms, they strived to secure all the minbars of North Africa and reinstitute the proper call to prayer.

In their promotion of the Maliki *madhhab* the Andalusi Umayyads distinguished themselves from all other caliphal dynasties. In their commitment to one particular rite of Islam, they opposed the unity of Fatimid rule and Isma'ili doctrine with a clear alternative. They developed a community of rule with the Maliki *'ulamā* of al-Andalus not characteristic of the government of their ancestors in Syria and, more significantly, established an authority over religion and judicial practice that their Abbasid rivals had failed to achieve. The efforts of the Abbasid caliph al-Ma'mūn to impose uniformity of belief and practice in the early ninth century had only contributed to the intensification of disunity in the east. In contrast, because the Maliki *madhhab* predominated in al-Andalus and North Africa, the Andalusi Umayyads could claim a unity of faith in their realm.[24]

The Andalusi Umayyads represented their campaigns and policies as evidence of their fulfillment of the mandate of the caliphate and their achievements as signs of their divine favor. The conjunction of 'Abd al-Raḥmān III's successes with the apparent weakness of the Abbasid caliphs of the same period provided the basis for the revival of the Umayyad caliphate and the denial of the significance of the Abbasid revolution. 'Abd al-Raḥmān III suppressed rebellion, restored the community, and proved victorious in holy war. In contrast, the Abbasid caliph was powerless in Baghdad as the lands in the east were rent by factionalism and overrun by infidels. Who was the true Commander of the Faithful and Champion of the Religion of God?

While in the middle of the eighth century the overthrow of Umayyad rule in Syria may have looked like divine judgment and the close of an era, as the Abbasids proclaimed, by the tenth century the Andalusi Umayyads could declare the vindication of their right to rule and promote a cyclical view of the past that brought them back into a position to assert their authority and suppress the latest *fitna* to tear the community apart.

The Andalusi Umayyads upheld the "traditions of their ancestors" in a changed world, redefining those traditions in the process, according to the political culture of their era and the immediate circumstances of their rule. All historical claimants to the authority of the caliphate, particularly when concerned to assert their legitimacy, invoked an idealized model of the past and employed a common stock of metaphors, adapted to their own interests.[25] The Andalusi Umayyads defined themselves in opposition to the Fatimids and the Abbasids in terms, and through means, they all shared, but signified and nuanced differently. So even as 'Abd al-Raḥmān III directed his armies against the Fatimids and their promulgation of new and disturbing ideas about the attributes of the true imam and the definition of the faith, he appropriated the idea of the *mahdī* as a metaphor for his own rule. Furthermore, we have seen that the construction of a new capital city had become a sign of independent authority and a necessary symbol for a new caliphate and how Madīnat al-Zahrā' visibly expressed the Andalusi Umayyad caliphal claim and challenge in pan-Islamic terms, at the same time that it spoke to the local context.

In articulating the legitimacy of the newly proclaimed caliphate, 'Abd al-Raḥmān III echoed and appropriated the revolutionary language used by both the Abbasids and the Fatimids when they justified their assaults against established authority in the name of a return to the original principles of the faith and the golden age of the Prophet. He claimed to have renewed the faith in al-Andalus with his triumph over *fitna* and in North Africa with the eradication of Isma'ili influences. In his support for the Maliki *madhhab,* in particular, he expressly associated the revival of the Umayyad caliphate with the return to the true faith, as exemplified by the Prophet and the early community. 'Abd al-Raḥmān III, however, did not direct himself to the overthrow of the established order in the manner of his rivals. He did not propose radical political, social, or religious changes to support his cause, in contrast to the Fatimids, who elaborated a distinct cosmology, theology, and system of law and set out to conquer the Islamic world. With the ideology of his caliphate, 'Abd al-Raḥmān III instead secured his dynasty's continued rule of al-Andalus and fostered its interests abroad. As we have seen, he articulated his legitimacy and promoted his authority in terms, symbols, monuments, ceremonies, and actions that helped bind political relationships and impressed a wide constituency. In so doing, he restored a family honor that had been lost, most recently in the decades of anarchy on the Iberian peninsula and historically as a consequence of the Abbasid revolution.

In both the exercise of his power and the elaboration of his legitimacy, 'Abd al-Raḥmān III provided a model for his successors. Al-Ḥakam II benefitted from the experience of his father's reign and followed his precedent, but his heir came to power at a vulnerable age, and the caliphate became subject to the manipulation of the politically savvy chamberlain, al-Manṣūr, who demonstrated his own appreciation for the model of the Andalusi Umayyad caliphs in the definition of his rule. The history of the Andalusi Umayyad caliphate in effect turned out to be a history of three generations, and yet the span of years between 'Abd al-Raḥmān III's ascendance and Ḥishām II's disappearance (912–1013) comprised a full century and actually exceeded the length of the first Umayyad caliphate (661–750).

Endnotes

NOTES TO INTRODUCTION

1. Cited in Ibn Ḥayyān, *al-Muqtabis fi akhbār balad al-Andalus,* ed. A. A. Hajji (Beirut, 1965), 163–164, Spanish translation *Anales palatinos del califa de Córdoba al-Ḥakam II por 'Īsā Ibn Aḥmad al-Rāzī,* trans. Emilio García Gómez (Madrid, 1967), 203. Citations that follow refer to the Arabic edition as *Muqtabis VII* and include corresponding pages in the Spanish edition.
2. Sunni theories of the caliphate were elaborated much later. The most famous formulations by al-Māwardī and al-Ghazālī date to the eleventh century. See A.K.S. Lambton, *State and Government in Medieval Islam* (London, 1981), for a survey of political thought expounded by Sunni jurists.
3. Moshe Sharon, *Black Banners from the East: The Establishment of the 'Abbasid State—Incubation of a Revolt* (Jerusalem and Leiden, 1983); Jacob Lassner, *The Shaping of Abbasid Rule* (Princeton, 1980); *Lassner, Islamic Revolution and Historical Memory: Abbasid Apologetics and the Art of Historical Writing* (New Haven, 1986); Lassner, "The Abbasid *Dawla*: An Essay on the Concept of Revolution in Early Islam," in F. M. Clover and R. S. Humphreys, eds., *Tradition and Innovation* (Madison, 1989); Elton Daniel, "The Anonymous History of the Abbasid Family and Its Place in Islamic Historiography," *International Journal of Middle Eastern Studies* 14 (1982), 419–434.

4. See Farhad Daftary, *The Isma'ilis: Their History and Doctrines* (Cambridge, 1990), and Heinz Halm, *The Empire of the Mahdi: The Rise of the Fatimids,* trans. Michael Bonner (Leiden, 1996).
5. Patricia Crone and Martin Hinds, *God's Caliph: Religious Authority in the First Centuries of Islam* (Cambridge, 1986); Wadad al-Qadi, "The Religious Foundation of Late Umayyad Ideology and Practice," in *Saber religioso y poder politico en el Islam. Actas de simposio internacional (Granada, 15–18 Octubre, 1991)* (Madrid, 1994), 231–273; Khalid Yahya Blankinship, *The End of the Jihād State: The Reign of Hishām Ibn 'Abd al-Malik and the Collapse of the Umayyads* (Albany, 1994).
6. For discussion of the lack of interest of the eastern writers, see Charles Pellat, "La España musulmana en las obras de al-Mas'ūdī," *Actas del primer congreso de estudios árabes e islámicos* (Madrid, 1964), 257–264, in Charles Pellat, ed., *Études sur l'histoire socio-culturelle de l'Islam (VIIe–XVes)* (London, 1976). Writers in the Abbasid domains were more concerned with the Fatimids than with the Andalusi Umayyads, who were at a geographical remove. In contrast, Fatimid partisans did treat the Andalusi Umayyads as ideological rivals. For example, they lambasted the Umayyads for their role in the martyrdom of Ḥusayn, the second imam, in the seventh century. See Marius Canard, "L'imperialisme des Fatimides et leur propagande," *Annales de l'Institut d'Études Orientales de la Faculté des Lettres d'Alger* 6 (1942–1947): 162–169, in Marius Canard, ed., *Miscellanea orientalia* (London, 1973); M. Yalaoui, "Controverse entre le fatimide al-Mu'izz et l'omeyyade al-Nāṣir, d'après le 'Kitāb al-majālis w-al-musāyarāt' du cadi Nu'mān," *Cahiers de Tunisie* 26 (1978): 7–33; Heinz Halm, "La réfutation d'une note diplomatique du calife 'Abdarraḥmān III par la cour du calife fatimide al-Mu'izz," *Saber religioso y poder politico en el Islam* (Madrid, 1994), 117–125; David Wasserstein, *The Caliphate in the West* (Oxford, 1993), 13–15.
7. Francesco Gabrieli cites al-Mas'ūdī (d. 956) to suggest that the Andalusis themselves could not have considered the Andalusi Umayyads true caliphs because they did not rule over the holy sites. Francesco Gabrieli, "Omayyades d'Espagne et Abbasides," *Studia Islamica* 31 (1970), 98. David Wasserstein argues in his book *The Rise and Fall of the Party Kings* (Princeton, 1986), 27–37, that 'Abd al-Raḥmān III's adoption of caliphal titles and prerogatives may

have been supported by "an ideological substructure" but that this was fundamentally undermined by the contradiction between the universal claims of the caliphate and the limited geographical extent of Andalusi Umayyad domains. In the first chapter of *Caliphate in the West* Wasserstein reiterates this view: "Under 'Abd al-Raḥmān III and al-Ḥakam II, the caliphal title seems to have been simply one means by which these rulers sought to increase their own magnificence; void of any but the most normative of religious content, and lacking any of the attributes usually associated with the command of the faithful, the Umayyad caliphal title came under these two rulers to be little more than a local Iberian variant of the title *amir*" (17). His analysis of numismatic evidence, however, demonstrates the enduring significance of Umayyad dynastic legitimacy in al-Andalus in the period of the Party Kings.

8. Miguel Asín Palacios, *Abenḥazam de Córdoba y su historia crítica de las ideas religiosas* (Madrid, 1932), 5:12; see A. Turki, "L'engagement politique et la théorie du califat d'Ibn Ḥazm," *Bulletin d'Études Orientales* 30 (1978), 221–251.
9. Hugh Kennedy, *Muslim Spain and Portugal: A Political History of al-Andalus* (London, 1996).
10. Pierre Guichard, *Structures sociales "orientales" et "occidentales" dans l'Espagne musulmane* (Paris, 1977), and *La España musulmana. Al-Andalus omeya (s. VIII-XI)*, vol. 7 of Historia 16 (Madrid, 1995); Manuel Acién Almansa, *Entre el feudalismo y el Islam: 'Umar ibn Ḥafṣūn en los historiadores, en las fuentes y en la historia* (Jaen, 1994); Eduardo Manzano Moreno, *La frontera de al-Andalus en época de los omeyas* (Madrid, 1991), Manzano Moreno, "The Creation of a Medieval Frontier: Islam and Christianity in the Iberian Peninsula, Eighth to Eleventh Centuries," in Daniel Power and Naomi Standen, eds., *Frontiers in Question: Eurasian Borderlands 700–1700* (New York, 1999), 32–54; Mohamad Meouak, *Pouvoir souverain, administration centrale et élites politiques dans l'Espagne umayyade (II–IVe/VIIIe–Xe siécles)* (Helsinki, 1999).
11. Wasserstein, *Caliphate in the West;* François Clément, *Pouvoir et légitimité en Espagne musulman à l'époque des taifas (Ve–XIe siècle): Imām fictif* (Paris, 1997).
12. Evariste Lévi-Provençal, *Histoire de l'Espagne musulmane,* 3 vols. (Paris, 1950–1953).

13. M. Isabel Fierro, "Sobre la adopción del título califal por 'Abd al-Raḥmān III al-Nāṣir," *Sharq al-Andalus* 6 (1989), 33-42; Miquel Barceló, "El califa patente: el ceremonial omeya de Córdoba o la enscenificación del poder," in Reyna Pastor, Ian Kieniewica, Eduardo García de Enterría, et al., eds., *Estructuras y formas del poder en la historia* (Salamanca, 1991), 51–71; Antonio Vallejo Triano, "Madīnat al-Zahrā': The Triumph of the Islamic State," in Jerrilynn D. Dodds, ed., *Al-Andalus: The Art of Islamic Spain* (New York, 1992), 27–39; Manuel Acién Almansa, "Madīnat al-Zahrā' en el urbanismo musulmán," *Cuadernos de Madīnat al-Zahrā'* 1 (1978), 11–26; Christine Mazzoli-Guintard, "Remarques sur le fonctionnement d'une capitale a double polarité: Madīnat al-Zahrā'-Cordoue," *Al-Qantara* 18 (1997), 43–64; Jerrilynn D. Dodds, "The Great Mosque of Córdoba," in Dodds, ed., *Al-Andalus: The Art of Islamic Spain* (New York, 1992), 11–25; D. Fairchild Ruggles, "Madīnat al-Zahrā's Constructed Landscape: A Case Study in Islamic Garden and Architectural History," Ph.D. diss., University of Pennsylvania, 1991; Nuha Khoury, "The Great Mosque of Córdoba in the Tenth Century," *Muqarnas* 13 (1996), 80–98.
14. Gabriel Martínez-Gros, *L'idéologie omeyyade: la construction de la legitimité du califat du Cordoue (X–XI siècles)* (Madrid, 1992).
15. Clifford Geertz, "Ideology as a Cultural System," in *The Interpretation of Cultures* (New York, 1973), 207. Geertz's definition of ideology as a cultural system—a system of ideas and symbols—explains how people communicate, cooperate, and clash within the framework of a common understanding of politics.
16. Ibn Ḥafṣūn's rebellion has been a subject of interest for generations of historians, as Manuel Acién Almansa describes and analyzes in his *Entre el feudalismo y el Islam,* 13–51. Sources describe Ibn Ḥafṣūn's rebellion as a movement of *muwalladūn*—that is, local converts to Islam and their progeny—which suggests that the *muwalladūn* had recognizable grievances. Thomas F. Glick, *Islamic and Christian Spain in the Early Middle Ages* (Princeton, 1979), 40, 188–189, proposes that the rebellion, occurring at the height of the conversion curve, was directed against the privileged status of the Muslims of preconquest lineage and expressed the *muwalladūn*'s desire to be integrated into society and the regime. Acién Almansa provides a nuanced view of the period of rebellion,

demonstrating that alliances cut across ethnic and religious affiliations among those who opposed and those who supported the rule of Cordoba. He argues, in contrast to Glick, that Ibn Ḥafṣūn and the rebels were fighting to resist the Islamization of Umayyad rule (here defined as centralization) and to defend the last vestiges of the Visigothic "feudal" system (55–101). Maribel Fierro takes issue with this last point and argues that Ibn Ḥafṣūn and the other rebels were not fighting to defend Visigothic feudalism per se. She supports Glick's view that the rebellions expressed frustration with the regime and sees the rebels as adventurers who took advantage of opportunities to establish themselves as local lords. See Maribel Fierro, "Cuatro preguntas en torno a Ibn Ḥafṣūn," *al-Qantara* 16 (1995), 221–257.

17. Ibn 'Abd Rabbihi, *al-'Iqd al-Farīd,* 2nd ed., Muhammad Sa'id al-'Aryan (Orien) (Cairo, 1953), 1:6.
18. Ibn 'Abd Rabbihi included a chapter on rulership ("al-Sulṭān") in his *al-'Iqd al-Farīd* ("The Unique Necklace"), a compendium of *adab*. The chapter does not take the form of a treatise but rather reads as a collection of verses and reports, drawn from a variety of sources, that pertain to matters of good government. While many of the excerpts that comprise the chapter emphasize the importance of obedience to the imām or ruler, many more suggest the ruler's responsibility to his subjects and the different ways in which he depends on them and their good will (1:5–66).

    This text, unfortunately, can tell us little specifically about 'Abd al-Raḥmān III's caliphate. We can appreciate that he referred to the models of the past in shaping his own rule and to the books of manners and etiquette patronized by the Abbasids. Most, if not all, of the text draws on mirrors for princes by eastern authors (in turn based on Sassanian models), such as the chapter on rulership in Ibn Qutayba's *'Uyūn al-Akhbār* and the *Kitāb al-Tāj* (unattributed), both written in the ninth century.
19. See Sally F. Moore and Barbara Myerhoff, eds., *Secular Ritual* (Assen, 1977), 3–24, for their essay, "Secular Ritual: Form and Meanings."
20. Clifford Geertz demonstrates the importance of "competitive display" as a legitimating device in his study *Negara: The Theater State in Nineteenth-Century Bali* (Princeton, 1980).

21. A number of scholars have discussed why the amirs of al-Andalus did not recognize the authority of the Abbasids (except perhaps briefly) or assume the caliphal dignity themselves. Discussion of ʻAbd al-Raḥmān III's decision to do so in 929 tends to emphasize the effects of changes in external circumstances. See Lévi-Provençal, *Histoire de l'Espagne musulmane* (*H.E.M.*), 1:132–133, 2:113–114; Gabrieli, "Omayyades d'Espagne," 93–100; Mikel de Epalza, "Problemas y reflexiones sobre el califato en al-Andalus," *Anuario de Historia del Derecho Español* (1983), 569–581; Fierro, "Sobre la adopción," 33-42; Wasserstein, *Caliphate in the West,* 8–10.
22. Pierre Guichard describes ʻAbd al-Raḥmān III's entourage as "a kind of microcosm of high-ranking people of various origins" in his essay "The Social History of Muslim Spain," in Salma Khadra Jayyusi, ed., *The Legacy of Muslim Spain* (Leiden, 1994), 2:690. Meouak, *Pouvoir souverain,* 69–227, identifies the elites in adminstrative service to the Umayyad regime (this does not include *ʻulamā'*) and their ethnic backgrounds. His study suggests that in the tenth century families of Arab origin continued to dominate the political and military administration along with a growing number of "Slavs" (*ṣaqāliba*) who were slaves or former slaves and clients of the dynasty. While Berbers were incorporated to a lesser extent in the upper ranks of the administration, the *muwalladūn* were largely restricted to provincial posts.

NOTES TO CHAPTER 1

1. Verses attributed to Ibn ʻAbd Rabbihi, cited in Ibn Ḥayyān, *al-Muqtabas V,* ed. P. Chalmeta, F. Corriente, and M. Subh (Madrid, 1976), 57, Spanish translation *Crónica del califa Abdarraḥmān III an-Nāṣir entre los años 912 y 942 (al-Muqtabis V),* trans. María Jesus Viguera and Federico Corriente (Zaragoza, 1981), 54. Citations that follow refer to the Arabic text as *Muqtabis V* and provide page numbers to both the Arabic edition and the Spanish translation. Ibn ʻIdhārī cites a variation in *Al-Bayān al-mughrib fī akhbār al-Andalus w-al-Maghrib* (Bayān 1 & 2), ed. E. Lévi-Provençal and G. S. Colin, after R. Dozy's 1849 ed. (Leiden, 1948–1951), 2:227, French translation *Histoire de l'Afrique et de l'Espagne intitulée al-Bayāno l-Mogrib,* trans. E. Fagnan (Algiers,

1901–1904), 2:377. Citations that follow refer to the text as *Bayān* and give page numbers for the Arabic edition and French translation.

2. Lévi-Provençal, *H.E.M.* 2: 113–114, reports that the limited epigraphical evidence dating before the tenth century confirms the discreet usage of titles such as "Amīr," "Malik," and "Banū al-Khalā'if" by 'Abd al-Raḥmān III's predecessors in al-Andalus.
3. For discussion of the *khuṭba* or *du'ā* and the *sikka,* see Emile Tyan, *Institutions du droit publique musulman* (Paris, 1954), 1:474–483.
4. George C. Miles, *The Coinage of the Umayyads of Spain* (New York, 1950), 28–29, reports that the first known gold dinar struck by 'Abd al-Raḥmān III dates from the year 317 H. (929–930 C.E.) and is inscribed on the reverse "Muḥammad rasūl Allāh li Amīr al-Mu'minīn 'Abd al-Raḥmān." The next year, the name of the Prophet was shifted to the obverse to make room for the title of "imām" and the caliph's *laqab,* so the reverse read "al-Imām al-Nāṣir li-Dīn Allāh 'Abd al-Raḥmān Amīr al-Mu'minīn," which became standard.
5. In addition to Miles, *Coinage of the Umayyads of Spain,* see Michael L. Bates, "The Islamic Coinage of Islamic Spain," in Jerrilynn D. Dodds, ed., *Al-Andalus. The Art of Islamic Spain* (New York, 1992), 384–391; Wasserstein, *Caliphate in the West,* 9–10, for a discussion of the numismatic evidence; and Miquel Barceló, "El hiato en las acuñaciones de oro en al-Andalus, 127–316/744(5)–929," *Moneda y Crédito* 132 (1975), 33–71, on the economic context of the change in specie.
6. Wasserstein, *Caliphate in the West,* 17.
7. For a recent political history of the Umayyad caliphate, see Joaquin Vallvé, *El califato de Córdoba* (Madrid, 1992).
8. Ibn Ḥayyān, *Muqtabis V,* 227 (Spanish 174).
9. The Abbasids initiated the use of *alqāb* (s. *laqab*) or regnal names, and the Fatimids, in asserting their claims to the leadership of the community, assumed *alqāb* as well. 'Abd al-Raḥmān III's choice of regnal name asserted his active role as God's agent and as a fighter for the faith. Prior to this, no other claimant to caliphal authority had used this *laqab;* however, in the pro-Umayyad traditions circulating in the east in the ninth and tenth centuries, Mu'āwiya was anachronistically said to have used the *laqab* al-Nāṣir li-Ḥaqq Allāh. Perhaps 'Abd al-Raḥmān III intended to evoke associations

with this important ancestor. See "Lakab," *Encyclopedia of Islam*, 2nd ed.; Bernard Lewis, "The Regnal Titles of the First Abbasid Caliphs," in *Dr. Zakir Husain Presentation Volume* (New Delhi, 1968), 13–22; Tyan, *Institutions du droit publique musulman* 1:486–487; Charles Pellat, "Le culte de Mu'āwiya au III siècle de l'Hegire," in Charles Pellat, ed. *Etudes sur l'histoire socio-culturelle de l'Islam (VIIe–XVes)*, Variorium Reprints (London, 1976).

10. *Crónica anónima de 'Abd al-Raḥmān III al-Nāṣir*, ed. and trans. E. Lévi-Provençal and E. García-Gómez (Madrid, 1950), 79 (Spanish 152–153).
11. Ibid.
12. *La crónica de 'Arīb sobre al-Andalus*, ed. Juan Castilla Brazales (Granada, 1992), 202; Ibn Ḥayyān, *Muqtabis V*, 216–217 (Spanish 166). Maribel Fierro, "Cuatro preguntas en torno a Ibn Ḥafṣūn," *al-Qantara* 16 (1995), 244–246, discusses the problem of Ibn Ḥafṣūn's "conversion" to Christianity and underscores the indistinctness of religious divisions for those moving between the two faiths in this period of accelerated conversion.
13. Ibn Ḥayyān, *Muqtabis V*, 219–220, 234 (Spanish 168, 179). Ibn Ḥayyān's history of the reign of the Amīr 'Abd Allāh, citing 'Īsā al-Rāzī, also reports that 'Umar ibn Ḥafṣūn pursued a liaison with the Abbasids early in his revolt. Ibn Ḥayyān, *al-Muktabis. Tome troisième. Chronique du règne du calife Umaiyade 'Abd Allāh à Cordoue (Muqtabis III)*, ed. P. Melchor M. Antuña (Paris, 1937), 93.
14. Ibn Ḥayyān, *Muqtabis V*, 228, 230, 233 (Spanish 75, 176, 178).
15. Ibid., 226–231 (Spanish 173–177).
16. Ibid., 233 (Spanish 178).
17. Ibid., 59, 89 (Spanish 55–56, 78). See also Ibn 'Abd Rabbihi, *'Iqd*, 5:223–224. Panegyric poetry served as propaganda for the caliphate of al-Andalus as it did in the courts of the rival caliphates. Ibn Ḥayyān recognized the importance of poetry as a form of propaganda in the introduction of his account of 'Abd al-Raḥmān III's reign (*Muqtabis V*, 40–50 [Spanish 46–51]) and included verses in his text to give emphasis to the historical narrative. His chronicle of al-Ḥakam II's reign (*Muqtabis VII*), largely a redaction from the tenth-century historian 'Īsā al-Rāzī's no longer extant chronicle,

does the same and informs us that in 972 al-Ḥakam II arrested disrespectful poets and gossipers, recognizing their potential for trouble-making (73–75 [Spanish 96–97]).

18. Ibn Ḥayyān, *Muqtabis V,* 137 (Spanish 112).
19. Ibid., 221 (Spanish 170).
20. Ibid., 226–228 (Spanish 173–174).
21. Ibid., 174–177 (Spanish 136–139).
22. Fierro makes similar observations in her article "Sobre la adopción" (39–42), although she approaches the correspondence with a different question.
23. Halm, *Empire of the Mahdi,* 147.
24. Ibid., 159. See also Farhat Dachraoui, *Le califat Fatimide au Maghreb (296–365 H/909–975 Jc)* (Tunis, 1981), 139–160.
25. M. Isabel Fierro Bello, *La heterodoxia en al-Andalus durante el período Omeya* (Madrid, 1987), 118–124; M. A. Makki, "Al-tashayyu' fī-l-Andalus," *Revista del Instituto Egipcio de Estudios Islámicos* 2 (1954), 111–116.
26. Ibn Ḥayyān notes that some of the Berber chiefs were won over by genuine loyalty to 'Abd al-Raḥmān III's dynasty and his cause, while benefitting from his gifts and support against the Shi'is, but others were simply hypocrites who played one power against the other. Ibn Ḥayyān, *Muqtabis V,* 256–257 (Spanish 194–195).
27. Ibid., 210, 302 (Spanish 235, 228). See Halm, *Empire of the Mahdi,* 203–204, 272, for boasts by the Fatimid heir-designate, al-Qā'im, of his intention to march to "Egypt and Syria, to Khurasan and the two Iraqs" (citing Ibn al-Haytham's *Sīrat al-Mahdī* in 'Imād al-Dīn Idrīs, *'Uyūn al-akhbār,* ed. M. Ghālib [Beirut, 1975], 5:128, 139–51). See also Canard, "L'imperialisme des Fatimides," 158–160.
28. For examples of 'Abd al-Raḥmān III's self-representation in these terms, see Ibn Ḥayyān, *Muqtabis V,* 312, 327–330, 350–351 (Spanish 235, 246–248, 263–264). For similar references by his correspondents, see *Muqtabis V,* 259–260, 263, 300–305, 310, 373 (Spanish 197, 199–200, 227–230, 234, 279). As a traitor to the faith and community (*al-mubaddil li-dīn, al-khārij 'an millat al-muslimīn*), the Fatimid imām is often referred to as "the Jew" (e.g., 263, 302–304, 329, 350, 385, 415 (Spanish 199–200, 227–229, 248, 263, 288, 311).

29. Ibid., 306, 310–312, 328–329 (Spanish 231, 234–235, 247–248).
30. Ibid., 311 (Spanish 235).
31. Ibid., 312 (Spanish 235). Fierro remarks on this in "Sobre la adopción," 39–40.
32. Ibn Ḥayyān, *Muqtabis V,* 312 (Spanish 235). In another letter to his Berber allies, 'Abd al-Raḥmān III identifies the Fatimid imām as the enemy of God, an impostor and unbeliever who intends to introduce error and doubt into the faith of the Berber tribes and break up the community. Ibid., 327–330 (Spanish 246–248).
33. Ibn Ḥayyān's summary (*Muqtabis V,* 257) [Spanish 195]); 'Abd al-Raḥmān III's letter to Berber allies in 933 (327 [Spanish 246–247]); Ibn Khazar's response to 'Abd al-Raḥmān III's appeal (266–267 [Spanish 202–203]); and praise for 'Abd al-Raḥmān III's ancestors, "whose faces will shine on the Day of Resurrection" (302–303 [Spanish 227–228]).
34. Ibid., 305, 306, 311, 371 (Spanish 230, 231, 235, 277).
35. Ibid., 266 (Spanish 202).
36. Ibid., 302 (Spanish 228).
37. Fierro's article "Sobre la adopción" argues that Abbasid weakness afforded 'Abd al-Raḥmān III the opportunity to assert his dynastic claims to the caliphate because, unlike his predecessors, he could hope to establish his authority over the holy cities of Mecca and Medina.
38. In a letter to Ibn Khazar, 'Abd al-Raḥmān III expressed his hope that God would honor him with the protection of His sacred house, referring to its recent violation. Ibn Ḥayyān, *Muqtabis V,* 306 (Spanish 231).
39. As 'Abd al-Raḥmān III wrote to Ibn Khazar, "The caliph is now free from his preoccupations in al-Andalus, after achieving all his objectives against his enemies. . . . He now concentrates his resolve and dedicates the struggle for his cause to the east." Ibn Ḥayyān, *Muqtabis V,* 306 (Spanish 231).
40. Ibid., 301 (Spanish 227).
41. Halm, *Empire of the Mahdi,* 20–21, 159. The term *fitna* (meaning temptation or trial) is used to designate political disorder on the scale of the civil wars of the first century of Islam and is highly charged with apocalyptic connotations (political disorder leads to chaos).
42. Ibn Ḥayyān, *Muqtabis V,* 27 (Spanish 32).

43. See, for example, verses in Ibn 'Abd Rabbihi, *'Iqd,* 19:49–51, and Ibn Ḥayyān, *Muqtabis V,* 45–46, 48–49, 57 (Spanish 47, 49, 54).
44. See Ibn 'Abd Rabbihi's *urjūza* celebrating 'Abd al-Raḥmān III's campaigns in *'Iqd,* 5:225–246, English translation *Hispano Arabic Poetry,* James T. Monroe trans. (Berkeley, 1974) 74–128, verses 26, 163, 238, 244; 18, 29, 199. Poets typically described 'Abd al-Raḥmān III as a moon or a sun or other source of light—for example, Ibn 'Abd Rabbihi, *'Iqd,* 5:223, 224, 225; Ibn Ḥayyān, *Muqtabis V,* 41, 43, 44, 46–47, 57, 59, 89, 102, 114, 337, 365 (Spanish 44–46, 48, 54–56, 78, 87, 138, 253, 273).
45. *Urjūza,* verses 36, 81–82.
46. Ibn Ḥayyān, *Muqtabis V,* 64, 89 (Spanish 59, 78).
47. Ibid., 277, 89 (Spanish 210, 78). Poets of the Fatimid court celebrated the divine illumination of the Fatimid imāms in similar terms. Canard, "L'imperialisme des Fatimides," 161–162.
48. Maribel Fierro, "Mahdīsme et eschatologie en al-Andalus," *Mahdisme, crise et changement dans l'histoire de Maroc,* ed. Faculté des Lettres et des Sciences Humaines de Rabat (Casablanca, 1994), 47–51.
49. 'Abd al-Malik ibn Ḥabīb, *Kitāb al-ta'rīkh (Kitāb al-Tarīj),* ed. Jorge Aguadé (Madrid, 1991). Report 403 predicts twenty-five rulers for al-Andalus between its conquest and its destruction; report 442 lists the Amir 'Abd Allāh as the twenty-fifth.
50. Crone and Hinds, *God's Caliph,* 34–38.
51. Ibn Ḥayyān, *Muqtabis V,* 226–228 (Spanish 173–174).
52. Ibid., 20–24 (Spanish 25–30) (attribution to "al-Rāzī" in the Spanish edition, without specifying either Aḥmad or 'Īsā; Ibn Ḥayyān cites both in his history but occasionally simply cites "al-Rāzī" or reports "*qāla*"). Some of Ibn Masarra's writings are extant and have been published. See *Min qaḍāyā-l-fikr al-islāmī,* ed. Muhammad Kamal Ibrahim Ja'far (Cairo, 1978), 310–360. For a description, see Emilio Tornero, "Noticia sobre la publicacion de obras ineditas de Ibn Masarra," *al-Qantara* 14 (1993), 47–64). For a discussion of Ibn Masarra's thought and a critique of the scholarship on him, see Claude Addas, "Andalusī Mysticism and the Rise of Ibn 'Arabī," in Salma Khadra al-Jayyusi, ed., *The Legacy of Muslim Spain* (Leiden, 1994), 2: 912–919. On 'Abd al-Raḥmān III's persecution of the sect, see M. Cruz Hernandez, "La persecución anti-massarí durante el reinado de 'Abd al-Raḥmān

al-Nāṣir li-Dīn Allāh, según Ibn Ḥayyān," *al-Qantara* 2 (1981), 51–67, and Fierro, *Heterodoxia,* 113–118, 132–140.

53. Ibn Ḥayyān, *Muqtabis V,* 24–25, 30 (Spanish 30–31, 35).
54. Ibid., 25–30 (Spanish 31–35).
55. In the Bobastro circular 'Abd al-Raḥmān III cites sura 59:2 and sura 11:102 to represent himself as God's scourge. Ibn Ḥayyān, *Muqtabis V,* 227, (Spanish 174). In his circular on Ibn Masarra's *firqa* he cites the following verses on the same theme: 43:13, 12:87, 40:69–70, 22:8–9, 3:7, 3:118, 11:76. Ibid., 25–30 (Spanish 31–35). Translation of sura 40:69–70 is from N. J. Dawood, *The Koran with a Parallel Arabic Text* (London, 1990).
56. Maria Isabel Fierro, "Heresy in al-Andalus," *Legacy,* 2:897, associates 'Abd al-Raḥmān III's proclamation of Malikism as the official doctrine of his reign with the execution of his traitorous son 'Abd Allāh, a Shafi'ī, in 950. The important point is that the caliph not only declared an official doctrine but demonstrated his intention to enforce compliance. See also Fierro, *Heterodoxia,* 145–147.
57. Ibn Ḥayyān, *Muqtabis V,* 25 (Spanish 30–31).
58. Ibid., 22 (Spanish 28).
59. Ibid., 22–23 (Spanish 28–29). Al-Rāzī thus charged the Abbasids with the very neglect they originally condemned the Umayyads for in the eighth century and upheld the Umayyads as, after all, the true upholders of the principles of the faith. On Abbasid propaganda against the Syrian Umayyads, see Sharon, *Black Banners of the East,* 19–27, 83–84.
60. Ibn Ḥayyān, *Muqtabis V,* 23 (Spanish 29).
61. Ibid., 23–24 (Spanish 29–30).
62. R. Stephen Humphreys discusses the Qur'anic myth of covenant, betrayal, and redemption as a conceptual theme in ninth- and tenth-century Arabic historiography. See Humphreys, "Qur'anic Myth and Narrative Structure in Early Islamic Historiography," in F. M. Clover and R. S. Humphreys, eds., *Tradition and Innovation in Late Antiquity* (Madison, 1989), 271–290.
63. Ibn 'Idhārī, *Bayān,* 2:220, 221 (French 2:366). Incidentally, Ibn 'Idhārī makes no mention of 'Abd al-Raḥmān III's efforts to establish diplomatic contacts with the Fatimids subsequently, which were sharply rebuffed by the imam al-Mu'izz. See Halm, *Empire of the Mahdi,* 396–397.

64. Ibn 'Idhārī, *Bayān* 2:210, 214 (French 2:348, 354–355). Eduardo Manzano Moreno discusses the historical independence of the frontier regions from Cordoba and describes 'Abd al-Raḥmān III's efforts to dominate the frontier lords until his defeat at Alhandega. Although Ibn 'Idhārī describes 'Abd al-Raḥmān III's continued commitment to the security of the frontier, Manzano Moreno argues that after 939 the caliph essentially entrusted this responsibility to the local aristocracy. He observes that the Umayyads were more successful in using their campaigns to support their claims to be defenders of the Muslims than in actually controlling the frontiers. See Manzano Moreno, *Frontera de al-Andalus* and "Medieval Frontier."
65. Ibn 'Idhārī mentions several occasions in the latter half of 'Abd al-Raḥmān III's reign when news of victories was read to the public in the great mosques of the capital. See *Bayān* 2:214, 217–220 (French 2:356, 361, 363, 365).
66. See Fierro, *Heterodoxia*, 149–155, and "Accusations of '*Zandaqa*' in al-Andalus," *Quaderni di studi Arabi* 5–6 (1987–1988); see also *Tres documentos sobre procesos de herejes en España musulmana*, ed. M.A.W. Khallaf (Cairo, 1981), 57–100, for the accusations made against Abū Khayr.
67. Ibn 'Idhārī, *Bayān*, 2:234, 236 (French 2:387, 389–390). Manzano Moreno, *Frontera de al-Andalus*, 63–64, 371, suggests that Ibn Idhārī's reports of these campaigns were fabricated to enhance the caliph's prestige, observing that we have no descriptions of them. This is to support his argument that al-Ḥakam II continued his father's policy regarding the frontier after 'Abd al-Raḥmān III's experience at the battle of Alhandega in 939. From then on the caliph no longer led campaigns in person and gave up trying to assert direct control over the frontier lords. We do not have enough evidence for most of al-Ḥakam II's reign to accept this argument as more than a theory. The reported refortification of the frontier suggests al-Ḥakam II did take an active interest in the north. His command that Yaḥyā Ibn Muḥammad al-Tujībī (a frontier lord of the Ebro valley) participate in the ceremonial life of the court and his appointment of al-Tujībī to the position of wazīr and then commander demonstrate an effort to strengthen bonds with the frontier lords and suggest a continued interest in their incorporation into the regime.

68. Ibn ʿIdhārī reports that envoys from Abū Yazīd came to Cordoba with news of his capture of Qayrawān and Raqqāda and assurances that Abū Yazīd recognized ʿAbd al-Raḥmān III's authority and accepted him as imam. *Bayān* 2:212 (French 2:352).
69. Ibn Ḥayyān, *Muqtabis VII,* 96–100, 130–131, 134–136 (Spanish 124–128, 165–166, 169–171).
70. Ibid., 130–131 (Spanish 165–166).
71. Ibid., 178–180 (Spanish 217–219).
72. Ibid., 180 (Spanish 219).
73. Ibid., 180–183 (Spanish 219–221).
74. Ibid., 179–180 (Spanish 218–219).
75. Ibid., 135–136 (Spanish 170).
76. In a few instances, caliphal texts referred to the sunna and then elaborated, explicitly mentioning the sunna of the Prophet and the sunna of the *rashīdūn,* "who made legal judgments following the consensus of their predecessors" (*ʿalā sabīl ijmāʿ aslāfihim*). Ibid., 181, 80 (Spanish 219, 103).
77. Ibid., 174, (Spanish 212–213).
78. Ibid., 174–175 (Spanish 213).
79. Ibid., 111–114 (Spanish 142–145).
80. Ibid., 126–127 (Spanish 160–161).
81. Ibid., 138 (Spanish 173).
82. See, for example, al-Khushanī's preface to his *Kitāb al-quḍāt bi-Qurṭuba* (*Historia de los jueces de Córdoba,*) ed. and trans. Julián Ribera (Madrid, 1914), 7 (Spanish 6). Al-Nubāhī records al-Ḥakam II's words of investiture to a newly appointed judge and thus demonstrates the caliph's concern for the proper administration of the law. See Al-Nubāhī, *Kitāb al-marqaba al-ʿulyā,* ed. E. Lévi-Provençal (Cairo, 1948), 75.
83. For example, Al-Nubāhī, *Marqaba,* 69–70.
84. Maribel Fierro, "Qāsim b. Asbag y la licitud de recibir regalos," in *Homenaje al Profesor José María Fórneas Besteiro* (Granada, 1994), 2:977–981.
85. Maribel Fierro, "Caliphal Legitimacy and Expiation," in Muhammed Khalid Masud, Brinkley Messick, and David S. Powers, eds., *Islamic Legal Interpretation: Muftis and Their Fatwas* (Cambridge, Mass., 1996), 55–62.
86. E. García Gomez highlights the territorial ambitions expressed in the verses cited in al-Rāzī's text in his article "La poesie politique

sous le califat de Cordoue," *Revue des Études Islamiques* 1949, 5–11.

87. Ibn Ḥayyān, *Muqtabis VII,* 165 (Spanish 204).
88. Ibid., 232–233 (Spanish 274–275).
89. Ibid., 231 (Spanish 273–274).
90. Ibid., 54–56 (Spanish 72–74).
91. Ibid., 160 (Spanish 200).
92. Ibid., 86 (Spanish 109).
93. Ibid., 84 (Spanish 108). It is possible that the 'Umar referred to here was (also) 'Umar ibn 'Abd al-'Azīz (r. 717–720), who had a reputation for being pious and upright.
94. Ibid., 122 (Spanish 155).
95. Ibid., 84, 61–62, 31, 60, 156 (Spanish 108, 83–84, 53, 82, 198).
96. Ibid., 55 (Spanish 72).
97. Ibid., 232, 95 (Spanish 274, 119). The caliphal circular announcing the surrender of Ḥasan ibn Qannūn represents all the caliphs who followed the prophets as chosen from Muhammad's family tree (*dawḥa*) (180 [Spanish 219]). The Umayyads could represent themselves as members of the Prophet's family or house (*ahl al-bayt*) if they traced their common descent back to 'Abd Manaf or Quraysh. See Moshe Sharon, "The Umayyads as Ahl al-Bayt," *Jerusalem Studies in Arabic and Islam* 14 (1991), 115–149.
98. Ibn Ḥayyān; *Muqtabis VII,*, 54, 138, 161–162 (Spanish 72, 172, 201–202).
99. Ibid., 163–164 (Spanish 203). On the image of the sun rising in the west as a sign of the eschaton, see Jane Idleman Smith and Yvonne Haddad, *The Islamic Understanding of Death and Resurrection* (Albany, 1981), 69. See also Halm, *Empire of the Mahdi,* 159. For an example of the Fatimid caliph al-Mahdī's representation as the sun risen in the west, see W. Ivanow's excerpt of *Zahr al-ma'ānī* by 'Imād al-Dīn Idrīs in *Ismaili Tradition Concerning the Rise of the Fatimids* (London, Calcutta, Bombay, 1942), Arabic 51 (English 238).
100. Ibn Ḥayyān, *Muqtabis VII,* 60, 120, 205, 31, 62 (Spanish 82, 153, 245, 53, 84).
101. Ibid., 161 (Spanish 154).
102. Ibid., 31, 85 (Spanish 53, 108).
103. Ibid., 216–217, 232 (Spanish 256–258, 274).

104. Ibid., 231 (Spanish 273). Al-Qasṭallī anticipated the arrival of Hishām's cavalry in Egypt and Syria (Ibn 'Idhārī, *Bayān* 2:275 [French 2:456–457]).
105. Ibn Ḥayyān, *Muqtabis VII,* 138, 231 (Spanish 172, 273).

NOTES TO CHAPTER 2

1. Ibn 'Idhārī, *Bayān,* 2:223 (French 2:371).
2. Ibn 'Idhārī, *Bayān,* 2:209, 231 (French 2:347, 381), and al-Maqqarī, *Nafḥ al-ṭīb min ghuṣn al-Andalus al-raṭīb,* ed. Ihsan 'Abbas (Beirut, 1968), 1:565, report that construction of Madīnat al-Zahrā' began in 325 H. (936), but Ibn Ḥayyān, *Muqtabis V,* 437–438 (Spanish 327–328) reports that the caliph turned to monumental construction after the battle of al-Khandaq (Alhandega).
3. Ibn Ḥayyān, *Muqtabis V,* 437–438 (Spanish 327–328).
4. Pedro Chalmeta, "Simancas y Alhandega," *Hispania* 36 (1976), 391–396; Manzano Moreno, "Medieval Frontier," 50.
5. Chalmeta, "Simancas y Alhandega," 391–392, describes the caliph's revised strategy in dealing with the Christian frontier in terms of a shift from frontal attacks to multidirectional and continuous harassment.
6. Chalmeta, "Simancas y Alhandega," 391–392, argues that 'Abd al-Raḥmān III constructed Madīnat al-Zahrā' for defensive reasons and that the defeat of Alhandega caused him to create and retreat into this last bastion.
7. al-Maqqarī, *Nafḥ al-ṭīb,* 1:565.
8. See Jere L. Bacharach, "Marwānid Umayyad Building Activities: Speculations on Patronage," *Muqarnas* 13 (1996), 38–39, on the identification of Damascus as the Umayyad capital even though the caliphs often did not reside there.
9. H. P. L'Orange, *Studies in the Iconography of Cosmic Kingship* (Cambridge, 1953), 12–14; Charles Wendell, "Baghdad: *Imago Mundi,* and Other Foundation Lore," *International Journal of Middle Eastern Studies* 2 (1971), 99–128; Jacob Lassner, *The Topography of Baghdad in the Early Middle Ages: Text and Studies (Detroit, 1970), 132–137; Lassner, Shaping of Abbasid Rule,*

169–183; Christian Beckwith, "The Plan of the City of Peace: Central Asian Iranian Factors in Early Abbasid Design," *Acta Orientalia Academiae Scientiarium Hung.* 38 (1984), 143–164.

10. See Manuel Acién Almansa, "Madīnat al-Zahrā' en el urbanismo musulmán," *Cuadernos de Madīnat al-Zahrā'* 1 (1987), 13–15, for discussion of the foundation of cities as a symbol of sovereignty that developed under the Abbasids.
11. Jonathan Bloom, "The Origins of Fatimid Art," *Muqarnas* 3 (1985), 23–24.
12. Alexandre Lézine, *Mahdīya: Recherches d'archéologie islamique* (Paris, 1965).
13. Halm, *Empire of the Mahdi,* 218, on the palace plans; Bloom, "Origins of Fatimid Art," 22–23, and Bloom, *Minaret: Symbol of Islam* (Oxford, 1989), 99–103, on the congregational mosque of al-Mahdīyya and the Fatimids' deliberate rejection of the tower minaret as an impious innovation.
14. Bloom, "Origins of Fatimid Art," 28–29.
15. D. Fairchild Ruggles, "The Gardens of the Alhambra and the Concept of the Garden in Islamic Spain," in Jerrilynn D. Dodds, ed., *Al-Andalus: The Art of Islamic Spain* (New York, 1992), 164; D. Fairchild Ruggles, "Madīnat al-Zahrā's Constructed Landscape: A Case Study in Islamic Garden and Architectural History," Ph.D. diss., University of Pennsylvania, 1991, 270–276, 288–289.
16. Acién Almansa, "Madīnat al-Zahrā'," 17; Christine Mazzoli-Guintard, "Remarques sur le fonctionnement d'une capitale a double polarité: Madīnat al-Zahrā'-Cordoue," *al-Qantara* 18 (1997), 43–50.
17. Ibn Ḥayyān, as cited by al-Maqqarī, *Nafḥ al-ṭīb,* 1:566–568.
18. Ruggles, "Madīnat al-Zahrā's Constructed Landscape, "chs. 3–4, notes the discrepancy between the information provided by the historical texts and the archeological excavations and treats each separately. She discusses the history of the excavations of Madīnat al-Zahrā' in D. Fairchild Ruggles, "Historiography and the Rediscovery of Madīnat al-Zahrā'," *Islamic Studies* 30 (1991), 129–141. Antonio Vallejo Triano discusses the state of the excavations, and of the caliph's *majlis* in particular, in "El salón de 'Abd al-Raḥmān III: problemática de una restauración," *Madīnat al-Zahrā': el salón de 'Abd al-Raḥmān III* (Cordoba, 1995), 11–40.

19. Vallejo Triano, "Madīnat al-Zahrā': The Triumph of the Islamic State," 27–30.
20. D. Fairchild Ruggles, "The Mirador in Abbasid and Hispano-Umayyad Garden Typology," *Muqarnas* 7 (1990), 75–79; Ruggles, "The Gardens of the Alhambra," 164–166; Ruggles, "Madīnat al-Zahrā's Constructed Landscape," 317–323, 329–339.
21. Ruggles, "Mirador," 73–82; Ruggles, "Gardens of the Alhambra," 164; Ruggles, "Madīnat al-Zahrā's Constructed Landscape," 304–306. Vallejo Triano, "Madīnat al-Zahrā': The Triumph of the Islamic State," 30, notes the "absence of rigid symmetry that characterizes Abbasid palace complexes" and associates the high elevation of the caliph's residence with al-Mahdīyya.
22. Ruggles, "Madīnat al-Zahrā's Constructed Landscape," 228 discusses the "communication network" of the city.
23. al-Maqqarī, *Nafḥ al-ṭīb,* 1:565, makes the favorable comparison to the constructions of the kings of the past.
24. Christian Ewert, "Elementos decorativos en los tableros parietales del Salón Rico de Madīnat al-Zahrā'," *Cuadernos de Madīnat al-Zahrā'* 1 (1987), 41–58; Vallejo Triano, "Madīnat al-Zahrā': The Triumph of the Islamic State," 34; Manuel Acién Almansa, "Materias e hipótesis para una interpretación del salón de 'Abd al-Raḥmān al-Nāṣir," *Madīnat al-Zahrā': el salón de 'Abd al-Raḥmān III,* 177–195.
25. Bloom, "Origins of Fatimid Art," 29, refers to paradisiacal gardens as part of Islamic palatine vocabulary by this period. Ruggles identifies the quadripartite garden facing the *majlis* as the earliest surviving garden of its type in al-Andalus and the Maghrib ("Gardens of the Alhambra," 165).
26. al-Maqqarī, *Nafḥ al-ṭīb,* 1:566.
27. Ibid., 1: 523–524. The flourishing of "al-Zahrā'" contrasted with the barren *al-ṣaḥrā'* (literally, desert) that served as pasturage outside Cordoba. For reference to this *ṣaḥrā'*, see Ibn Ḥayyān, *Muqtabis III,* 139.
28. See Nasser Rabbat, "Al-Azhar Mosque: An Architectural Chronicle of Cairo's History," *Muqarnas* 13 (1996), 53, for his discussion of the name of the al-Azhar mosque in Cairo. He notes that the honorific name of Faṭīma, the Prophet's daughter and eponym of the Fatimid dynasty, was al-Zahrā' but is skeptical about the argu-

ment that al-Azhar represented a masculinization of the name. He suggests that the Fatimids used names such as *al-azhar* and *al-zāhira* to convey the idea of the imam's divine light. It is possible that 'Abd al-Raḥmān III was similarly motivated, challenging the Fatimid belief in the imam's inspiration while appropriating the metaphors of their representation, and that he was also aware that the name al-Zahrā' signified Fāṭima. Note that his palace-city predated the first al-Azhar mosque in al-Manṣūriyya, so 'Abd al-Raḥmān III may have initiated a contest of names.

Rosario Castejon, "Madīnat al-Zahrā'en los autores árabes," *al-Mulk* 1 (1959–1960), 74, suggests an astrological explanation for the naming of 'Abd al-Raḥmān III's palace-city. She identifies the name of al-Zahrā' with the Arabic name for Venus (*al-zuhara*), proposes that the statue above the Bāb al-Ṣūra represented the classical Venus, but does not provide compelling evidence to support this hypothesis.

29. Ibn Ḥayyān, *Muqtabis VII,* 60.
30. Ibid., 84.
31. Acién Almansa, "Madīnat al-Zahrā'," 22. Mazzoli-Guintard, "Madīnat al-Zahrā'-Cordoue," describes the two cities as a single capital, an urban center with a "double polarity."
32. Ibn Ḥayyān, *Muqtabis V,* 23–24 (Spanish 29–30). See Robert Hillenbrand, "Medieval Córdoba as a Cultural Centre," in Salma Khadra Jayyusi, ed., *The Legacy of Muslim Spain* (Leiden, 1994), 1:112–135, for a description of Cordoba in this period and its representation by contemporary, and especially later, sources.
33. Ibn Ḥayyān, *Muqtabis VII,* 64–65, 67–68, 70–71, 207 (Spanish 77–78, 89–90, 93, 247); Ibn 'Idhārī, *Bayān* 2:240 (French 2:397).
34. al-Maqqarī, *Nafḥ al-ṭīb,* 1:560–561.
35. M. Ocaña, "La basilica de San Vincente y la gran mezquita de Córdoba," *al-Andalus* 7 (1942), 347–366, discusses contradictions in references to the church of Cordoba and the story of its division, raising considerable doubts about the latter.
36. Rodrigo Amador de los Ríos y Villata, *Inscripciones árabes de Córdoba,* 2nd ed. (Madrid, 1880), 186–187. The full inscription on the "Sagrario" gate, dating from the rule of the *ḥājib* al-Manṣūr, reads: "In the name of God, the Merciful and Compassionate, God bears witness that there is no god but Him, and so do the angels and the sages. He is the Executor of Justice, the Mighty,

the Wise One. The only true faith in God's sight is Islam. Those to whom the scriptures were given disagreed among themselves" (sura 3:16–17). I have relied on Dawood's *Koran with a Parallel Arabic Text* to render the Qur'anic verses.

37. This is the inscription on the "Puerta de la Ventana," dating from al-Ḥakam II's reign (Amador de los Ríos y Villalta, *Inscripciones,* 185–186).
38. Here I am following Irene Bierman's treatment of public inscriptions in the eastern Mediterranean from the sixth to tenth centuries (*Writing Signs: The Fatimid Public Text* [Berkeley, 1998], chap. 2, "Signing the Community," 28–59).
39. Amador de los Ríos y Villata, *Inscripciones,* 182–183.
40. Ibid., 183–185.
41. Ibid., 178–180.
42. Ibid., 206–213.
43. Nuha N. N. Khoury, "The Great Mosque of Cordoba in the Tenth Century," *Muqarnas* 13 (1996), 86–88, argues that the inscriptions are ideologically compatible with dogma espoused by the Syrian Umayyad caliph 'Abd al-Malik when he sought to unite the community.
44. Amador de los Ríos y Villalta, *Inscripciones,* 213.
45. See Erika Cruikshank Dodd and Shereen Khairallah, *The Image of the Word: A Study of Quranic Verses in Islamic Architecture* (Beirut, 1981), vol. 2 (Indexes), 3. They note the inscriptional use of the *fātiḥa* in only these two examples (al-Walīd's mosque at Medina and the Great Mosque of Cordoba) before the eleventh century, but Klaus Brisch, "Observations on the Iconography of the Great Mosque of Damascus," in Priscilla P. Soucek, ed., *Content and Context of Visual Arts in the Islamic World* (University Park, Penn., 1988), 13–23, notes that, according to textual evidence, the Great Mosque of Damascus was also decorated with a mosaic inscription of the opening verses of the Qur'an.
46. Other inscriptions inside the mosque that relate to prayer and ritual purification are emblematic of the caliph's role as guide. He reminds the Muslims of their ritual obligations and provides them with a place for congregational worship. See Amador de los Ríos y Villalta, *Inscripciones,* 215–216, 227–231.

47. Amador de los Ríos y Villalta, *Inscripciones,* 218–221; Evariste Lévi-Provençal, *Inscriptions árabes d'Espagne* (Leiden, 1931), 15–16.
48. Amador de los Ríos y Villalta, *Inscripciones,* 222–223; Lévi-Provençal, *Inscriptions,* 12–14.
49. Amador de los Ríos y Villalta, *Inscripciones,* 223–224.
50. On the lamp, and especially the mosaic decorations, see Henri Stern, *Les mosaiques de la Grande Mosquée de Cordoue* (Berlin, 1976). Oleg Grabar observes that the *miḥrāb* as a room, rather than a niche, resembles a doorway into the light when it is illuminated or into the darkness when it is not. Grabar, "Notes sur le Miḥrāb de la Grande Mosquée de Cordoue," in Alexandre Papadoulu, ed., *Le miḥrāb dans l'architecture e la religion musulmanes: Actes du colloque internationale: Formes symboliques et formes esthetiques dans l'architecture religieuse musulmane: le miḥrāb, Paris, 1980* (Leiden, 1988), 115. As a gateway into the beyond, the *miḥrāb* may evoke associations with the Judgment Day, with the caliph as gatekeeper. On the cosmological associations of the octagonal shape of the *miḥrāb* room (recalling the octagonal shape of the Dome of the Rock in Jerusalem) and the dome capping it, see Alexandre Papadopoulu's remarks in response to Grabar ("Notes sur le Miḥrāb," 120–121). Hillenbrand, "Córdoba as Cultural Centre," 133–134. discusses the themes of light and paradise in the mosque.
51. Dodds, "Great Mosque of Córdoba," 11–19. Khoury, "Great Mosque of Cordoba," 83–84, points out that no one sought to correct the misalignment of the *qibla* out of a desire to maintain historical continuity with the original mosque.
52. Dodds, "Great Mosque of Córdoba," 17.
53. Dodds, "Great Mosque of Córdoba," 20–21, suggests al-Ḥakam II's addition adapted the tripartite basilical plan of contemporary Mozarabic churches, appropriating the "rhetorical force of Christian liturgical building."
54. Maria Isabel Fierro, "En torno a la decoración con mosaicos de las mezquitas omeyas," *Homenaje al prof. Jacinto Bosch Vilá* (Universidad de Granada, Departmento de Estudios Semíticos, Granada, 1991), 131–144.

55. See Khoury, "Great Mosque of Cordoba," 83. Khoury develops an argument for a particular association between al-Ḥakam II's mosque and al-Walīd's Great Mosque of Medina, constructed on the site of the Prophet's house (the original place of congregation and worship for the Muslim community). This is an interesting idea, given the importance of the Mālikī *madhhab* to the Andalusi Umayyad caliphs.
56. Grabar, "Notes sur le Miḥrāb," 115–122; Jerrilynn D. Dodds, *Architecture and Ideology in Early Medieval Spain* (University Park, Penn., 1990), 94–106.
57. Ibn 'Idhārī, *Bayān* 2:237 (French 2:392), reports that al-Ḥakam commanded the Byzantine emperor to send mosaics and a skilled mosaicist as al-Walīd had done when undertaking the construction of the Great Mosque of Damascus.
58. Bloom, *Minaret,* 109–111.
59. We find this metaphor in verse when the poet Aḥmad ibn Sulaymān al-Bayyānī referred to the caliph al-Ḥakam II as the minaret of divine guidance, cited in Ibn Ḥayyān, *Muqtabis VII,* 214 (Spanish 254).
60. Halm, *Empire of the Mahdi,* 415–416; Paula Sanders, *Ritual, Politics, and the City in Fatimid Cairo* (Albany, 1994), 40–42.
61. Vallejo Triano, "Madīnat al-Zahrā': The Triumph of the Islamic State," 35; Vallejo Triano, "El salón de 'Abd al-Raḥmān III," 16; Dodds, "Great Mosque of Córdoba," 21.
62. Mazzoli-Guintard, "Madīnat al-Zahrā'-Cordoue," 57–61.
63. Sanders, *Fatimid Cairo,* provides a model for understanding the relationship between public or processional ceremony and urban space.
64. For discussion of the possible Roman and Visigoth origins of the office of the *ṣāḥib al-madīna* and its history and functions in the Umayyad period, see J. Vallvé, "El Zalmedina de Córdoba," *al-Qantara* 2 (1981), 277–318. As Vallvé discusses, the amir 'Abd al-Raḥmān II has been credited with the formal establishment of the office. By the caliphal period, the *ṣāḥib al-madīna* had become the most important officer of the regime after the *ḥājib* or chief minister. He was the chief officer responsible for maintaining law and order in the city, accountable directly to the caliph.
65. See Moore and Myerhoff, *Secular Ritual,* 3–24, for their discussion of ritual as a traditionalizing instrument.

66. Ibid. See also Stanley Jeyaraja Tambiah, "A Performative Approach to Ritual," in his *Culture, Thought, and Social Action* (Cambridge, Mass., 1985), 123–166, and M. E. Combs-Schilling, *Sacred Performances: Islam, Sexuality, and Sacrifice* (New York, 1989), 29–37, for summary discussions of ritual and different approaches to understanding ritual. Ritual, of course, is a subject of long-standing anthropological interest with an extensive bibliography, and historians interested in political culture have made their own contributions.
67. See Sanders, *Fatimid Cairo,* chap. 2, "The Ceremonial Idiom."
68. al-Maqqarī, *Nafḥ al-ṭīb,* 1:212–213.
69. Ibn 'Idhārī, *Bayān* 2:91 (French 2:148).
70. For a brief account of the swearing of the *bay'a,* or oath of loyalty, see *Crónica anónima de 'Abd al-Raḥmān III,* 2 (Spanish 91–93). P. Melchor M. Antuña traces the history of the *bay'a* in al-Andalus and provides a glimpse of the ceremony as practiced by the amirs in his article "La jura en el califato de Córdoba," *Anuario de historia del derecho español* 6 (1930), 108–140.
71. Extensive descriptions of caliphal receptions for visiting embassies and dignitaries recorded by late sources, in particular, may exaggerate, embellish, or invent in order to glorify the past. See Fernando de la Granja, "A propósito de una embajada cristiana en la corte de 'Abd al-Raḥmān III," *Al-Andalus* 39 (1974), 391–406. For Andalusi Umayyad diplomatic history, see A. al-Hajji, *Andalusian Diplomatic Relations with Western Europe during the Umayyad Period* (Beirut, 1970); A. al-Hajji, "The Andalusi Diplomatic Relations with the Vikings during the Umayyad Period (A.H. 138–366/A.D. 755–966)," *Hesperis-Tamuda* 8 (1967), 67–110; A. al-Hajji, "Al-Alāqāt al-diblūmāsiyya bayna al-Andalus wa-l-Bīzanṭa hattā nihāyat al-qarn al-rābi' al-hijrī," *Revista del Instituto Egipcio de Estudios Islámicos* 23 (1982–1983), 53–91.
72. Ibn 'Idhārī, *Bayān,* 2:215 (French 2:357).
73. Ibid., 2:213 (French 2:353).
74. al-Maqqarī, *Nafḥ al-ṭīb,* 1:364–365, 366–371.
75. Ibid., 368–371. Al-Maqqarī notes that the text of al-Ballūṭī's speech was preserved by Ibn Ḥayyān and others and here cites Ibn Khāqān's *Maṭmaḥ* (d. 1137). See also al-Nubāhī, *Kitāb al-marqaba,* 66–68. Al-Ballūṭī did not refrain from chastising the caliph on other occasions. Al-Nubāhī, *marqaba,* 69–70.

76. Barceló, "El califa patente," 53–56, discusses the problem of the sources and draws similar conclusions.
77. Ibn Ḥayyān, *Muqtabis VII.*
78. See Michael McCormick, "Analyzing Imperial Ceremonies," *Jahrbuch der Österreichischen Byzantinistik* 35 (1985), 1–20, for discussion of such methodological problems.
79. The word *ḥājib*—generally translated as "chamberlain" or defined, in terms of the Andalusi court, as an official of the highest rank who controlled access to the caliph and was in charge of protocol—derives from the same root as words signifying veiling, covering, or screening. See Barceló, "El califa patente," 52–53, for a discussion of the absence of a curtain (*sitr*) to obscure the caliph from view.
80. See Ibn Ḥayyān, *Muqtabis VII,* 22, 52, 151–152 (Spanish 45, 70, 192), for examples.
81. Barceló, "El califa patente," 57–65.
82. For a contemporary almanac and insight into the schedule for the collection of resources to support and equip the military, see Reinhardt Dozy, ed., *Le calendrier de Cordoue,* new ed. in Arabic and Latin with French trans. by Charles Pellat (Leiden, 1961).
83. Ibn Ḥayyān, *Muqtabis VII,* 79, 102, 106, 219, 221 (Spanish 102, 130, 135, 259, 261). 'Abd al-Raḥmān III's armies probably departed the capital in fanfare as well. In his reports on the campaigns of 'Abd al-Raḥmān III's reign, Ibn 'Idhārī indicates that the caliph held a military parade or review (*burūz*) usually about a month before the army departed. See Ibn 'Idhārī, *Bayān* 2:175–176, 180, 182–183, 185, 193, 196, 202, 206, 221. One report suggests that the men, women, and children of Cordoba customarily attended the spectacle. Ibid., 2:222 (French 2:368).
84. Ibn 'Idhārī refers to the customary Umayyad ceremony for the tying of the banners in his account of the rule of the *ḥājib* al-Muẓaffar (al-Manṣūr's successor) in *Kitāb al-Bayān al-Mughrib. tome troisième. Histoire de l'Espagne musulmane au XIe siécle* (*Bayān III*), ed. E. Lévi-Provençal (Paris, 1930), 5–6.
85. Ibn Ḥayyān, *Muqtabis VII,* 25–26 (Spanish 48–50).
86. Ibid.
87. Ibid., 102 (Spanish 130).
88. Ibid., 219–222 (Spanish 259–262).
89. Ibid., 220–221 (Spanish 261).

90. Ibid., 142–143 (Spanish 180–181).
91. Ibid., 225 (Spanish 266). 'Abd al-Raḥmān III's commanders and allies had also sent trophies to Cordoba, including the heads of slain enemies, as well as banners, drums, crosses, and bells, which were all displayed at the gate of the *qaṣr*. We can imagine, but do not have descriptions of, their parade through the city. For examples, see Ibn 'Idhārī, *Bayān* 2:218 (French 362, 363).
92. Ibn 'Idhārī, *Bayān* 2:213, 215 (French 2:353, 357); Ibn Ḥayyān, *Muqtabis VII*, 22, 168 (Spanish 45, 207).
93. Ibn Ḥayyān, *Muqtabis VII*, 22–23 (Spanish 46). See also E. García Gómez, "La poesie politique sous le califat de Cordoue," *Revue des Études Islamiques* (1949), 8.
94. See Janina M. Safran, "Ceremony and Submission: The Symbolic Representation and Recognition of Legitimacy in Tenth-Century al-Andalus," *Journal of Near Eastern Studies* 58 (1999), 191–201.
95. Ibn Ḥayyān, *Muqtabis VII*, 32–38 (Spanish 54–59).
96. Ibid., 194–202 (Spanish 235–242).
97. According to Muḥammad ibn Yūsuf ibn 'Abd Allāh al-Warrāq, as cited in Ibn Ḥayyān's text, Ja'far and his brother Yaḥyā were descendants of a Syrian family settled in al-Andalus for many generations and loyal to the Umayyads until their father, Tha'alaba, settled in North Africa after performing the pilgrimage and marrying a woman of the Kutāma tribe. There he was converted and renamed 'Ali by the Shi'ī *dā'i* who conquered Ifriqiyya (area of Tunisia) for the first Fatimid caliph. Thereafter, he advanced in the service of al Mahdī and his heir. Ibid., 32–35 (Spanish 54–56).
98. Ibid., 79–80, 135–136 (Spanish 102–103, 170). 'Abd al-Raḥmān III had pursued the same policy at home and in North Africa, even extending his mercy to the Banū Ḥafṣūn. See *Crónica anónima de 'Abd al-Raḥmān III*, 57 (Spanish 148); Ibn Ḥayyān, *Muqtabis V*, 213 (Spanish 164).
99. Ibn Ḥayyān, *Muqtabis VII*, 41 (Spanish 61–62).
100. Ibid., 39–40 (Spanish 60–61).
101. Ibid., 41–43 (Spanish 62–64).
102. Ibid., 44–45 (Spanish 64–65). Al-Rāzī reports that as soon as the caliph learned of the disembarkation of Yaḥyā and the Banū Khazar, he alerted the district commanders and governors of the

peninsula to send the men of reputation and prominence of their regions to the capital to attend their arrival. Ibid., 41 (Spanish 61).

103. Ibid., 45–46 (Spanish 65–66).
104. Ibid., 46 (Spanish 66).
105. Ibid., 38–39 (Spanish 59).
106. Ibid., 57 (Spanish 75).
107. Ibid., 46–47 (Spanish 66–67).
108. Ibid., 47–50 (Spanish 67–69).
109. Emilio García Gómez, "Armas, banderas, tiendas de campaña, monturas y correos en los 'annales de al-Ḥakam II' por 'Īsā Rāzī," *Al-Andalus* 32 (1967), 163–174, discusses the banners briefly and surmises that the banner named *al-Shataranj* looked like a chessboard.
110. Ibn Ḥayyān, *Muqtabis VII,* 47–50 (Spanish 67–69).
111. Ibid., 51–52 (Spanish 70).
112. See Barceló, "El califa patente," 56–62, 66–71, for a description of the participants and a mapping of their places in the *majlis* for the caliph's *'īd* receptions, as reported by al-Rāzī.
113. Ibn Ḥayyān, *Muqtabis VII,* 50–51 (Spanish 69).
114. Ibid., 52 (Spanish 70–71).
115. Ibid.
116. See Suzanne Pinckney Stetkevych, "The *Qaṣīdah* and the Poetics of Ceremony: Three *'Id* Panegyrics to the Cordoban Caliphate," in Ross Brann, ed., *Languages of Power in Islamic Spain* (Bethesda, 1997), 1–48 for her discussion of the ceremonial function of *qaṣā'id*; Stetkevych, "Abbasid Panegyric and the Poetics of Political Allegiance: Two Poems of al-Mutannabi on Kafur," in Stefan Sperl and Christopher Shackle, eds., *Qaṣīdah Poetry in Islamic Asia and Africa* (Leiden, 1996), 1:35–63; Stetkevych, "Abbasid Panegyric: The Politics and Poetics of Ceremony: Al-Mutanabbi's 'Id-poem to Sayf al-Dawlah," in J. R. Smart, ed., *Tradition and Modernity in Arabīc Language and Literature* (Surrey, 1996), 119–143.
117. Ibn Ḥayyān, *Muqtabis VII,* 54–56 (Spanish 72–74).
118. Ibid., 56–57 (Spanish 74–75).
119. Tambiah, "A Performative Approach to Ritual," 129–131.
120. Combs-Schilling discusses the story of Abraham's covenant and sacrifice as "Islam's central orienting myth" on a number of lev-

els. See, for example, *Sacred Performances,* 56–58, 223–244. The book demonstrates how the Sharifi kings of Morocco used (and still use) the ritual of the sacrifice to legitimize their rule.

121. Ibn Ḥayyān, *Muqtabis VII,* 28–31, 59–62, 81–86, 93–95, 119–123, 136–138, 155–169, 184–187, 229–233 (Spanish 51–53; 80–84, 105–109, 117–119, 152–156, 171–172, 196–206, 222–226, 271–275).
122. Stetkevych, "The *Qaṣīdah* and the Poetics of Ceremony," 21.
123. Ibn Ḥayyān, *Muqtabis VII,* 28–30 (Spanish 51–53).
124. Ibid., 59–60 (Spanish 81).
125. Ibid., 100, 131 (Spanish 128, 165).
126. There is a discrepancy in the sources here. Ibn ʿIdhārī reports that when Ghālib returned to Cordoba he brought Ḥasan ibn Qannūn and his Idrisid partisans, as well as the Idrisid shaykh Ḥannūn, with him. *Bayān,* 2:248 (French 2:410). Ibn Ḥayyān's text, based on al-Rāzī, indicates that Ḥasan ibn Qannūn's arrival preceded Ghālib's return (with Ḥannūn).
127. Ibn Ḥayyān, *Muqtabis VII,* 155 (Spanish 196).
128. Ibid., 160–161 (Spanish 201), English trans. in Stetkevych, "The *Qaṣīdah* and the Poetics of Ceremony," 8.
129. Ibn Ḥayyān, *Muqtabis VII,* 155 (Spanish 196–197).
130. Recognizing the end of Ramadan by the sight of the new moon, and not by calculation, was one of al-Ḥakam II's formal requirements for all the North African chiefs or rulers who renounced loyalty to the Fatimids and professed obedience to the Umayyad caliphate. See Ibn Ḥayyān, *Muqtabis VII,* 111–114 (Spanish 141–145).
131. Ibid., 155–156 (Spanish 196–197).
132. Ibid., 158–159 (Spanish 199–200), English trans. Stetkevych, "The *Qaṣīdah* and the Poetics of Ceremony," 6.
133. Ibid., 159–160 (Spanish 200), English trans. in Stetkevych, "The *Qaṣīdah* and the Poetics of Ceremony," 7.
134. Ibid., 156–158 (Spanish 198–199), English trans. in Stetkevych, "The *Qaṣīdah* and the Poetics of Ceremony," 5.
135. According to al-Rāzī's account, Ghālib had previously ordered the Idrisid shaykh and his companions to travel to the caliphal court and seek al-Ḥakam II's favor. They arrived in the port city of Algeciras at the same time that al-Ḥakam II called Ghālib back to the capital. The Idrisid notables, received in Algeciras by

officials sent from Cordoba with tents and furnishings, must have been kept waiting for Ghālib's escort. See Ibn Ḥayyān, *Muqtabis VII,* 176–177 (Spanish 214–215).

136. Ibid., 194–202 (Spanish 235–242).
137. Ibid., 198 (Spanish 239).
138. Ibid., 132 (Spanish 166).
139. Ibid., 199 (Spanish 240).
140. Ibid., 199–200 (Spanish 240–241).
141. Ibid., 200–202 (Spanish 241–242).
142. Ibid., 184–187 (Spanish 222–226).
143. Ibid., 184 (Spanish 223).
144. *Crónica anónima de 'Abd al-Raḥmān III,* 2 (Spanish 91).
145. See Stetkevych, "The *Qaṣīdah* and the Poetics of Ceremony," 16–18, on *a'yad.* According to Ibn 'Idhārī, al-Ḥakam II held a formal ceremony in 976 to secure the oath of loyalty (*bay'a*) for Hishām, requiring both oral and written oaths from his officials. He then had the oath taken publicly in the congregational mosques of the capital and the provinces and ordered that Hisham be named as caliphal heir-designate in the *khuṭba. Bayān,* 2:249 (French 2:412).
146. See Combs-Schilling, *Sacred Performances,* 56–62, 233–244.
147. Ibn Ḥayyān, *Muqtabis VII,* 93 (Spanish 117). On Fatimid practice see Halm, *Empire of the Mahdī,* 220, 353–354, and Sanders, *Fatimid Cairo,* 47. Evidence suggests the caliphs attended, at least on occasion, the Friday prayers at the congregational mosque of Cordoba or Madīnat al-Zahrā'. From an elevated place on the *qaṣr* of Cordoba they could also observe, and in this way participate in, prayers conducted on the *muṣallā,* as 'Abd al-Raḥmān III did on an occasion when Mundhir ibn Sa'īd al-Ballūṭī led the prayers for rain. See al-Nubāhī, *Marqaba,* 69–70.
148. Ibn Ḥayyān, *Muqtabis VII,* 220–221, 223, 233–234 (Spanish 261, 264, 275–276).
149. al-Maqqarī, *Nafḥ al-ṭīb,* 3:93. According to Muhammad Manazir Ahsan, the *qalansuwa ṭawīla,* a tall cap with a turban generally wrapped around it, became popular head wear in the Abbasid period. See Ahsan, *Social Life under the Abbasids* (London, 1979), 30.
150. On the contrasting Fatimid experience, see Sanders, *Fatimid Cairo.*

151. See Ibn Ḥayyān, *Muqtabis VII,* 151 (Spanish 192).
152. Ibid., 207–209 (Spanish 247–249). This generous act was also a way for al-Ḥakam II to express his gratitude to God; it followed his manumission of 100 slaves and establishment of a pious foundation to support the education of the poor. Ibid., 206–207 (Spanish 246–247).
153. Ibid., 211 (Spanish 251).
154. Ibid., 215 (Spanish 252).
155. Ibid.
156. Ibid., 212–213 (Spanish 252–253).
157. Ibid., 213–215 (Spanish 253–255).
158. Ibid., 213 (Spanish 254).

NOTES TO CHAPTER 3

1. For a narrative history of ʻĀmirid rule and the collapse of the caliphate and centralized rule in al-Andalus, see Lévi-Provençal, *H.E.M.,* 2:196–345; Wasserstein, *Party Kings,* 55–81; Kennedy, *Muslim Spain and Portugal,* 109–129; Joaquín Vallvé, *El califato de Córdoba* (Madrid, 1992), 227–265. For a more extended recent analysis of the politics of the period and discussion of the sources, see Peter C. Scales, *The Fall of the Caliphate of Cordoba* (Leiden, 1994). The discussion in this chapter of Muḥammad ibn Abī ʻĀmīr's manipulation of the legitimacy of the Umayyad caliphate relies primarily on evidence found in Ibn ʻIdhārī's *Bayān,* which is largely based on Ibn Ḥayyān's history of Amirid rule, no longer extant. Cristina de la Puente discusses the sources for a study of al-Manṣūr and argues that they all derive from Ibn Ḥayyān. Thus much of the material Ibn ʻIdhārī presents can be found verbatim in other geographical and historical texts, such as al-Ḥimyarī, *La péninsule Ibérique au moyen-age d'après le Kitāb al-Rawḍ al-miʻṭār fi ḥabar al-aqṭār,* Arabic ed. and French trans. E. Lévi-Provençal (Leiden, 1938), and al-Maqqarī's *Nafḥ al-ṭīb.* See Cristina De la Puente, "La caracterización de Almanzor: entre la epopeya y la historia," *Estudios onomastico-biograficos de al-Andalus* 8 (1997), 369–374.
2. One of ʻAbd al-Raḥmān III's grandsons. The translation is from Ibn Saʻīd al-Maghribī, *The Banners of the Champions,* trans.

James A. Bellamy and Patricia Owen Steiner (Madison, 1989), 136.

3. Ibn ʻIdhārī, *Bayān,* 2:249, 254 (French 2:412, 419–420). For discussion of the *bay'a,* see María Luisa Ávila Navarro, "La proclamación (*Bay'a*) de Hišam II. Año 976 d.C.," *al-Qantara* 1 (1980), 79–114.
4. Ibn ʻIdhārī, *Bayān,* 2:276–277, 278 (French 2:459–460, 462).
5. Ibid., 2:272 (French 452). See also Ibn Khaldūn, *The Muqaddimah,* trans. Franz Rosenthal (1958; London, 1986), 1:378.
6. Ibn ʻIdhārī, *Bayān,* 2:275–277 (French 2:457–462).
7. Ibid., 2:251–252 (French 2:415–416).
8. Ibid., 2:257–258 (French 2:429–430).
9. Ibn Ḥayyān, cited by al-Maqqarī, *Nafḥ al-ṭīb,* 1:398, reports that Ibn Abī ʻĀmir undertook fifty-six campaigns against the Christians and never met with defeat. Ibn Sa'īd reports fifty-two (ibid., 1:402).
10. Ibn ʻIdhārī, *Bayān* 2:264 (French 2:439).
11. Ibid., 2:265–266 (French 2:440–441).
12. Ibid., 2:267 (French 2:443).
13. Ibid., 2:275–277 (French 2:457–462). On the Great Mosque of al-Zāhira as a subject of controversy among some of the *fuqahā',* see Avila Navarro, "La Proclamación de Hišam II," 107–109.
14. Ibn ʻIdhārī, *Bayān,* 2:275–277 (French 2:457–462).
15. Ibid., 2:278 (French 2:462).
16. Ibid., 2:279 (French 2:465). Pierre Guichard points out that Ibn Abī ʻĀmir assumed a *laqab* styled after those of the caliphs but stopped short of using the name of God as part of his honorific name. All the available numismatic, epigraphic, and textual evidence suggests he was "al-Manṣūr" and not "al-Manṣūr Billāh" (in contrast to "al-Nāṣir li-Dīn Allāh" and "al-Mustanṣir Billāh"). See Pierre Guichard, "*Al-Manṣūr* ou *al-Manṣūr bi-Llāh*? Les *laqab*s des Amirids d'après la numismatique et les documents officiels," *Archeologie islamique* 5 (1995), 47–53.
17. Ibn Khaldūn, cited by al-Maqqarī, *Nafḥ al-ṭīb,* 1:397–398.
18. Ibn ʻIdhārī, *Bayān,* 2:279–280 (French 2:465).
19. Ibid., 2:293 (French 2:489).
20. Ibid., 2:294 (French 2:491).

21. Ibid., 2:277 (French 2:461).
22. Ibid., 2:267 (French 2:444).
23. Hillenbrand, "Córdoba as Cultural Centre," 133, suggests that al-Manṣūr may have wanted to "outflank" al-Ḥakam II's *miḥrāb* and "set his own personal seal on this continually evolving monument, the symbol *par excellence* of Muslim al-Andalus."
24. Ibn 'Idhārī, *Bayān,* 2:286–288 (French 2:477–481).
25. Ibid., 2:292 (French 2:487).
26. Ibn 'Idhārī, *Bayān* 2:257 (French 2:426–427), describes al-Manṣūr's education and notes his learning approached that of al-Ḥakam II.
27. Ibid., 2:280 (French 2:465).
28. Ibid., 2:293 (French 2:488).
29. Ibid., 2:293 (French 2:488), verses attributed to 'Abd al-'Azīz al-Khaṭīb.
30. The translator of the French edition of Ibn 'Idhārī's *Bayān,* E. Fagnan, doubts the veracity of the report on the basis of what he sees as a false attribution of the verses (2:488 n. 6). It is worth considering the possibility that al-Manṣūr's panegyrist consciously recited Ibn Hāni's verses or that the historian who inserted them into the record intended to criticize al-Manṣūr's pretensions.
31. Ibid., 2:281 (French 2:467–468).
32. Ibid., 2:281–282 (French 2:468).
33. Ibid., 2:281 (French 2:468).
34. De la Puente observes that the historiographical idealization of al-Manṣūr grew over time. See her discussion of al-Manṣūr's representation in Andalusi texts, "Caracterización de Almanzor,"382–401.
35. Ibn Khaldūn, *Muqaddimah,* 1:380.
36. The text of the document(s) of nomination, as recorded by Ibn Ḥayyān, is preserved in a number of sources, including the third volume of Ibn 'Idhārī's history, *Kitāb al-Bayān al-Mughrib, tome troisième. Histoire de l'Espagne Musulmane au XIe siècle (Bayān III),* ed. E. Lévi-Provençal (Paris, 1930), 44–46; for English translations and analysis, see Scales, *Fall of the Caliphate,* 43–52, and Wasserstein, *Caliphate in the West,* 19–27.
37. This is the subject of Wasserstein, *Caliphate in the West,* and Clément, *Pouvoir et légitimité.*

NOTES TO INTRODUCTION, PART TWO: HISTORIOGRAPHY

1. See Anwar Chejne, *Muslim Spain: Its History and Culture* (St. Paul, 1974). See also Hillenbrand, "Córdoba as a Cultural Centre," Pierre Cachia, "Andalusi Belles Lettres," Salma Khadra Jayyusi, "Andalusi Poetry: The Golden Period," and other contributions in al-Jayyusi, *Legacy of Muslim Spain.*
2. Hillenbrand, "Córdoba as Cultural Centre," 120–123. Hillenbrand notes that al-Manṣūr purged the library in his effort to forge ties with the *'ulamā'*.
3. Abū 'Ali al-Qālī, famous philologist from Baghdad, was invited to move to the Andalusi court in 941 and there had a significant impact on high culture. 'Arīb ibn Sa'īd, who served as 'Abd al-Raḥmān III's governor in Osuna and then as secretary to the heir-presumptive, al-Ḥakam II, added the history of al-Andalus and North Africa to his summary and extension of al-Ṭabarī's *History of the Prophets and Kings.* See *La crónica de 'Arīb,* ed. Castilla Brazales, for an introduction to 'Arīb and his work and a Spanish translation of the extant portion of this text (903–932) that is devoted to al-Andalus. M. J. de Goeje provides an Arabic edition and Latin translation of the section devoted to the history of the Abbasids in *Ṣilat ta'rīkh al-Ṭabarī* (Tabari Continuatus) (Leiden, 1897).
4. Reinhardt Dozy bemoaned the fact that all Andalusī historians of the tenth century were clients and partisans of the Umayyad family. See his introduction to Ibn 'Idhārī's *al-Bayān al-mughrib (Al-Bayāno'l-Mogrib),* ed. R. Dozy (Leiden, 1848–1851), 16–27.
5. Acién Almansa, *Entre el feudalism y el Islam,* discusses how the Arabic accounts of 'Umar ibn Ḥafṣūn's revolt are ideologically colored, particularly in their treatment of his character and motivations. He is particularly concerned to go beyond the texts' schematic application of ethnic identities in certain contexts.
6. See Ibn Ḥayyān's volume on the history of the amir 'Abd Allāh's reign (especially where he cites 'Īsā al-Rāzī and Ibn al-Qūṭiyya). Ibn Ḥayyān, *Muqtabis III,* 9, 50, 52–53, 82–83, 89, 93, 104, 107–108, 128, 139–140.
7. Ibid., 9.
8. Ibn al-Qūṭiyya as cited by Ibn Ḥayyān, *Muqtabis III,* 129.

9. Ibn al-Qūṭiyya, *Ta'rīkh iftitāḥ al-Andalus* (*Historia de la conquista de España de Abenalcotia el Cordobés*), ed. and trans. Julián Ribera (Madrid, 1926), 90–94 (Spanish 76–79). See María Isabel Fierro, "La obra histórica de Ibn al-Qūṭiyya," *al-Qantara* 10 (1989), 485–512, for discussion of the composition, sources, and features of the text.
10. Ibn al-Qūṭiyya, *Tarīkh iftitah al-Andalus,* 90–94 (Spanish 76–79).
11. Fierro, "Cuatro preguntas en torno a Ibn Ḥafṣūn," 250–252, suggests that Ibn Ḥafṣūn became the focus of messianic expectations. She also notices a parallel between the story of Ibn Ḥafṣūn's stay in Tahart and the prediction of his rule and a story about 'Abd al-Raḥmān I, founder of Umayyad rule in al-Andalus (253–254). We discuss this story in Chapter 4.

NOTES TO CHAPTER 4

1. *Akhbār majmū'a fī fath al-Andalus* (*Ajbar machmua*), ed. and Spanish trans. Emilio Lafuente y Alcantara (Madrid, 1867); Ibn al-Qūṭiyya, *Ta'rīkh iftitāḥ al-Andalus* (*Historia de la conquista de España de Abenalcotia el Cordobés*), ed. and Spanish trans. Julián Ribera (Madrid, 1926).
2. The authorship and date of the composition of *Akhbār majmū'a* are not known and remain a matter of some dispute. The form and quality of the text as a whole, and the fact that it ends with a brief account of 'Abd al-Raḥmān III's reign, suggest it is contemporary with Ibn al-Qūṭiyya's (d. 977) history. These two texts are distinctly different from extant histories dating to either the ninth or the eleventh century. Martínez-Gros, *L'idéologie omeyyade,* 52, shares this assessment, and he and Pedro Chalmeta, *Invasión e islamización: la sumisión de Hispania y la formación de al-Andalus* (Madrid, 1994), 50, consider *Akhbār majmū'a* a tenth-century work. Luis Molina, however, compares the dynastic history presented in *Akhbār majmū'a* with later texts and argues that our anonymous text was composed after Ibn Ḥayyān's *Muqtabis.* While he establishes clear connections among the texts he compares, it is difficult to establish a chronological relationship when *Akhbār majmū'a* does not cite its sources and we do not know all the sources in circulation in a given period. See Luis Molina, "Los

Ajbar maŷmū'a y la historiografía árabe sobre el periodo omeya en al-Andalus," *al-Qantara* 10 (1989), 513–542.

3. *Akhbār majmū'a* and Ibn al-Qūṭiyya present coherent narratives of the conquest of al-Andalus and the foundation of the amirate, in contrast to the treatment by later historians such as Ibn 'Idhārī or al-Maqqarī, who present multiple versions of events and legends culled from earlier sources, acknowledge that their accounts are contradictory, and question the veracity of some of the reports they reproduce.
4. *Akhbār majmū'a,* 3 (Spanish 17).
5. *Akhbār majmū'a,* 2–3 (Spanish 15–17).
6. For a survey of opinions about Julian's identity, see Julia Hernández Juberīas, *La península imaginaria, Mitos y leyendas sobre al-Andalus* (Madrid, 1996), 184–194.
7. *Akhbār majmū'a,* 4–6 (Spanish 18–20).
8. Ibid., 5–9 (Spanish 19–22).
9. Ibid., 9–15 (Spanish 23–28).
10. Ibid., 15–20 (Spanish 28–31).
11. Ibid., 29–30 (Spanish 41–42).
12. Albrecht Noth demonstrates how histories of the period of the *rashīdūn* caliphs and the early conquests employed literary forms, topoi, and schema in part to convey the idea "that in the early Islamic state everything took place on the orders of the central authority of the 'caliphal court'. " Noth, *The Early Arabīc Historical Tradition,* 2nd ed., with Lawrence I. Conrad, trans. from German by Michael Bonner (Princeton, 1994), 81 and all. We can recognize the same interest here.
13. *Akhbār majmū'a,* 22 (Spanish 33).
14. Ibid., 22–24 (Spanish 33–35).
15. Ibid., 23 (Spanish 34).
16. Ibid., 24–28 (Spanish 35–39).
17. Ibid., 28–45 (Spanish 39–54).
18. Ibid., 45–46 (Spanish 54).
19. During this period, the text relates, the Galicians recovered some of their lost territory in the north. The Muslims of the region either converted back to Christianity, fled, or were killed. At the same time, famine spread through the region, causing the population to seek sustenance in North Africa. *Akhbār majmū'a,* 62 (Spanish 66–67).

20. Ibid., 59 (Spanish 64).
21. Ibid., 117–118 (Spanish 106–107).
22. Ibid.
23. Ibid., 46–50 (Spanish 55–58).
24. Ibid., 46–47 (Spanish 55).
25. See Sabatino Moscati, "Le massacre des Umayyades," *Archiv Orientalni* 18 (1950), 88–115, for brief descriptions of the Abbasid massacres of the Umayyads as found in a variety of historical and verse sources.
26. *Akhbār majmū'a*, 48–49 (Spanish 57). The story of the banquet turned bloodbath is a topos found in numerous historical narratives,used to suggest the ruthlessness of the host and sometimes, as here, his treachery. See Eduardo Manzano-Moreno, "Oriental 'Topoi' in Andalusian Sources," *Arabica* 39 (1992), 49–56, for discussion of another such tale in Andalusi historiography.
27. Ibid., 48 (Spanish 56–57).
28. Ibid., 50 (Spanish 58).
29. Ibid., 51–52 (Spanish 59). Al-Maqqarī, *Nafḥ al-tīb,* 1:62–63, records another version of this account. The first Umayyad amir recollects that he had in mind his uncle's prediction that he would "one day revive the dynasty after its fall" when he arrived in al-Andalus.
30. *Akhbār majmū'a,* 52–54 (Spanish 59–61).
31. *Akhbār majmū'a,* 54–55 (Spanish 61–62). According to the account, Ibn Ḥabīb later produced false testimony against two sons of the caliph al-Walīd ibn Yazīd and killed them, appropriating their riches. He similarly turned against other members of the Umayyad family who had sought refuge in his province, and it became clear, in spite of the anecdote above, that he meant to betray 'Abd al-Raḥmān I as well, so 'Abd al-Raḥmān and his family took shelter with the Nafza Berbers, his mother's kin.
32. Ibid., 63–64 (Spanish 67–68).
33. Ibid., 67 (Spanish 70).
34. Ibid., 119 (Spanish 108). Although 'Abd al-Raḥmān's domination over the civil war established him as ruler of al-Andalus, in fact, the rest of the account of his life and reign is largely a record of a long series of rebellions against his authority and his successful suppression of them.

35. ‘Abd al-Raḥmān’s foundation of a new epoch of Umayyad rule in al-Andalus is represented in the development of a new symbol—a banner—which is then carefully preserved by subsequent rulers until it eventually disintegrates. *Akhbār majmū‘a,* 84–85 (Spanish 82–83).
36. *Akhbār majmū‘a,* 118–119 (Spanish 107–108). Contemporary eastern sources generally do not paint the Umayyads in such a favorable light. Al-Mas‘ūdī, for example, relates another anecdote in which al-Manṣūr discusses the Umayyads with his associates and declares: “Abd al-Malik was an arrogant tyrant who did not care what he did. Sulaimān’s only ambition lay in his belly and his balls. Umar ibn Abd al-Azīz was like a one-eyed man among the blind. The only great man of the dynasty was Hishām.” Al-Mas‘ūdī, *Les prairies d’or,* Arabic ed. and French trans., C. Barbier de Meynard and Pavet de Courteille (Paris, 1861–1877), 6:161–165, English translation al-Mas‘ūdī, *The Meadows of Gold,* ed. and trans. Paul Lunde and Caroline Stone (London, 1989), 24.
37. Julius Wellhausen compares the situation that ‘Abd al-Malik faced to Mu‘āwiya’s situation after the murder of ‘Uthmān. In both cases, “Syria alone stood opposed to the whole rest of the Islamic world.” J. Wellhausen, *The Arab Kingdom and Its Fall,* trans. Margaret Graham Weir (Beirut, 1963), 184. ‘Abd al-Raḥmān’s situation is represented as comparable in this anecdote, but the text makes clear that the seat of Umayyad power has shifted to al-Andalus.
38. The representation of ‘Abd al-Raḥmān I can be seen in many instances as colored by, or a projection backward of, ‘Abd al-Raḥmān III’s attributes and ambitions. As al-Maqqarī, *Nafḥ al-ṭīb,* 1:333, describes, ‘Abd al-Raḥmān I overcame challengers to his rule in al-Andalus, raided the Christian territories, and intended to renew the *dawla* of the Banū Marwān in the Mashriq but died without doing so.
39. Martínez-Gros notes this relationship between the representation of ‘Abd al-Raḥmān I and the caliphate of ‘Abd al-Raḥmān III and argues that the idea of exile and return was a kind of metatheme in Andalusi texts that was repeatedly signified in a number of ways. He observes that this theme recalled the story of the Prophet’s exile from Mecca and triumphant return and also had suggestive parallels in the Shi‘i idea of the hidden imam and his expected return.

See the introduction to Martínez-Gros, *L'idéologie omeyyade*, 17–24.

40. Ibn al-Qūṭiyya, *Ta'rīkh iftitāḥ al-Andalus*, 26–27 (Spanish 20). Marj Rāhiṭ was a touchstone in Umayyad historiography. References recur in poetry and historical texts as in Muḥammad ibn Shukhayṣ's verses comparing al-Ḥakam II to Marwān on the day of the battle of Marj Rāhiṭ or Ibn 'Idhārī's comparison of the *ḥājib* al-Manṣūr to that celebrated caliph on the same fateful battle day (Ibn Ḥayyān, *Muqtabis VII*, 55; and Ibn 'Idhārī, *Bayān*, 2:298).
41. See Francisco Pons Boigues, *Los historiadores y geógrafos Arabīgo-españoles* (1898; Amsterdam, 1972), 83–88.
42. The bonds between the two families were still close during 'Abd al-Raḥmān III's reign. Ibn Ḥayyān, *Muqtabis V*, 69–81, describes Ibn al-Qūṭiyya's father's involvement in the negotiations between 'Abd al-Raḥmān III and the town of Seville and his responsibility for securing a peaceful settlement between them. Ibn al-Qūṭiyya served in the Umayyad court, notably under al-Ḥakam II, and was renowned for his mastery of Arabic and lexicography.
43. Ribera argues that the sole manuscript of the chronicle was actually compiled from notes by one of Ibn al-Qūṭiyya's students, perhaps either his son 'Umar Abū Ḥafṣ or a nephew, 'Abd al-Malik, but insists that the text is essentially Ibn al-Qūṭiyya's. Ibn al-Qūṭiyya, *Ta'rīkh iftitāḥ al-Andalus*, xx–xxii. See Fierro, "Obra de Ibn al-Qūtiyya," 486–494, for further discussion.
44. Ibn al-Qūṭiyya, *Ta'rīkh iftitāḥ al-Andalus*, 3 (Spanish 1–2).
45. Ibid., 3–4 (Spanish 2–3).
46. Ibid., 8 (Spanish 6).
47. Ibid., 11 (Spanish 8).
48. Introduction to Ibn al-Qūtiyya, *Ta'rīkh iftitāḥ al-Andalus*, xxiii.
49. A range of legends about Witiza, Roderick, and Julian exist in Arabic, Latin, and European language sources from the ninth to the twentieth centuries. Some of the early Latin sources attribute the fall of the Visigoth kingdom to Witiza's moral corruption rather than to Roderick's. For descriptions and discussions of the early sources, see Reinhardt Dozy, *Recherches sur l'histoire et la littérature de l'Espagne pendant le moyen age* (Leiden, 1860), 1: 5–23; Juan Menéndez-Pidal, *Leyendas del último godo* (Madrid, 1906); Ramon Menéndez-Pidal, *Floresta de leyendas heróicas españolas* (Madrid, 1925), vol. 1; Menéndez-Pidal, *El rey Rodrigo*

en la literatura (Madrid, 1925); and more recently, Hernández Juberías, *Peninsula imaginaria,* 171–181.

50. Ibn al-Qūṭiyya, *Ta'rīkh iftitah al-Andalus,* 7 (Spanish 5). A version of this story can be found in numerous Arabic texts dating from as early as the ninth century. See Hernández Juberías, *Península imaginaria,* 194–208, for a discussion of the story's possible origins, differences among the Arabic versions, and the story's diffusion into the historiography of the Christian kingdoms.
51. Ibn al-Qūṭiyya's later description of 'Abd al-Raḥmān I's respect for Yūsuf al-Fihri's wife and daughters contrasts noticeably with the behavior of this illegitimate king. Ibn al-Qūṭiyya, *Ta'rīkh iftitah al-Andalus,* 28 (Spanish 22).
52. Ibid., 8 (Spanish 5–6).
53. Ibid., 5–6 (Spanish 3–4).
54. Ibid., 36–37 (Spanish 28–29).
55. 'Abd al-Raḥmān I here becomes associated with traditions of Visigoth legitimacy through his ties with Witiza's family. In contrast, *Akhbār majmū'a* represents 'Abd al-Raḥmān as someone who supplanted Visigoth rule. Through the successive use of the metaphor of the mount as throne—'Abd al-Raḥmān I was placed on Maslama's mount, King Roderick was felled from his jewel-bedecked mount—we understand that 'Abd al-Raḥmān ascended the mount (throne) Roderick left vacant with his mysterious disappearance. See *Akhbār majmū'a,* 9, 51, 119 (Spanish 22, 59, 108).
56. *Akhbār majmū'a,* 101–103 (Spanish 95–97).
57. Ibn al-Qūṭiyya, *Ta'rīkh iftitah al-Andalus,* 32–35 (Spanish 25–26).
58. Ibid., 15 (Spanish 11). The last Umayyad caliph, Marwān, was defeated on the banks of the Great Zab in Mesopotamia on the eleventh of Jumāda, 132 H. (January 25, 749). The boundary between Abbasid and Umayyad territory, although perhaps nominally fixed, actually fluctuated.
59. *Akhbār majmū'a,* 165 (Spanish 142).
60. Other sources suggest a less smooth transition. Ibn 'Idhārī, for example, mentions that some controversy prevailed over whether the authority of the Umayyad dynasty was temporarily interrupted by the Abbasid revolution and reconstituted by 'Abd al-Raḥmān I or whether the Umayyads reigned continuously from the caliphate of 'Uthmān until 1032 (*Bayān* 2:39 [French 2:58]). He and other

sources, such as al-Maqqarī, even report that 'Abd al-Raḥmān I had the Abbasid caliph al-Manṣūr's name invoked in the *khuṭba* for some time before he decided to forbid it and ushered in the long period in al-Andalus when the title of Commander of the Faithful was not mentioned from the minbars. Iibid., 2:48 (French 75); *Nafḥ al-ṭīb,* 1:329.

NOTES TO CHAPTER 5

1. 'Abd al-Malik, Ibn Ḥabīb, *Kitāb al-Ta'rikh* (*Kitāb al-Tarīj*), ed. Jorge Aguadé (Madrid, 1991). Hamilton A. R. Gibb, "Tarikh," in his *Studies on the Civilization of Islam* (Princeton, 1982), 115–116, tells us that the earliest written redactions of literary works date from the early ninth century, following the introduction of paper production in Baghdad. He also describes universal histories as characteristic of the earliest stage of the development of historical narrative.
2. Ibid., 115. See also Tarif Khalidi, *Arabic Historical Thought in the Classical Period* (Cambridge, 1994), chap. 2, especially 65–67.
3. See Aguadé's introduction to Ibn Ḥabīb's *Kitāb al-Ta'rikh* for a description and synthesis of all the biographical literature on Ibn Ḥabīb.
4. Ibn Ḥabīb, *Kitāb al-Ta'rikh,* report no. 39.
5. The chapter dealing with the duration of the universe is entitled "The number [of years] between the Torah and the Psalms and the Gospels, and between the Gospels and the Qu'ran" (73–74). Ibn Ḥabīb recounts that the consensus among the *ahl al-ḥadīth* is that the world will endure seven thousand years. but that they differ over how many years are left. He here calculates that two hundred years remain, but elsewhere he describes the apocalypse as imminent. The chapter on the evaluation of one's fate on Judgment Day is entitled "How God will evaluate the people on the day of the Resurrection and reward or punish good and evil" (125–126).
6. Mahmud Makki notes that, according to Ibn al-Faraḍī, the first Andalusi text devoted to "successors" who went to al-Andalus was written by Ibn Ḥabīb and entitled *Ṭabaqāt al-fuqahā' wa-l-tābi'īn.* See Mahmud Makki, "Egipto y los orígenes de la historiografía

Arabigo-española," Revista del Instituto de Estudios Islamicos enMadrid 5 (1957), 164. Ibn Ḥabīb's account of the conquest contrasts with those of Ibn al-Qūṭiyya and *Akhbār majmūʿa* in its representation of Mūsā as the central hero. The conquest history of (Pseudo) Ibn Qutayba, presented in Julián Ribera's edition of Ibn al-Qūṭiyya's conquest history, *Taʿ rīkh iftitāḥ al-Andalus,* however, shares Ibn Ḥabīb's perspective and many of the same reports. See Makki, "Egipto y los orígenes de la historiografía Arabigo-española," for a discussion of the authorship of that account.

7. Ibn Ḥabīb, *Kitāb al-Ta'rikh,* report no. 397. The Egyptian hadīth scholar and contemporary of Ibn Ḥabīb, Ibn ʿAbd al-Ḥakam (d. 870 or 871), wrote a history of the conquests of Egypt, North Africa, and Spain. His account of the conquest of al-Andalus highlights the moral challenges posed by the conquest of a rich land and shares some anecdotal reports on this theme with Ibn Ḥabīb's text. See Ibn ʿAbd al-Ḥakam, *The History of the Conquest of Egypt, North Africa, and Spain, Known as the Futūh Miṣr of Ibn Abd al-Ḥakam,* ed. Charles C. Torrey (New Haven, 1922).
8. For example, Alexander is confronted with a shaykh's devotion to one who is greater than he, and Solomon begs God's forgiveness in a story based on sura 38, Ibn Ḥabīb, *Kitāb al-Ta'rikh,* nos. 166 and 180.
9. The person who delivers this message is one of the *ahl al-rāfiḍiyya.* Ibn Ḥabīb, *Kitāb al-Ta'rikh,* no. 388.
10. Ibid., no. 389.
11. Ibn Ḥabīb may have witnessed the "revolt of the suburbs" of Cordoba during the reign of al-Ḥakam I and perhaps witnessed the crisis of the Cordoban martyrs. See Aguade's introduction to Ibn Ḥabīb, *Kitāb al-Ta'rikh.*
12. Ibn Ḥabīb, *Ta'rikh,* no. 59.
13. Ibid., no. 422. Two hundred years from the conquest of Cordoba would put its destruction some fifty years after Ibn Ḥabīb's death.
14. Ibid., no. 403. See Hernández Juberías, *Peninsula imaginaria,* 195–208, for discussion of possible Egyptian origins for this story and its elaboration in later texts.
15. Ibn Ḥabīb, *Kitāb al-Ta'rikh,* no. 442. The description of ʿAbd Allāh's rule and the prediction about the Berbers are later interpolations, as Ibn Ḥabīb died before ʿAbd Allāh came to the throne

(r. 888–912). The prediction seems to anticipate the destruction of Cordoba by the Berbers in the early eleventh century but may possibly reflect anxiety about the revolt of 'Umar ibn Ḥafṣūn, which extended over most of al-Andalus during the reign of the amir 'Abd Allāh.

16. Ibid., nos. 447–449, 456–457, 460, 465–467.
17. Hadīth collections include a large corpus of reports describing the signs of the Final Hour, including *fitan* (political upheavals) and *malāḥim* (massacres), which were in circulation at the time. Aguadé compares Ibn Ḥabīb's predictions to the eschatological treatise of his contemporary, Nu'aym ibn Ḥammād (d. 842–843), based on such hadiths (*Kitāb al-fitan wa-l-malāḥim*). He also points out that predictions about the destruction of cities were not rare in the east. Al-Khaṭīb al-Baghdādī's history of Baghdad includes a chapter on predictions of the city's demise. See Aguadé's introduction to Ibn Ḥabīb, *Kitāb al-Ta'rikh,* 88–100. For a discussion of common themes in Jewish, Christian, and Muslim apocalyptic traditions, see Armand Abel, "Changements politiques et littérature eschatologique dans le monde musulman," *Studia Islamica* 2 (1954), 23–43; see also G. Van Vloten, *Recherches sur la domination arabe, le Chiitisme et les croyances messianiques sous le khalifat des Omayades* (Amsterdam, 1894) 54–70.
18. Ibid., no. 450.
19. Ibid., nos. 415, 419–420.
20. Ibid., no. 416.
21. Ibid., no. 420.
22. Ibid., nos. 418–419. Hernández Juberías, *Península imaginaria,* 33 ff., demonstrates how the legend of the "city of copper" and the legend of Solomon's jinn became more clearly linked in later literary narratives.
23. Ibn Ḥabīb, *Kitāb al-Ta'rikh,* nos. 415, 418–419. Hernández Juberías also discusses the "city of copper" as one of the markers, along with idols, rivers, mountains, and the ocean, of the boundary between the known and unknown worlds. She suggests that Islamic stories of travel to the unknown world had origins in the classical legends of Alexander the Great (generally identified as Dhū al-Qarnayn in Islamic tradition), but the protagonists changed to include Moses and the prophet Khidr. Sura 18 of the

Qur'an presents a notable example, describing a journey Moses took to the mysterious "land where the two seas meet." It seems likely Ibn Ḥabīb used this Qur'anic story as the basis of his account of Mūsā ibn Nuṣayr's conquest, reinforcing the historical event's cosmological significance.

24. Dozy, *L'Espagne pendant le moyen age,* 1:26–27.
25. See José Alemany-Bolufer, *La geografía de la península ibérica en los escritores árabes* (Madrid, 1921), 5, 13–14. Ibn Khurdadhbeh and Ibn Rusta tell the story of the "house of kings" in Toledo, the "house of locks," and how Roderick forced the latter open, bringing about the Muslim conquest (Ibn Ḥabīb, no. 403). Al-Hamadhānī describes Mūsā's attack against a copper city.
26. Ibn Ḥayyān, *Muqtabis V,* 56 (Spanish 53).
27. al-Maqqarī, *Nafḥ al-ṭīb,* 1:158.
28. The historians writing from the tenth century onward were interested in, and reported on, the ancient ruins found in al-Andalus, classifying what once was rendered as alien and even terrifying.
29. Hernández Juberías, *Península imaginaria,* 23–68; Alemany-Bolufer, *La geografía de la península ibérica,* 13.
30. Alemany-Bolufer, *La geografía de la península ibérica,* chap. 1.
31. Accounts of the strange wonders (*'ajā'ib*) of al-Andalus continued to be of interest for later writers who recounted these popular legends. In the later context, however, they stand out as anomalous, differing from the rest of the landscape described or represented.
32. Ibn Ḥabīb, *Kitāb al-Ta'rikh,* nos. 421, 409. Mūsā's men complained that he was leading them to the ends of the earth and asked him why he was not yet satisfied with his conquests. Mūsā remarked that had it not been for their impatience, he would have gone on to conquer Constantinople. The conquest of Constantinople, which eluded the Muslims for centuries, became a theme in eschatological hadiths. For example, see Ibn Kathīr, *Kitāb al-Nihāya,* ed. T. M. al-Zayni (Cairo, 1969), 2:53–58, 61–63.
33. Gibb, "Tarikh," 118–119.
34. The biographical dictionaries of local scholars and prominent men in this period were generally written by *'ulamā* or religious scholars. Two such dictionaries extant from the Umayyad period are: al-Khushanī's (d. 971) history of the judges of Cordoba, *Kitāb al-Quḍāt bi Qurtuba* (*Historia de los jueces de Cordoba por al-*

Joxani), ed. and trans. Julian Ribera (Madrid, 1914), and Ibn al-Faraḍī's (d. 1013) history of the *'ulamā* of al-Andalus, *Ta'rikh 'ulamā al-Andalus,* ed. F. Codera, 2 vols. (Madrid, 1890).

35. Thomas F. Glick discusses how a strange landscape is made culturally and historically intelligible (the process of "solving the landscape") in *From Muslim Fortress to Christian Castle* (Manchester, 1995), 49.
36. Ibn al-Qūṭiyya, *Ta'rīkh iftitāḥ al-Andalus* 9–10 (Spanish 6–7).
37. *Akhbār majmū'a fī fath al-Andulus* (Ajbar machmua), ed. and trans. Emilio Lafuente y Alcantara (Madrid, 1867), 6–9 (Spanish 20–23). The familiar identification of Gibraltar as *jabal Ṭāriq* (Ṭāriq's promontory) is made in numerous accounts but not in these two texts.
38. Ibid., 14–15 (Spanish 27–28).
39. Ibid., 15–19 (Spanish 28–31).
40. Ibid., 28 (Spanish 38–39). The Berber revolt and civil war that ensued gave the Christians of Galicia the opportunity to push the Muslims out of the region in the middle of the eighth century. Ibid., 61–62 (Spanish 67).
41. Ibid., 23–24 (Spanish 34).
42. Many of the accounts of the conquests of particular cities recorded in *Akhbār majmū'a* appear in Ibn 'Idhārī's *Bayān,* as reports attributed to al-Rāzī.
43. Ibid., 10 (Spanish 23).
44. Ibid., 16 (Spanish 28–29).
45. Ibid., 16 (Seville), 10–12 (Cordoba), 15–16 (Carmona) (Spanish 29, 23–25, 28).
46. Ibid., 12–13 (Tudmir), 16–18 (Merida) (Spanish 26, 29–30).
47. Many motifs in accounts of conquests of cities appear interchangeable in early historical writing, as Noth points out in *Early Arabic Historical Tradition,* 167–168. The accounts of the conquests of Andalusi cities discussed here are similarly contrived. Perhaps this mode of representation was meant to convey the idea that the conquests were predictable (given the Muslims' divine support) and conformed to a universal experience.
48. *Akhbār majmū'a* 9–10 (Spanish 23–24).
49. Ibid., 11–12 (Spanish 24–25).
50. Ibid., 13–14 (Spanish 26–27).

51. Ibid., 14 (Spanish 27). The Muslim conquerors typically charged the Jewish populations of the conquered cities with their defense and administration because they could ill-afford to leave much of a garrison behind as they proceeded with their conquests. See also ibid., 12, 16 (Spanish 25, 29).
52. Ibid., 21 (Spanish 32–33).
53. Mūsā and Mughīth's rivalry gets played out later (although the anecdote precedes this one in the text) when the three commanders—Ṭāriq, Mūsā, and Mughīth—depart for Damascus. According to the story, Mughīth intended to bring his royal captive with him to present to the caliph, but Musa ordered him to turn the prisoner over to him. Rather than surrender his trophy to Mūsā, Mughīth (who was a personal client of the caliph) executed him. *Akhbār majmū'a,* 19–20 (Spanish 31).
54. When 'Abd al-Raḥmān I set out to establish his authority in al-Andalus through force of arms, his supporters remarked that he did not have a banner to identify his forces and created one for him out of a turban and a lance. This banner acquired a certain prestige: succeeding amirs took it, or its remnants, to battle until it disintegrated entirely. *Akhbār majmū'a,* 84–85 (Spanish 82–83); Ibn al-Qūṭiyya, *Ta'rīkh iftitāḥ al-Andalus,* 26 (Spanish 20).
55. See *Akhbār majmū'a,* 138–139 (Spanish 122), for an account of 'Abd al-Raḥmān II's suppression of Merida's revolt.
56. Ibid., 16 (Spanish 29).
57. Ibid., 16–17 (Spanish 29).
58. Ibid., 17 (Spanish 29).
59. Ibid., 17–18 (Spanish 29–30).
60. Ibid., 18 (Spanish 30).
61. Ibn al-Qūṭiyya, *Ta'rīkh iftitāḥ al-Andalus,* 9 (Spanish 6).
62. For example, see ibid., 12, 21, 24–25, 27–28 (Spanish 9, 16–17, 19–21).
63. Ibid., 25–26, 28 (Spanish 19–21).
64. *Akhbār majmū'a, 67–96* (Spanish 70–91).
65. Ibid., 82–83 (Spanish 81).
66. Ibid., 73 (Spanish 74).
67. Ibid., 117 (Spanish 106–107).
68. Ibn Ḥayyān, *Muqtabis V,* 56.
69. Isḥāq ibn Maslama may be Isḥāq ibn Salāma al-Laythī, who wrote a history of al-Andalus for al-Ḥakam II. The description of Toledo

is by Sa'īd ibn Sa'īd (d. 1070), who served as *qāḍī* of the city and wrote a history of al-Andalus as well. See Pons Boigues, *Historiadores,* 82, 100, 139–140.

70. Ibn Ḥayyān, *Muqtabis V,* 280 (Spanish 212).
71. Ibid., 319 (Spanish 239–240).
72. Ibid, 272–273 (Spanish 206). The Spanish translation renders *Barbāṭ* as *Viriato.* Viriathus became leader of the Lusitanian revolt, annihilated the Roman forces arrayed against them, and killed the praetor c. 152 to 140 B.C.E. See J. S. Richardson, *The Romans in Spain* (Oxford, 1996), 64–66.
73. Ibn Ḥayyān, *Muqtabis V,* 273 (Spanish 206–207).
74. Ibid., 273–274 (Spanish 207).
75. Ibid., 274 (Spanish 207).
76. Ibid., 274–275 (Spanish 208). The English names of the Visigoth rulers and the following dates of their reigns come from Roger Collins, *Early Medieval Spain* (1983; reprint London, 1988), 300. Suinthila ruled 621 to 631, Sisenand 631 to 636, Chintila 636 to 639, Wamba 672 to 680, Ervig 680 to 687, Witiza 698 to 710, Roderick 710 to 711. Note that Ibn Maslama omits the reigns of several kings.
77. Ibn Ḥayyān, *Muqtabis V,* 275 (Spanish 208).
78. Ibid., 275–276 (Spanish 208–209).
79. Ibid., 276 (Spanish 209).
80. Ibid., 276–277 (Spanish 209–210).
81. Ibid., 277–278 (Spanish 210).
82. Ibn Sa'īd reports that Toledo was of ancient foundation and the former capital of the Goths, but he seems much more interested in its geographic orientation. He situates the city in the middle of the peninsula, ten days from the Mediterranean coast and thirteen from the Atlantic coast and devotes most of his description to the course of the Tagus River, from its source in the mountains to its outlet at Lisbon. The quoted passage closes with a brief mention of the city walls and the large number of *fuqahā'* and pious men who lived within it. Ibn Ḥayyān, *Muqtabis V,* 278–280 (Spanish 210–211).
83. Ibid., 282–284 (Spanish 212–214).
84. Ibid., 317–321 (Spanish 238–241).
85. Ibid., 226–237 (Spanish 173–181).
86. Ibid., 280 (Spanish 212).

87. Ibid., 318 (Spanish 238).
88. Ibid., 321–322 (Spanish 241–242).
89. Ibn Sa'īd lived and wrote in the thirteenth century. His *al-Mughrib fī ḥulā al-Maghrib* included the history and geography of al-Andalus from 1135 to 1243. Ibn Bashkuwāl wrote in the eleventh century and is best known for his biographical dictionaries; he had a reputation for being incomparable in his knowledge of the history of al-Andalus. See Pons Boigues, *Historiadores,* 306–310 (Ibn Sa'īd), 246–249 (Ibn Bashkuwāl).

   Ibn 'Idhārī's *Bayān* provides some of the same extensive reports on the building activity of the caliphs we find in *Nafḥ al-ṭīb,* particularly on the construction of the Great Mosque of Cordoba and Madīnat al-Zahrā', but does not attribute many of them to their sources.
90. al-Maqqarī, *Nafḥ al-ṭīb,* 3:160–161. See Pons Boigues, *Historiadores,* 62–66.
91. al-Maqqarī, *Nafḥ al-ṭīb,* 3:173.
92. E. Lévi-Provençal believes that Aḥmad al-Rāzī had the same impact on the geographical writing of al-Andalus that he had on its historiography and suggests that his description of al-Andalus was a basis for all subsequent Arabic descriptions of the peninsula, with the exception of the *Masālik* literature of eastern authors. See E. Lévi-Provençal, "La 'description de l'Espagne d'Aḥmad al-Rāzī'," *al-Andalus* 18 (1953), 51–108, for his discussion of al-Rāzī's work and a reconstruction of part of his description based on extracts in later Arabic texts and a fourteenth-century Portuguese translation transmitted through various Castilian translations. For discussion of the sources and a multitextual edition of the translations of Aḥmad al-Rāzī's geography and history, see *Crónica del Moro Rasis,* ed. Diego Catalán and M. Soledad de Andrés et al. (Madrid, 1975). For a critique of the *Crónica del Moro Rasis,* see Luis Molina, "Sobre la procedencia de la historia preislamica inserta en la crónica del moro Rasis," *Awraq* 5–6 (1982–1983), 133–139. Molina accepts the "authenticity" of the geographical section of the *Crónica* as al-Rāzī's but raises doubts about the pre-Islamic history.
93. Al-Maqqarī, *Nafḥ al-ṭīb,* 1:460.
94. Ibid., 1:481.

95. Ibid., 1:129–131. See also Lévi-Provençal, "Description de l'Espagne," 59–108.
96. Al-Maqqarī, *Nafḥ al-ṭīb,* 1:460.
97. Ibid., 1:470.
98. Ibid., 1:545. Other sources suggest that 'Abd al-Raḥmān I must have added to the ancient palace of Cordoba. See Ibn Bashkuwāl's report, *Nafḥ al-ṭīb,* 1:463–464. The *qaṣr* of Cordoba, the seat of the Umayyad government until 'Abd al-Raḥmān III moved it to Madīnat al-Zahrā', grew to be a complex of buildings. See Ruggles, "Madīnat al-Zahrā's Constructed Landscape," 115–122.
99. Al-Maqqarī, *Nafḥ al-tīb,* 1:560 presents al-Rāzī's description of the previous circumstances of worship in which Muslims and Christians shared a church and al-Rāzī's account of how the amir negotiated with the Christians to purchase the site, destroyed the old structure, and erected the new mosque.
100. Ibid., 1:545.
101. It is important to remember that the literary representation of the building is distinct from the actual structure. Other textual and epigraphic evidence ascribe the major expansions of the mosque to 'Abd al-Raḥmān II (completed by his son, Muḥammad), al-Ḥakam II, and the *ḥājib* al-Manṣūr. 'Abd al-Raḥmān III elaborated the courtyard and constructed the towerlike minaret. The contributions of the other Umayyad rulers were less dramatic: Muḥammad may have built a *maqṣūra,* al-Mundhir added a treasury, and 'Abd Allāh a covered walkway from the palace to the mosque. See Dodds, "Great Mosque of Cordoba," 11–25, for an overview of the history of the mosque.
102. Al-Maqqarī, *Nafḥ al-ṭīb,* 1:546.
103. Ibid., 1:466–467. See also 546, where al-Maqqarī, citing "some historians," reiterates this description of the gardens of al-Ruṣāfa.
104. Ibid., 1:467.
105. *Akhbār majmū'a,* 51–52 (Spanish 58–59).
106. In the same period the Abbasid caliph al-Manṣūr constructed a palace-complex outside the round city for his son, al-Mahdī, which he called al-Ruṣāfa. See Lassner, *Topography of Baghdad,* 149–154.

107. al-Maqqarī, *Nafḥ al-ṭīb,* 1:467. Ibn Ḥayyān recounts the story of the introduction and propagation of a certain kind of pomegranate. See Ruggles, "Madīnat al-Zahrā's Constructed Landscape," 88–99, on the influence of botanical gardens and caliphal patronage in the diffusion of new plant species, and 99–104, for her argument for a slow agricultural revolution in Umayyad al-Andalus that reached a peak in the eleventh century.
108. al-Maqqarī, *Nafḥ al-ṭīb,* 3:54.
109. Ibid., 1:523–524.
110. Ibid., 1:523.
111. Ibid., 1:567–568.
112. Ibid., 1:566.
113. Ibid., 1:568.
114. Ibid. Al-Maqqarī provides other estimates on the cost of construction as well.
115. Ibid., 1:566.
116. Ibid., 1:565–566.
117. Glick, *Islamic and Christian Spain,* discusses Christian and Muslim representations of the peninsula and notes the Muslims' perception of the Syrianization of al-Andalus (in particular, see 53–55).
118. Ibn al-Qūṭiyya, *Ta'rīkh iftitāḥ al-Andalus,* 20 (Spanish 15). For a discussion of how 'Abd al-Raḥmān I "syrianized" al-Andalus in social and political terms, see Pedro Chalmeta, "El nacimiento del estado neo-omeya Andalusī" *Homenaje a Manuel Ocaña Jimenez,* (Cordoba, 1990), 97–106.
119. Al-Maqqarī, *Nafḥ al-ṭīb,* 1:176.
120. Ibn Ḥabīb, *Kitāb al-Ta'rikh,* nos. 406–407, 418–419; *Akhbār majmū'a,* 15–16, 19, 29–30 (Spanish 27, 31, 41–42). Hernández Juberías, *Península imaginaria,* 208–248, discusses the different versions of the legend of Solomon's table.
121. Al-Maqqarī, *Nafḥ al-ṭīb,* 1:135, 161. Ibn Ḥayyān refutes the common attribution of the table to Solomon and describes it as a church treasure. Ibid., 232.
122. al-Maqqarī, *Nafḥ al-ṭīb,* 1:560–561. See Ocaña, "La Basilica de San Vicente y la gran mezquita," 344–366, for discussion of the dubious authenticity of this account.
123. al-Maqqarī, *Nafḥ al-ṭīb,* 1:563.

124. See Priscilla Soucek, "The Temple of Solomon in Islamic Legend and Art," in Joseph Gutmann, ed. *The Temple of Solomon* (Missoula, Montana, 1976), for Muslim accounts of the foundations of the Temple and the Dome of the Rock.

NOTES TO CONCLUSION: THE ANDALUSI-UMAYYAD CALIPHATE IN RETROSPECT

1. These verses about the Umayyads are from al-Shaqundī's *risāla* on the virtues of al-Andalus, as preserved in al-Maqqarī's *Nafḥ al-ṭīb,* 3:189.
2. This treatise has been preserved in al-Maqqarī, *Nafḥ al-ṭīb* chap. 7. For a French translation, see Charles Pellat, "Ibn Ḥazm: bibliographe e apologiste de l'Espagne musulmane," *al-Andalus* 19 (1954), 53–102.
3. See Chejne, *Muslim Spain,* 155–161, 277–278.
4. al-Maqqarī's *Nafḥ al-ṭīb* includes an entire volume devoted to the defense of Andalusi scholarship and literature (*al-bāb al-sabī'*). As al-Maqqarī explains in his introduction, he composed this work on al-Andalus at the behest of the ruler of Damascus, who was interested in the life and works of Lisān al-Dīn ibn al-Khaṭīb. Al-Maqqarī, who was born in Tlemcen and lived in Fez until he traveled east, explains that he took the opportunity to inform easterners of the history, literature, geography, religion, and learning of al-Andalus and the virtues of its land and people.
5. al-Maqqarī, *Nafḥ al-ṭīb,* 1:379.
6. Ibn Khaldūn, *Muqaddimah,* 1:356–357, 359–360.
7. See the account of Ibn Shuhayd's gift to al-Nāṣir in al-Maqqarī, *Nafḥ al-ṭīb,* 1:356–360.
8. al-Maqqarī, *Nafḥ al-ṭīb,* 1:455–456.
9. See, for example, al-Maqqarī, *Nafḥ al-ṭīb,* 1:459–461, 540, 558.
10. See Emilio García Gómez, "Algunas precisiones sobre la ruina de la Córdoba omeya," *al-Andalus* 12 (1947), 277–293, and Ruggles, "Madīnat al-Zahrā's Constructed Landscape," 469–480, for a discussion of responses to the ruins of the palace-city.
11. Ibn Sa'īd quotes these verses in his discussion of the folly of the *mulūk al-tawā'if* or petty kings. Al-Maqqarī, *Nafḥ al-ṭīb,* 1:215.

12. Ibn Sa'īd was born in 1214 in Qālat Ya'sub outside Granada and died in Damascus in 1274 (or Tunis in 1286 or 1287). He governed Algeciras for a time and served in the administration of the amir of Tunis. He traveled extensively in the east, seeking knowledge from the great scholars of the day and visiting the famous libraries. He is reputed to have written four hundred works. See Pons Boigues, *Historiadores,* 306–310.
13. Ibn Sa'īd takes care to refute all charges that the Andalusis had become cowardly and weak, spoiled by the abundance of the land and their prosperity. He asserts that the people of al-Andalus had always been famous for their readiness to fight the infidel, their constancy in upholding the tenets of the faith, and their endurance of the tribulations of war. Their rulers for centuries were brave and talented, which explained their long reigns. Al-Maqqarī, *Nafḥ al-ṭīb,* 1:210–212.
14. al-Maqqarī, *Nafḥ al-ṭīb,* 1:212–213, 455–456.
15. Ibid., 1:215–216.
16. Ibid., 1:212–213.
17. Ibid., 1:214–215.
18. Ibid., 1:214.
19. Ibid., 1:212–213.
20. See Blankinship, *End of the Jihād State,* for this characterization of the Syrian Umayyad state and discussion of its expansionary policy.
21. See al-Qadi, "Late Umayyad Ideology and Practice," 241–242, 252–273; W. Montgomery Watt, *The Formative Period of Islamic Thought* (Edinburgh, 1973), 83–84.
22. Crone and Hinds, *God's Caliph,* 30–42.
23. For more discussion of the Syrian Umayyad conception of the caliphate, see al-Qadi, "Late Umayyad Ideology and Practice, "and Crone and Hinds, *God's Caliph,* 4–42. See also Von Vloten, *Recherches,* 36, on the language used by Umayyad partisans.
24. On the introduction of Maliki teachings in al-Andalus, see M. A. Makki, *Ensayo sobre las aportaciones orientales en la España musulmana* (Madrid, 1968), 134–140. Jorge Aguadé, "Some Remarks about Sectarian Movements in al-Andalus," *Studia Islamica* 64 (1986), 53–77, discusses the predominance of the *madhhab* in al-Andalus. M. Isabel Fierro, "El derecho Mālikī en al-Andalus: siglos II/VIII–V/XI," *al-Qantara* 12 (1991), 119–132, traces its de-

velopment on the peninsula. H. Monès, "Le role des hommes de religion dans l'histoire de l'Espagne musulmane jusqu'à la fin du califat," *Studia Islamica* 20 (1964), 63–83, and Dominique Urvoy, "The 'Ulamā' of al-Andalus," in Salma Khadra Jayyusi, ed., *The Legacy of Muslim Spain* (Leiden; 1994), 2:849–877, discuss the relationship between the *'ulamā* and the state and the impact of the caliph's policy.

25. See Crone and Hinds, *God's Caliph*, 80–83, 99–105, for a discussion of how the Abbasids and Fatimids shared a common vocabulary of caliphal representation with the Umayyads and some idea of the caliph as deputy of God.

Bibliography

Abel, Armand. "Changements politiques et littérature eschatologique dans le monde musulman." *Studia Islamica* 2 (1954), 23–43.

———. "Un hadit sur la prise de Rome dans la tradition eschatologique de l'Islam." *Arabica 5 (1958), 1–14.*

———. "Le khalife, présence sacrée." *Studia islamica* 7 (1957), 29–45.

Acien Almansa, Manuel. *Entre el feudalismo y el Islam: 'Umar ibn Ḥafṣūn en los historiadores, en las fuentes y en la historia.* Jaen, Universidad de Jaen, 1994.

———. "Madīnat al-Zahrā' en el urbanismo musulmán." *Cuadernos de Madīnat al-Zahrā'* 1 (1978), 11–26.

———. "Materias e hipótesis para una interpretación del salón de 'Abd al-Rahman al-Nāṣir" in Antonio Vallejo Triano, ed., *Madīnat al-Zahrā': El Salón de 'Abd al-Raḥmān III.* Cordoba, Junta de Andalucía, Consejeria de Cultura, 1995, 177–191.

Addas, Claude. "Andalusī Mysticism and the Rise of Ibn al-'Arabī." In Salma Khadra Jayyusi, ed., *The Legacy of Muslim Spain. Leiden,* Brill, *1994,* 2:910–933.

Aguadé, Jorge. "Some Remarks about Sectarian Movements in Andalus." *Studia Islamica* 64 (1986), 53–77.

Ahsan, Muhammad Manazir. *Social Life under the Abbasids.* London, Longman, 1979.

Akhbār majmū'a fī fath al-Andalus (Ajbar machmua). Ed. and trans. Emilio Lafuente y Alcantara. Madrid, La Real Academia de la Historia, 1867.

Alemany-Bolufer, José. *La geografía de la península ibérica en los escritores árabes.* Madrid, El Defensor, 1921.

Amador de los Ríos y Villata, Rodrigo. *Inscripciones árabes de Córdoba,* 2nd ed. Madrid, Imprenta de Fortanet, 1880.

Antuña, P. Melchor M. "La Jura en el califato de Córdoba." *Anuario de historia del derecho español* 6 (1930), 108–140.

Arie, Rachel. *Historia de España: III, España musulmana (siglos VIII-XV),* Barcelona, Labor, 1989.

Arjona Castro, Antonio. *Anales de Córdoba musulmana 711–1008.* Cordoba, Publicaciones del Monte de Piedad y Caja de Ahorros de Córdoba, 1982.

Asín Palacios, Miguel. *Abenḥazam de Córdoba y su historia crítica de las ideas religiosas.* Madrid, Revista de Archivos 1927–1932.

Ávila Navarro, María Luisa. "La proclamación *(Bay'a)* de Ḥišam II. Año 976 d.C." *al-Qantara* 1 (1980), 79–114.

Bacharach, Jere L. "Marwanid Umayyad Building Activities: Speculations on Patronage." *Muqarnas* 13 (1996), 27–44.

Barceló, Miquel. "El califa patente: el ceremonial omeya de Córdoba o la enscenificación del poder." In Reyna Pastor, Ian Kieniewica, Eduardo García de Enterría, et al., eds., *Estructuras y formas del poder en la historia.* Salamanca, Ediciones Universidad de Salamanca, 1991, 51–71.

———. "El hiato en las acuñaciones de oro en al-Andalus, 127–316/ 774(5)—929." *Moneda y Crédito* 132 (1975), 33–71.

Bates, Michael L. "The Islamic Coinage of Islamic Spain." In Jerrilynn Dodds, ed., *Al-Andalus: The Art of Islamic Spain.* New York, The Metropolitan Museum of Art, 1992, 384–391.

Beckwith, Christian. "The Plan of the City of Peace: Central Asian Iranian Factors in Early Abbasid Design." *Acta Orientalia Academiae Scientiarium Hung.* 38 (1984), 143–164.

Bierman, Irene. *Writing Signs: The Fatimid Public Text.* Berkeley, University of California Press, 1998.

Blankinship, Khalid Yahya. *The End of the Jihād State: The Reign of Hishām Ibn 'Abd al-Malik and the Collapse of the Umayyads.* Albany, State University of New York Press, 1994.

Bloom, Jonathan. *Minaret: Symbol of Islam.* Oxford, Oxford University Press, 1989.

———. "The Origins of Fatimid Art." *Muqarnas* 3 (1985), 23–24.

Brisch, Klaus. "Observations on the Iconography of the Great Mosque of Damascus." In Priscilla P. Soucek, ed., *Content and Context of the Visual Arts in the Islamic World.* University Park, Penn., Pennsylvania State University Press, 1988, 13–23.

Brunschvig, Robert. "Ibn 'Abdalḥakam et la conquête de l'Afrique du Nord par les arabes." In Abdel Magid Turki, ed., *Études sur l'Islam classique et l'Afrique du Nord.* London, Variorum Reprints, 1986.

Bulliet, Richard. *Conversion to Islam in the Medieval Period,* Cambridge, Mass., Harvard University Press, 1979.

Cachia, Pierre. "Andalusi Belles Lettres." In Salma Khadra Jayyusi, ed., *The Legacy of Muslim Spain.* Leiden, Brill, 1994, 1:307–316.

Le Calendrier de Cordoue. New ed. based on R. Dozy in Arabic and Latin. French trans. Charles Pellat. Leiden, Brill, 1961.

Canard, Marius, "Le cérémonial fatimite et le cérémonial byzantin: essai de comparaison." *Byzantion* 21 (1951), 355–420.

———. "L'imperialisme des Fatimides et leur propagande." *Annales de l'Institut d'Ètudes Orientales de la Faculté des Lettres d'Alger* 6 (1942–1947), 156–193. Reprinted in Marius Canard, *Miscellanea orientalia.* London, Variorum Reprints, 1973.

Castejon, Rosario. "Madīnat al-Zahrā' en los autores árabes." *Al-Mulk* 1 (1959–1960), 63–106; 2 (1961–1962), 119–156.

Chalmeta, Pedro. "Concessiones territoriales en al-Andalus." *Cuadernos de historia* 6 (1975), 1–90.

———. *Invasión e islamización: la sumisión de Hispania y la formación de al-Andalus.* Madrid, MAPFRE, 1994.

———. "El nacimiento del estado neo-omeya andalusī." *Homenaje a Manuel Ocaña Jimenez.* Cordoba, Junta de Andalucía, Consejería de Cultura, 1990, 97–106.

———. "Simancas y Alhandega." *Hispania* 36 (1976), 359–444.

Chejne, Anwar. *Muslim Spain: Its History and Culture.* St. Paul, University of Minnesota Press, 1974.

Clément, François. *Pouvoir et légitimité en Espagne musulman à l'époque des taifas (Ve–XIe siècle): Imam fictif.* Paris, L'Harmattan, 1997.

Collins, Roger. *Early Medieval Spain.* London, MacMillan Education Ltd., 1988 (1983).

Combs-Schilling, M. E. *Sacred Performances: Islam, Sexuality, and Sacrifice*. New York, Columbia University Press, 1989.

Crone, Patricia, and Michael Hinds. *God's Caliph: Religious Authority in the First Centuries of Islam*. Cambridge, Cambridge University Press, 1986.

Crónica anónima de 'Abd al-Raḥmān III al-Nāṣir. Ed. and trans., E. Lévi-Provençal and E. García-Gómez. Madrid, Consejo Superior de Investigaciones Científicas, 1950.

La Crónica de Àrīb sobre al-Andalus. Ed. Juan Castilla Brazales. Granada, Impredisur, 1992.

Crónica del Moro Rasis. Ed. Diego Catalán, M. Soledad de Andrés, et al. Madrid, Editorial Gredos, 1975.

Cruz Hernandez, M. "La persecución anti-massarí durante el reinado de 'Abd al-Raḥmān al-Nāṣir li-Dīn Allāh, según Ibn Ḥayyān." *al-Qantara* 2 (1981), 51–67.

Dachraoui, Farhat. *Le califat Fatimide au Maghreb (296–365 H/909–975 JC)*. Tunis, S.T.D., 1981.

———. "Tentative d'infiltration ši'ite en Espagne musulmane sous le règne d'al-Ḥakam II." *al-Andalus* 23 (1958), 97–106.

Daftary, Farhad. *The Isma'ilis: Their History and Doctrines*. Cambridge, Cambridge University Press, 1990.

Daniel, Elton. "The Anonymous History of the Abbasid Family and Its Place in Islamic Historiography." *International Journal of Middle Eastern Studies* 14 (1982), 419–434.

———. *The Political and Social History of Khurasan under Abbasid Rule*, 747–820. Minneapolis, Bibliotheca Islamica, 1979.

Dawood, N.J. *The Koran with a Parallel Arabic Text*. London, Penguin, 1990.

De la Granja, Fernando. "A propósito de una embajada cristiana en la corte de 'Abd al-Raḥmān III." *Al-Andalus* 39 (1974), 391–406.

De la Puente, Cristina. "La caracterización de Almanzor: entre la epopeya y la historia." *Estudios onomastico-biograficos de al-Andalus* 8 (1997), 367–402.

Dodd, Erika Cruikshank, and Shereen Khairallah. *The Image of the Word: A Study of Quranic Verses in Islamic Architecture*. Beirut, American University Press, 1981.

Dodds, Jerrilynn D. *Architecture and Ideology in Early Medieval Spain.* University Park, Penn., Pennsylvania State University Press, 1990.

———. "The Great Mosque of Córdoba." In Jerrilynn D. Dodds, ed., *Al-Andalus: The Art of Islamic Spain.* New York, The Metropolitan Museum of Art, 1992.

Dozy, Reinhardt. *Recherches sur l'histoire et la littérature de l'Espagne pendant le moyen age.* Leiden, Brill, 1860.

Epalza, Mikel de. "Problemas y reflexiones sobre el califato en al-Andalus." *Anuario de Historia del Derecho Español (1983),* 569–581.

Ewert, Christian. "Elementos decorativos en los tableros parietales del Salón Rico de Madīnat al-Zahrā'." *Cuadernos de Madīnat al-Zahrā'* 1 (1987), 41–58.

Fierro (Bello), Maribel (M. Isabel). "Accusations of '*Zandaqa*' in al-Andalus." *Quaderni di studi arabi* 5–6 (1987–1988), 251–258.

——— "Caliphal Legitimacy and Expiation." In Muhammad Khalid Masud, Brinkley Messick, and David S. Powers, eds., *Islamic Legal Interpretation: Muftis and Their Fatwas.* Cambridge, Mass., Harvard University Press, 1996, 55–62.

———. "Cuatro preguntas en torno a Ibn Ḥafṣūn." *Al-Qantara* 16 (1995), 221–257.

———. "El derecho Mālikī en al-Andalus: siglos II/VIII–V/XI." *Al-Qantara* 12 (1991), 119–132.

———. *La heterodoxia en al-Andalus durante el período Omeya.* Madrid, Instituto Hispano-Árabe de Cultura, 1987.

———. "Mahdisme et eschatologie en al-Andalus." *Mahdisme, crise et changement dans l'histoire de Maroc.* Ed. Faculté des Lettres et des Sciences Humaines de Rabat. Casablanca, 1994, 47–70.

———. "La obra histórica de Ibn al-Qutiyya." *al-Qantara* 10 (1989), 485–512.

———. "Qasim b. Asbag y la licitud de recibir regalos." In *Homenaje al Profesor José María Fórneas Besteiro.* Granada, 1994, 2: 977–981.

———. "Sobre la adopción del título califal por 'Abd al-Raḥmān III al-Nāṣir." *Sharq al-Andalus* 6 (1989), 33–42.

———. "En torno a la decoración con mosaicos de las mezquitas omeyas." *Homenaje al prof. Jacinto Bosch Vilá.* Granada, Universidad de Granada, Departmento de Estudios Semíticos, 1991, 131–144.

Gabrieli, Francesco. "Consideraciones sobre el califato omeya del oriente." *Al-Andalus* 39 (1974), 407–430.

———. "Omeyyades d'Espagne et Abbasides." *Studia Islamica* 31 (1970), 93–100.

García Gómez, E. "Algunas precisiones sobre la ruina de la Córdoba omeya." *Al-Andalus* 12 (1947), 277–293.

———. "Armas, banderas, tiendas de campaña, monturas y correos en los 'annales de al-Hakam II' por 'Īsā Rāzī." *Al-Andalus* 32 (1967), 163–174.

———. "Notas de topografía cordobesa en los 'Anales de al-Hakam II' de 'Īsā Rāzī." *Al-Andalus* 30 (1965), 319–379.

———. "La poesie politique sous le califat de Cordoue." *Revue des Études Islamiques* (1949), 5–11.

Geertz, Clifford. "Ideology as a Cultural System." In Clifford Geertz, *The Interpretation of Cultures.* New York, Basic Books, 1973.

———. *Negara: The Theater State in Nineteenth Century Bali.* Princeton, Princeton University Press, 1980.

Gibb, Hamilton A. R. *Studies on the Civilization of Islam.* Princeton, Princeton University Press, 1982.

Glick, Thomas F., *From Muslim Fortress to Christian Castle.* Manchester, Manchester University Press, 1995.

———. *Islamic and Christian Spain in the Early Middle Ages.* Princeton, Princeton University Press, 1979.

Grabar, Oleg. "Notes sur le Mihrab de la Grande Mosquée de Cordoue." In Alexandre Papadopoulu, ed., *Le miḥrāb dans l'architecture e la religion musulmanes: Actes du colloque internationale: Formas symboliques et formes esthetiques dans l'architecture religieuse musulmane: le miḥrāb, Paris, 1980.* Leiden, Brill, 1988.

———. "Notes sur les ceremonies omayyades." In Myriam Rosen-Ayalon, ed., *Studies in Memory of Gaston Wiet.* Jerusalem, Institute of Asian and African Studies, Hebrew University of Jerusalem, 1977.

Guichard, Pierre. "*Al-Manṣūr* ou *al-Manṣūr bi-Llāh?* Les *laqab/s* des Amirids d'après la numismatique et les documents officiels." *Archeologie islamique* 5 (1995), 47–53.

———. "The Social History of Muslim Spain." In Salma Khadra Jayyusi, ed., *The Legacy of Muslim Spain*. Leiden, Brill, 1994, 2:579–708.

———. *Structures sociales "orientales" et "occidentales" dans l'Espagne musulmane*. Paris, Mouton, 1977.

Al-Hajji, A. "Al-Alāqāt al-diblūmasiyya bayna al-Andalus wa-l-Bīzanta ḥattā nihāyat al-qarn al-rābi' al-hijrī." *Revista del Instituto Egipcio de Estudios Islámicos*. 23 (1982–1983), 53–91.

———. "The Andalusian Diplomatic Relations with the Vikings during the Umayyad Period (A.H. 138–366/A.D. 755–966)." *Hesperis-Tamuda* 8 (1967), 67–110.

———. *Andalusian Diplomatic Relations with Western Europe during the Umayyad Period*. Beirut, Dar al-Irshad, 1970.

Halm, Heinz. *The Empire of the Mahdi: The Rise of the Fatimids*. Trans. Michael Bonner. Leiden, Brill, 1996.

———. "La réfutation d'une note diplomatique du calife 'Abdarraḥmān III par la cour du calife fatimide al-Mu'izz," *Saber religioso y poder politico en el Islam. Actas de simposio internacional (Granada 15–18 Octubre, 1991)*. Madrid, Agencia Española de Cooperación Internacional, 1994, 117–125.

Hernández Juberías, Julia. *La peninsula imaginaria. Mitos y leyendas sobre al-Andalus*. Madrid, Consejo Superior de Investigaciones científicas, 1996.

Hillenbrand, Robert. "Medieval Córdoba as a Cultural Centre." In Salma Khadra Jayyusi, ed., *The Legacy of Muslim Spain*. Leiden, Brill, 1994, 1:112–135.

Al-Ḥimyarī. *La péninsule Ibérique au moyen-age d'après le Kitāb al-Rawḍ al-mi'tār fī ḫabar al-aqṭār*. Arabic ed. and French trans., E. Lévi-Provençal. Leiden, Brill, 1938.

Humphreys, R. S. "Quranic Myth and Narrative Structure in Early Islamic Historiography." In F. M. Clover and R. S. Humphreys, eds., *Tradition and Innovation in Late Antiquity*. Madison, University of Wisconsin Press, 1989, 271–290.

Ibn 'Abd al-Ḥakam. *The History of the Conquest of Egypt, North Africa, and Spain, Known as the Futūh Miṣr of Ibn 'Abd al-Ḥakam.* Ed. Charles C. Torrey. New Haven, Yale University Press, 1922.

Ibn 'Abd Rabbihi. *al-'Iqd al-Farīd,* 2nd ed. Ed. Muhammad Sa'id al-'Aryan (Orien.) Cairo, al-Maktab al-Tijārī al-Kubrā, 1953.

Ibn al-Faqīh al-Hamadhānī. *Kitāb al-buldān.* In M. J. de Goeje, ed., *Biblioteca Geographorum Arabicorum,* vol. 5. Leiden, Brill, 1967.

Ibn al-Faraḍī. *Ta'rīkh 'ulamā al-Andalus.* Ed. F. Codera. Madrid, La Guirnalda, 1890.

Ibn Ḥabīb, 'Abd al-Malik. *Kitāb al-Ta'rīkh (Kitāb al-Tarīj).* Ed. Jorge Aguadé. Madrid, Consejo Superior de Investigaciones Científicas, 1991.

Ibn Hawqal. *Kitāb ṣurat al-ard.* In J. H. Kramers, ed., *Biblioteca Geographorum Arabicorum,* vol. 2. Leiden, Brill, 1967. French translation *Configuration de la terre,* trans. J. H. Kramers and G. Wiet. Paris, Maisonneuve & Larose, 1964.

Ibn Ḥayyān. *Al-Muktabis. Tome troisième. Chronique du règne du calife Umaiyade 'Abd Allah à Cordoue.* (Muqtabis III). Arabic ed. P. Melchor M. Antuña. Paris, P. Geunthner, 1937.

———. *al-Muqtabis V. de Ibn Hayyan* Ed. P. Chalmeta, F. Corriente, and M. Subh. Madrid, Instituto Hispano Árabe de Cultura, Facultad de Letras-Rabat, 1976. Spanish translation *Crónica del califa Abdarraḥmān III an-Nāṣir entre los años 912 y 942 (al-Muqtabis V),* trans. María Jesus Viguera and Federico Corriente. Zaragoza, Anubar: Instituto Hispano-Arabe de Cultura, 1981.

———. *al-Muqtabis fi akhbār balad al-Andalus (Muqtabis VII).* Ed. A. A. Hajji. Beirut, Dār al-Thaqāfā, 1965. Spanish translation, *Anales palatinos del califa de Córdoba al-Ḥakam II por 'Īsā Ibn Aḥmad al-Rāzī,* trans. Emilio García Gómez. Madrid, Sociedad de Estudios y Publicaciones, 1967.

Ibn 'Idhārī. *al-Bayān al-mughrib fī akhbār al-Andalus w-al-Maghrib (Bayān 1 & 2).* Ed. E. Lévi-Provençal and G. S. Colin, after R. Dozy's 1849 ed. Leiden, Brill, 1948–1951. French translation *Histoire de l'Afrique et de l'Espagne intitulée al-Bayano l-Mogrib,* trans. E. Fagnan. Algiers, 1901–1904.

———. *Kitāb al-Bayān al-Mughrib, tome troisième. Histoire de l'Espagne musulmane au XIe siècle (Bayān III).* Ed. E. Lévi-Provençal. Paris, P. Geuthner, 1930.

Ibn Kathīr. *Kitāb al-Nihāya.* Ed. T. M. al-Zayni. Cairo, Dār al-Kutub al-Ḥadītha, 1969.

Ibn Khaldūn. *The Muqaddimah.* Trans. Franz Rosenthal. London, Routledge and Kegan Paul, 1986.

Ibn Khurdādhbeh. *Kitāb al-masālik w–al-mamālik.* In M. J. de Goeje, ed., *Biblioteca Geographorum Arabicorum,* vol. 6. Leiden, Brill, 1967.

Ibn al-Qūṭiyya. *Ta'rīkh iftitāḥ al-Andalus (Historia de la conquista de España de Abenalcotia el Cordobés).* Ed. and trans. Julián Ribera. Madrid, Revista de Archivos, 1926.

Ibn Rusta. *'Alaq al-nafīsa.* In M. J. de Goeje, ed., *Biblioteca Geographorum Arabicorum,* vol. 7. Leiden, Brill, 1967.

Ibn Sa'īd, 'Arīb. *La Crónica de 'Arīb sobre al-Andalus.* Ed. Juan Castilla Brazalas. Granada, Impredisor 1992.

———. *Silat ta'rikh al-Ṭabarī (Tabari Continuos),* Ed. M. J. de Goeje. Leiden, Brill, 1897.

Ibn Sa'īd al-Maghribī. *The Banners of the Champions.* Trans. James A. Bellamy and Patricia Owen Steiner. Madison, Hispanic Seminary of Medieval Studies, 1989.

Ibn Sa'īd al-Maghribī. *Kitāb al-mughrib.* In Shawqi Dayf, ed., *Dhakhā'ir al-'arab,* vols. 9–10. Cairo, Dār al-Ma'ārif, 1953.

Ivanow, W. *Ismaili Tradition Concerning the Rise of the Fatimids.* London, Oxford University Press, 1942.

Ja'far, Muhammad Kamal Ibrahim, *Min qaḍāyā-l-fikr al-islāmī.* Cairo, Maktabat Dār al-'Ulūm, 1978.

Jayyusi, Salma Khadra. "Andalusi Poetry: The Golden Period." In Salma Khadra Jayyusi, ed., *The Legacy of Muslim Spain.* Leiden, Brill, 1994, 1:317–366.

Kennedy, Hugh. *Muslim Spain and Portugal: A Political History of al-Andalus.* London, Longman, 1996.

Khalidi, Tarif. *Arabic Historical Thought in the Classical Period.* Cambridge, Cambridge University Press, 1994.

Khoury, Nuha N. N. "The Great Mosque of Córdoba in the Tenth Century." *Muqarnas* 13 (1996), 80–98.

al-Khushānī. *Kitāb al-quḍāt bi Qurṭuba (Historia de los jueces de Córdoba)*. Ed. and trans. Julián Ribera. Madrid, Maestre, 1914.

Lambton, A.K.S. *State and Government in Medieval Islam*. Oxford, Oxford University Press, 1981.

Lassner, Jacob. "The Abbasid *Dawla:* An Essay on the Concept of Revolution in Early Islam." In F. M. Clover and R. S. Humphreys, eds., *Tradition and Innovation*. Madison, University of Wisconsin Press, 1989.

———. *Islamic Revolution and Historical Memory: Abbasid Apologetics and the Art of Historical Writing*. New Haven, American Oriental Society, 1986.

———. *The Shaping of Abbasid Rule*. Princeton, Princeton University Press, 1980.

———. *The Topography of Baghdad in the Early Middle Ages: Text and Studies*. Detroit, Wayne State University Press, 1970.

Lévi-Provençal, Evariste, "La description de L'Espagne d'Aḥmad al-Rāzī.'," *Al-Andalus* 18 (1953), 51–108.

———. *L'Espagne musulmane au Xe siécle: institutions et vie sociale*. Paris, Larose, 1932.

———. *Histoire de l'Espagne musulmane (H.E.M.),* 3 vols. Paris, Maisonneuve, 1950–1953.

———. *Inscriptiones árabes d'Espagne*. Leiden, Brill, 1931.

———. "La politica africana de 'Abd al-Raḥmān III." *Al-Andalus* 11 (1946), 351–378.

Lewis, Bernard. *The Origins of Ismailism*. Cambridge, W. Heffer, 1940.

———. *The Political Language of Islam*. Chicago, University of Chicago Press, 1988.

———. "The Regnal Titles of the First Abbasid Caliphs." *Dr. Zakir Husain Presentation Volume*. New Delhi, Dr. Zakir Husain Presentation Volume Committee, 1968, 13–22.

Lézine, Alexandre. *Mahdiya: Recherches d'archéologie islamique*. Paris, Klincksieck, 1965.

L'Orange, H. P. *Studies in the Iconography of Cosmic Kingship*. Cambridge, Mass., Harvard University Press, 1953.

MacDonald, John. "The Day of Judgement in Near Eastern Religions." *Indo-Iranica* 14 (1961), 33–53.

———. "The Day of Resurrection." *Islamic Studies* 5 (1966), 129–197.

———. "The Preliminaries to the Resurrection and Judgment." *Islamic Studies* 4 (1965), 137–179.

Makki, M. A. "Egipto y los orígenes de la historiografía arabigo-española." *Revista del Instituto de Estudios Islamicos en Madrid* 5 (1957), 157–248.

———. *Ensayo sobre las aportaciones orientales en la España musulmana.* Madrid, Instituto de Estudios Islámicos, 1968.

———. "Al-tashayyu' fi-l-Andalus." *Revista del Instituto Egipcio de Estudios Islámicos* 2 (1954), 93–149.

Manzano Moreno, Eduardo, "The Creation of a Medieval Frontier: Islam and Christianity in the Iberian Peninsula, Eighth to Eleventh Centuries." In Daniel Power and Naomi Standen, eds., *Frontiers in Question: Eurasian Borderlands 700–1700.* New York, St. Martin's Press, 1999, 32–54.

———. "Oriental 'Topoi' in Andalusian Sources." *Arabica* 39 (1992), 42–58.

———. *La frontera de al-Andalus en época de los omeyas.* Madrid, Consejo Superior de Investigaciones Científicas, 1991.

al-Maqqarī. *Nafḥ al-tīb min ghuṣn al-Andalus al-raṭīb.* Ed. Ihsan Abbas. Beirut, Dār Ṣādir, 1968. Partial English translation with reorganization of the text, Pascual de Gayangos, *The History of the Mohammedan Dynasties in Spain.* London, W. H. Allen & Co., 1840–1843.

Martinez Antuña, P. Melchor. "La jura en el califato de Córdoba." *Anuario de historia del derecho español* 6 (1930), 108–140.

Martínez-Gros, Gabriel. *L'idéologie omeyyade: la construction de la legitimité du califat de Cordoue (X–XI siècles).* Madrid, Casa de Velazquez, 1992.

al-Mas'ūdī. *Les prairies d'or.* Arabic ed. and French trans., C. Barbier de Meynard and Pavet de Courteille. Paris, Imprimerie imperiale, 1861–1877. English translation from al-Mas'ūdī, *The Meadows of Gold,* ed., and trans. Paul Lunde and Caroline Stone. London, Kegan Paul International, 1989.

Mazzoli-Guintard, Christine, "Remarques sur le fonctionnement d'une capitale a double polarité: Madīnat al-Zahrā'-Cordoue." *Al-Qantara* 18 (1997), 43–64.

McCormick, Michael. "Analyzing Imperial Ceremonies." *Jahrbuch der Österreichischen Byzantinistik* 35 (1985), 1–20.

Menéndez-Pidal, Juan. *Leyendas del último godo.* Madrid, Revista de Archivos, 1906.

Menéndez-Pidal, Ramon. *Rodrigo, el último godo.* Madrid, Ediciones de "La Lectura," 1925.

Meouak, Mohamed. *Pouvoir souverain, administration centrale et élites politiques dans l'Espagne umayyade (IIe-IVe/VIIIe–Xe siècles).* Helsinki, Academia Scientiarum Fennica, 1999.

Miles, George C. *The Coinage of the Umayyads of Spain.* New York, American Numismatic Society, 1950.

Molina, Luis. "Los *Ajbar maymu'a* y la historiografía árabe sobre el periodo omeya en al-Andalus." *Al-Qantara* 10 (1989), 513–542.

———. "Sobre la procedencia de la historia preislamica inserta en la crónica del moro rasis." *Awrāq* 5–6 (1982–1983), 133–139.

Monés, H. "Le role des hommes de religion dans l'histoire de l'Espagne musulmane jusqu'à la fin du califat." *Studia Islamica* 20 (1964), 63–83.

———. "The Umayyads of East and West: A Study in the History of a Great Arab Clan." *Der Orient in der Forschung.* Weisbaden, 1967.

Monroe, James T., *Hispano Arabic Poetry.* Berkeley, University of California Press, 1974.

———. "La poesía hispanoárabe durante el califato de Córdoba: teoría y práctica." *Estudios Orientales* 4 (1971), 113–151.

Moore, Sally F., and Barbara Myerhoff, eds., *Secular Ritual.* Assen, The Netherlands, Van Gorcum, 1977.

Moscati, Sabatino. "Le massacre des Umayyades." *Archiv Orientalni.* 18 (1950), 88–115.

Noth, Albrecht. *The Early Arabic Historical Tradition,* 2nd ed. With Lawrence I. Conrad and trans. Michael Bonner. Princeton, Darwin Press, 1994.

al-Nubāhī. *Kitāb al-Marqaba al-'ulyā.* Ed. E. Lévi-Provençal. Cairo, Scribe Egyptien, 1948.

Ocaña, M. "La basilica de San Vincente y la gran mezquita de Córdoba." *Al-Andalus* 7 (1942), 347–366.

Pellat, Charles. "La España musulmana en las obras de al-Mas'ūdī" and "Le culte de Mu'awiya au III siècle de l'Hegire." In Charles Pellat, ed., *Ètudes sur l'histoire socio-culturelle de l'Islam (VIIe–XVes)*. London, Variorum Reprints, 1976.

———. "Ibn Ḥazm: bibliographe e apologiste de l'Espagne musulmane." *Al-Andalus* 19 (1954), 53–102.

Pons Boigues, Francisco. *Los historiadores y geógrafos arabigo-españoles.* Amsterdam, Philo Press, 1972 (1898).

al-Qadi, Waddad. "The Religious Foundation of Late Umayyad Ideology and Practice." In *Saber religioso y poder politico en el Islam. Actas de simposio internacional (Granada, 15–18 Octubre, 1991).* Madrid, Agencia Española de Cooperación Internacional, 1994, 231–273.

Al-Qālī. *Kitāb al-amālī.* Beirut, al Maktab al-Tijārī, n.d.

Rabbat, Nasser. "Al-Azhar Mosque: An Architectural Chronicle of Cairo's History." *Muqarnas* 13 (1996), 45–67.

Ribera y Tarrago, Julian. *Disertaciones y opúsculos.* Madrid, E. Maestre, 1928.

Richardson, J. S. *The Romans in Spain.* Oxford, Blackwell, 1996.

Rosenthal, Franz. *A History of Muslim Historiography.* Leiden, Brill, 1968.

Ruggles, D. Fairchild. "The Gardens of the Alhambra and the Concept of the Garden in Islamic Spain." In Jerrilynn Dodds, ed., *Al-Andalus: The Art of Islamic Spain.* New York, The Metropolitan Museum of Art, 1992, 163–171.

———. "Historiography and the Rediscovery of Madīnat al-Zahrā." *Islamic Studies* 30 (1991), 129–141.

———. "Madīnat al-Zahrā's Constructed Landscape: A Case Study in Islamic Garden and Architectural History." Ph.D. diss., University of Pennsylvania, 1991.

———. "The Mirador in Abbasid and Hispano-Umayyad Garden Typology." *Muqarnas* 7 (1990), 73–82.

Sachedina, Abdulaziz Abdulhussein. *Islamic Messianism.* Albany, State University of New York Press, 1981.

Safran, Janina M., "Ceremony and Submission: The Symbolic Representation and Recognition of Legitimacy in Tenth-Century al-Andalus." *Journal of Near Eastern Studies* 58 (1999), 191–201.

———. "The Command of the Faithful in al-Andalus: A Study in the Articulation of Caliphal Legitimacy." *International Journal of Middle East Studies* 30 (1998), 183–198.

Sanders, Paula. *Ritual, Politics, and the City in Fatimid Cairo*. Albany, State University of New York Press, 1994.

Scales, Peter. *The Fall of the Caliphate of Cordoba*. Leiden, Brill, 1994.

Sharon, Moshe. *Black Banners form the East: The Establishment of the 'Abbasid State—Incubation of a Revolt*. Jerusalem, Magnes Press, Hebrew University, 1983.

———. "The Umayyads as Ahl al-Bayt." *Jerusalem Studies in Arabic and Islam* 14 (1991), 115–149.

Smith, Jane Idleman, and Yvonne Haddad, *The Islamic Understanding of Death and Resurrection*. Albany, State University of New York Press, 1981.

Soucek, Priscilla. "The Temple of Solomon in Islamic Legend and Art." In Joseph Gutmann, ed., *The Temple of Solomon*. Missoula, Scholars Press, 1976.

Sourdel, D. "Questions de cérémonial 'Abbaside." *Revue des Études Islamiques* (1960), 121–148.

Stern, Henri. *Les mosaiques de la Grand Mosquée de Cordoue*. Berlin, Walter de Gruyter & Co., 1976.

Stetkevych, Suzanne Pinckney. "Abbasid Panegyric and the Poetics of Political Allegiance: Two Poems of al-Mutannabi on Kafur." In Stefan Sperl and Christopher Shackle, eds., *Qaṣīda Poetry in Islamic Asia and Africa*. Leiden, Brill, 1996, 1:35–63, 2:92–105.

———. "Abbasid Panegyric: The Politics and Poetics of Ceremony: Al-Mutanabbi's 'Id-poem to Sayf al-Dawlah." In J. R. Smart, ed., *Tradition and Modernity in Arabic Language and Literature*. Surrey, Curzon, 1996, 119–143.

———. "The *Qaṣīdah* and the Poetics of Ceremony: Three 'Id Panegyrics to the Cordoban Caliphate." In Ross Brann, ed., *Languages of Power in Islamic Spain*. Bethesda, Md., CDL Press, Occasional Publications of the Department of Near Eastern Studies and the Program of Jewish Studies, Cornell University, 1997, 1–48.

Tambiah, Stanley Jeyaraja. *Culture, Thought, and Social Action*. Cambridge, Mass., Harvard University Press, 1985.

Tornero, Emilio. "Noticia sobre la publicacíon de obras ineditas de Ibn Masarra." *al-Qantara* 14 (1993), 47–64.

Tres documentos sobre procesos de herejes en España musulmana. Ed. M.A.W. Khallaf. Cairo, al-Markaz al-ʻArabī al–Duwalī li-l-ʻilām, 1981.

Turki, A. "L'engagement politique et la théorie du califat d'Ibn Ḥazm." *Bulletin d'Études Orientales* 30 (1978), 221–251.

Tyan, Emile. *Institutions du droit publique musulman*. Paris, Recueil Sirey, 1954.

Urvoy, Dominique. "The ʻUlamā' of al-Andalus." In Salma Khadra Jayyusi, ed., *The Legacy of Muslim Spain*. Leiden, Brill, 1994, 2:849–877.

Vallejo Triano, Antonio. "Madīnat al-Zahrā': The Triumph of the Islamic State." In Jerrilynn D. Dodds, ed., *Al-Andalus: The Art of Islamic Spain*. New York, Metropolitan Museum of Art, 1992, 27–39.

———. "El Salón de ʻAbd al-Raḥmān III: problemática de una restauración." *Madīnat al-Zahrā': El Salón de ʻAbd al-Raḥmān III*. Cordoba, Junta de Andalucía, Consejería de Cultura, 1995, 11–40.

Vallvé, J., *El califato de Córdoba*. Madrid, MAPFRE, 1992.

———. "El Zalmedina de Córdoba." *al-Qantara 2 (1981), 277–318.*

Van Vloten, G. *Recherches sur la domination arabe, le chiitisme et les croyances messianiques sous le khalifat des Omayades*. Amsterdam, J. Muller, 1894.

Wasserstein, David, *The Caliphate in the West*. Oxford, Clarendon Press, 1993.

———. *The Rise and Fall of the Party Kings*. Princeton, Princeton University Press, 1986.

Watson, Andrew. *Agricultural Innovation in the Early Islamic World*. Cambridge, Cambridge University Press, 1983.

Watt, W. Montgomery. *The Formative Period of Islamic Thought*. Edinburgh, Edinburgh University Press, 1973.

———. with Pierre Cachia. *A History of Islamic Spain*. Edinburgh, Edinburgh University Press, 1973.

Wellhausen, Julius. *The Arab Kingdom and Its Fall*. Trans. Margaret Graham Weir. Beirut, Khayats, 1963.

Wendell, Charles. "Baghdad: Imago Mundi, and Other Foundation Lore." *International Journal of Middle Eastern Studies* 2 (1971), 99–128.

Yalaoui, M. "Controverse entre le fatimide al-Mu'izz et l'omeyyade al-Nāṣir, d'après le 'Kitāb al-majālis w-al-musāyarāt' du cadi Nu'mān." *Cahiers de Tunisie* 26 (1978), 7–33.

Index

HARVARD MIDDLE EASTERN MONOGRAPHS

1. *Syria: Development and Monetary Policy,* by Edmund Y. Asfour. 1959.
2. *The History of Modern Iran: An Interpretation,* by Joseph M. Upton. 1960.
3. *Contributions to Arabic Linguistics,* Charles A. Ferguson, Editor. 1960.
4. *Pan-Arabism and Labor,* by Willard A. Beling. 1960.
5. *The Industrialization of Iraq,* by Kathleen M. Langley. 1961.
6. *Buarij: Portrait of a Lebanese Muslim Village,* by Anne H. Fuller. 1961.
7. *Ottoman Egypt in the Eighteenth Century,* Stanford J. Shaw, Editor and Translator. 1962.
8. *Child Rearing in Lebanon,* by Edwin Terry Prothro. 1961.
9. *North Africa's French Legacy: 1954-1962,* by David C. Gordon. 1962.
10. *Communal Dialects in Baghdad,* by Haim Blanc. 1964.
11. *Ottoman Egypt in the Age of the French Revolution,* Translated with Introduction and Notes by Stanford J. Shaw. 1964.
12. *The Economy of Morocco: 1912-1962,* by Charles F. Stewart. 1964.
13. *The Economy of the Israeli Kibbutz,* by Eliyahu Kanovsky. 1966.
14. *The Syrian Social Nationalist Party: An Ideological Analysis,* by Labib Zuwiyya Yamak. 1966.
15. *The Practical Visions of Ya'qub Sanu',* by Irene L. Gendizier. 1966.
16. *The Surest Path: The Political Treatise of a Nineteenth-Century Muslim Statesman,* by Leon Carl Brown. 1967.
17. *High-Level Manpower in Economic Development: The Turkish Case,* by Richard D. Robinson. 1967.

18. *Rebirth of a Nation: The Origins and Rise of Moroccan Nationalism, 1912-1944,* by John P. Halsted. 1967.

19. *Women of Algeria: An Essay on Change,* by David C. Gordon. 1968.

20. *The Youth of Haouch El Harimi, A Lebanese Village,* by Judith R. Williams. 1968.

21. *The Problem of Diglossia in Arabic: A Comparative Study of Classical and Iraqi Arabic,* by Salih J. Al-Toma. 1969.

22. *The Seljuk Vezirate: A Study of Civil Administration,* by Carla L. Klausner. 1973.

23. and 24. *City in the Desert,* by Oleg Grabar, Renata Holod, James Knustad, and William Trousdale. 1978.

25. *Women's Autobiographies in Contemporary Iran,* Afsaneh Najmabadi, Editor. 1990.

26. *The Science of Mystic Lights,* by John Walbridge. 1992.

27. *Political Aspects of Islamic Philosophy: Essays in Honor of Muhsin S. Mahdi,* by Charles E. Butterworth. 1992.

28. *The Muslims of Bosnia-Herzegovina: Their Historic Development from the Middle Ages to the Dissolution of Yugoslavia,* Mark Pinson, Editor. 1994.

29. *Book of Gifts and Rarities: Kitāb al-Hadāyā wa al-Tuḥaf.* Ghāda al Hijjāwī al-Qaddūmī, Translator and Annotator. 1997.

30. *The Armenians of Iran: The Paradoxical Role of a Minority in a Dominant Culture: Articles and Documents.* Cosroe Chaqueri, Editor. 1998.

31. *In the Shadow of the Sultan: Culture, Power, and Politics in Morocco,* edited by Rahma Bourqia and Susan Gilson Miller. 1999.

32. *Hermeneutics and Honor: Negotiating Female "Public" Space in Islamic/ate Societies,* edited by Asma Afsaruddin, 1999.

33. *The Second Umayyad Caliphate: The Articulation of Caliphal Legitimacy in al-Andalus,* by Janina M. Safran. 2000.